Praise for *Howard Thurman: Reflections on a Luminous Life*

"To witness the spiritual brilliance of two extraordinary iconic souls in one book is a gift from the heavens! I predict this publication shall be read, re-read, highlighted, "dog eared," and quoted by a village of spiritual seekers for years to come."

Otis Moss III, Senior Pastor,
Trinity United Church of Christ, Chicago, Illinois

"In addition to insights on Howard Thurman's spirituality, this book portrays Thurman's influence on Massey as a prominent religious thinker. Their relationship is an inspiring sign that beloved community is not reliant on theological conformity."

Luther E. Smith, Jr., author of *Howard Thurman: The Mystic as Prophet*

"James Earl Massey was one of the most perceptive of Howard Thurman's protégés, and his hitherto unpublished biography and study of the great religious thinker and teacher is a treat and treasure for all of Thurman's many admirers, and a fascinating addition to the Thurman literature. Of particular value are the chapters on Thurman as a preacher, theologian, and practical mystic, followed by an illuminating 1971 interview between the two men. Massey's volume is filled with deep insights into Thurman the man and his abundant spiritual gifts."

Peter Eisenstadt, Affiliate Professor of History at Clemson University
and author of *Against the Hounds of Hell: A Life of Howard Thurman*

"If the highest form of flattery is imitation, then Dr. Curtiss DeYoung's imitation of the imitable Dr. James Earl Masey as he tells the story of his mentor, Dr. Howard Thurman, is the pinnacle of honor. DeYoung serves as a guide through Dr. James Earl Massey's inside view of his progenitor's life. By joining their journey, readers hear the voice of Massey share the timeless wisdom of Thurman in words that speak of justice, education, and equality today. DeYoung shares these organized voices from the past to encourage generations for the future. It is more than a must read, it is a must consume!"

Robert Smith, Jr., Distinguished Professor of Divinity,
Beeson Divinity School, Samford University

"James Earl Massey's account of Howard Thurman's life and work reveals the depth of vocation and theological imagination that energized Thurman's spiritual impact upon the church, the academy, and the civil rights movement. Massey's framing of Thurman's legacy is brought to light in a volume skillfully edited by Curtiss Paul DeYoung, a devoted advocate for racial reconciliation and social change who has embraced the mantle as Massey's protégé and literary executor. The result is a compelling portrayal of the intertwined lives of two Black luminaries—one a mentor and the other his protégé—that discloses the vulnerabilities and victories they shared in ministry while navigating the turbulent waters of racial discrimination and economic injustice. A must read for anyone who cherishes the legacy of Thurman's witness against the disparities that continue to hamper human flourishing in the twenty-first century."

Cheryl J. Sanders, Professor of Christian Ethics at Howard University School of Divinity and Presiding Elder of the National Association of the Church of God

"James Earl Massey served as a mentor to many, myself included, and his impact continues to shape contemporary Christian thought. In this remarkable volume, Curtiss DeYoung has gifted the church with a previously unpublished work by Massey, thereby opening access to two legendary contributors to Christian theology. Through Massey's rich engagement with Howard Thurman, these reflections offer both a compelling window into Christian theology and a powerful witness to the life-giving importance of mentoring. This eye-witness account of the 20th century speaks with prophetic clarity to the 21st century church, making this book a timely and deeply needed contribution."

Joy J. Moore, Visiting Scholar, Litfin Divinity School at Wheaton College

"There are books that allow us to see a person. There are books that allow us to understand a period. There are books that allow us to gain new or clearer perspectives. Whenever that happens, we are the better for having read it. This book is one the few books that allows us to do all the above. In this book we are given the privilege of "seeing" two of the great Divines of the 20th-century church, and more specifically of the Black Church in America. These two men, Dr. Howard Thurman and Dr. James Earl Massey, were bright stars in the constellation of Preaching. We meet these men, not only as colleagues but also as collaborators, mentor, mentee, student, teacher. The periods this book covers were some of most seminal and significant times in America and in the world. We see in this book those periods through the lens of Dr. Thurman and Dr. Massey, and they show us how

to 'serve this present age.' Finally, we are given a new perspective into the lives and relationship of these two men. We see the honesty, the openness, the safety of their relationship. From this alone we can learn how to be honest, faithful, corrective, and supportive in our relationships.
I salute my brother, Dr. Curtiss DeYoung, for putting pen to paper and editing this book that instructs, informs, and inspires."

Bishop Timothy J. Clarke,
Pastor of First Church of God in Columbus, OH

"Thoughtfully curated by Curtiss Paul DeYoung, this eye-opening volume invites us to consider how relationships themselves become instruments of transformation and repair. In tracing the connection between Howard Thurman and James Earl Massey, we encounter a model of intellectual and spiritual companionship grounded in purpose. In his effort to render Thurman's life, Massey offers something more revealing—not simply a biography, but a portrait of a life forged in faith, animated by justice, and sustained through shared calling. In excavating that relationship, DeYoung gives us a gift: not only Massey's unpublished reflections on Thurman, but a testament to the enduring power of their friendship."

Yohuru Williams, Distinguished University Chair
and Professor of History, Founding Director of
the Racial Justice Initiative, University of St. Thomas

"*Howard Thurman: Reflections on a Luminous Life* brings to light an unpublished manuscript on the life and thought of Howard Thurman by noted preacher and scholar James Earl Massey. Edited by Curtiss Paul DeYoung, the volume is enriched by insightful editorial commentary and a fascinating account of Massey and Thurman's close relationship, drawn from a wealth of primary sources. Students and teachers of preaching will especially value the chapter on Thurman's preaching, along with an interview that offers a window into his early formation and sermons. A valuable contribution to the growing field of Thurman studies."

E. Trey Clark, Assistant Professor of Preaching and
Spiritual Formation, Fuller Seminary

HOWARD THURMAN

HOWARD THURMAN

REFLECTIONS ON A LUMINOUS LIFE

JAMES EARL MASSEY

EDITED BY CURTISS PAUL DEYOUNG

Foreword by Walter Earl Fluker

Friendship Press™

Howard Thurman

Reflections on a Luminous Life

Print ISBN: 978-1-961088-41-2
Ebook ISBN: 978-1-961088-42-9

Table of Contents

Foreword
The Soul's Quiet Speech

By Walter Earl Fluker

How beautiful on the mountains
are the feet of the messenger
who brings good news,
The good news of peace and salvation,
the news that the God of Israel reigns!
Isaiah 52.7 (NLT, 2007)

There was a time when men wrote tender and intimate letters to one another—speaking of their friendship and desire as an extension of the soul's quiet speech. This was not romantic sentimentality; rather, it was a disciplined tenderness—a language through which men bore witness to one another's inner lives. Whether it be Paul the Apostle writing to his "dear son" in the ministry, Timothy, from the shadow of Nero's prison while awaiting imminent execution: *"I thank God, whom I serve, as my ancestors did, with a clear conscience, as night and day I constantly remember you in my prayers. Recalling your tears, I long to see you, so that I may be filled with joy. I am reminded of your sincere faith . . ."* (2 Timothy 1:3-5 NIV)

Or Henry David Thoreau writing to his mentor and beloved friend Ralph Waldo Emerson: *"I had not spoken of writing to you, but as you say you are about to write to me when you get my letter, I make haste on my part in order to get yours the sooner."(Concord, MA, January 24, 1843).*[1]

Or a young Howard Thurman writing to Mordecai Wyatt Johnson, the man who would become his long-time mentor and

1. Franklin Benjamin Sanborn, "The Emerson-Thoreau Correspondence," *The Atlantic Monthly*, May 1892.

colleague, after hearing him speak for the first time: "*Do not be surprised at hearing from me. . . . I let you slip into my heart and occupy the place of a precious friend. . . . I admired your eloquence, bowed humbly before your sympathy, and rejoiced to know that you cared. I wanted to know you and wanted you to know me; I longed for a cheering word from a man like you . . .*"[2]

This fading tradition of emotional openness and tender correspondence finds one of its most luminous expressions in Howard Thurman's letter to his mentee, friend, and "son in the spirit," James Earl Massey. Writing on Massey's twenty-fifth year of ordained ministry, Thurman gives voice to a love that is at once disciplined, discerning, and deeply personal: "*But such is the mystery of Grace that our paths have crossed, and to the delight of our spirits it is as if we had been companions of the Way from the beginning. . . . You have the neatness of mind that is only matched by your neatness in dress. . . . Yours, however, is a neatness that is paradoxically exuberant, lush, creative. . . . On this occasion, therefore, I salute you as a blood brother of the mind AND of the spirit.*" And then, with a tenderness that borders on the sacred: "*If it had been my portion to have had a son . . . he would be a young man like you. I say no more; no more is necessary to say.*" This indeed is the quiet language of the soul's longing to find home in the other's heart.

And so it was between the two principals of this rich and timely publication of the late James Earl Massey's biography of his beloved mentor, *Reflections on a Luminous Life*, edited by Curtiss Paul DeYoung. Dr. DeYoung is no stranger to this mentor–friend relationship; indeed, he was entrusted by Massey to steward his papers—among them this hidden scroll that sheds light on lesser-known fragments of Thurman's life, mentors, struggles, and spiritual evolution.

In this volume, DeYoung offers readers a gift—one that enriches, surprises, and invites deeper reflection. In the early 1970s, Massey

---

2. Howard Thurman, letter to Mordecai Wyatt Johnson, July 17, 1918, in *The Papers of Howard Washington Thurman*, vol. 1, *My People Need Me*, ed. Walter Earl Fluker (Columbia: University of South Carolina Press, 2009), 1-4; see also Howard Thurman, "Eulogy for Mordecai Wyatt Johnson," September 12, 1976, in *The Papers of Howard Washington Thurman*, vol. 5, *The Wider Ministry*, ed. Walter Earl Fluker (Columbia: University of South Carolina Press, 2017), 278-280.

undertook the ambitious task of writing a critical biography of Thurman—a project fruitful, yet ultimately unfinished. DeYoung's editorial framing and careful curation of correspondence reveal not only the depth of a forty-year relationship between these two extraordinary preachers and scholars, but also the reasons the manuscript remained unpublished.

Massey's reflections on Thurman's preaching, theology, and mysticism provide rare insight into a vast corpus of writings, meditations, and sermons that prior to his investigation had received only minimal attention, primarily from a small ensemble of Black scholars. These biographical reflections include high moments of effulgent praise from a disciple who has found his teacher; yet with scholarly dissent and characteristic gentility, Massey offers critique alongside admiration, noting: *"It is at the point of Christology that Howard Thurman's theology is weakest and problematic. Measured against the essential nature and substance of New Testament preaching and teaching, Thurman's preaching and theology are admittedly non-kerygmatic."* Among the volume's most significant contributions are Massey's interview with Thurman (chapter 8), which includes an extended reflection on Thurman's admiration for Mary McLeod Bethune and a closing meditation (chapter 9) capturing Massey's thoughts in the years following Thurman's death. DeYoung has midwifed this remarkable achievement in its present form, offering it to a burgeoning cavalcade of Thurman scholars, interpreters, readers, and seekers at this critical impasse in the history of this nation and the world.

Finally, I cannot fail to name the role that James Earl Massey played in my own life. Beyond his role on the advisory board of the Howard Thurman Papers Project, for nearly forty years, he served as mentor and guide to me in ways that echoed his relationship with Thurman. We did not write many letters, as I recall—but thanks be to God for his timely, late-evening phone calls. Sometimes, out of the blue—when my soul was weary and the oil in my lamp was running low—the phone would ring. And on the other end was that familiar voice, always *neat, exuberant, lush, creative, and healing*:

> *"Dear Dr. Fluker, this is James Earl Massey. I've been thinking of you. How are you doing? How's your spirit? I'm praying for you."*

Sometimes I could say, *"All is well."* At other times, I found it difficult to speak at all, for there was no path, no light—only darkness. And still, he would call and the light would return. During some of the most tumultuous periods of the Howard Thurman Papers Project—where I continue to serve as editor and steward—it was Dr. Massey who found me, who spoke again that quiet language of the soul, giving me strength for another day.

In 2011, I was invited to offer a tribute to Dr. Massey who had been selected to receive *The Beautiful Are The Feet Award* from the Samuel Dewitt Proctor Conference, Inc. in February 2012 (I hasten to add that my wife and I are the now proud 2026 recipients of that honor). I chose to write my tribute as a personal letter, which was later included as part of an elegiac reflection at his memorial service in 2018. The words are as true now as they were when I first wrote them:

> Thank you, my dear friend and mentor, for finding me like the shepherd who left the ninety-nine others and went looking for me; like the woman who swept tirelessly until she found the lost coin; and like the father who waited and still waits for me to come home. Thank you for the late-night calls to simply say, "I'm praying for you" or "I've been thinking about you" or "How is your spirit?" Much like our common mentor, Howard Thurman, who provided the occasion for our initial meeting and who also asked probing, disturbing and off-setting questions in soft and considerate tones, you have kept watch with me through long nights and brought good news!
>
> I admired your early work on Thurman, providing me with the first bibliography on the master; and then, your own interviews and constructive biography on Thurman that I still pray will one day reach publics beyond the narrow confines of scholars. You, like him, are never intrusive, but ever insistent that we dive deep into the interior where real questions lead us to the center of ourselves. Quiet counselor, wise guide and disciplined man of letters and practice, you leave a well-trodden path for the young runners who are coming!
>
> I congratulate those at the Samuel DeWitt Proctor Conference who made the wise choice to select you for this prestigious honor. Who best exemplifies the beautiful feet of the runner

who brings the good news that captivity is ceased; that grace has rescued us; and that love still rules in a sometimes ugly and grotesque existence?

My prayer for you, and the lovely Mrs. Gwendolyn Massey, is that you will continue to run on, majestically and quietly, until we all see how beautiful it is on the mountains!

With love and gratitude,

Walter Earl Fluker
Atlanta, Georgia
March 30, 2026

Acknowledgments

I am honored to edit this book on Howard Thurman written by James Earl Massey, and unpublished for fifty years. This editorial process has allowed me the wonderful opportunity to step back in history into the dynamic relationship between Thurman and Massey, and to finally publish the book that my mentor Dr. Massey wrote about his mentor, Dr. Thurman. Thank you to James Earl Massey and his wife Gwendolyn Massey for their love and support through the years, and for preserving the book manuscript, correspondence, and other papers.

I express my overflowing gratitude to the Massey family, especially Placidia (Cyd) Frierson for organizing and donating the papers of James Earl Massey to Anderson University, and for their blessing of the publication of this book. Rev. Kervin Jones, the Masseys' pastor in Greensboro, Alabama, and I put in a lot of hours with Cyd to complete the sorting, boxing, and delivering of over fifty boxes of the James Earl Massey papers. It was a labor of love.

Nathan Willowby (Dean of the School of Theology), Nic Don Stanton-Roark (Archivist), and Jeff Frymire (Director of the James Earl Massey Center for Preaching) at Anderson University have been particularly generous in their support of the James Earl Massey papers, archiving them and making them available for this book project and for future researchers.

I am delighted and honored that Friendship Press embraced the opportunity to publish this volume. Publisher and CEO Brian Sigmon has been a joy to work with. I am grateful for the encouragement of Thurman scholars: Walter Earl Fluker (and his wonderful foreword to this book), Luther Smith, and Peter Eisenstadt.

We are blessed to have the permission of grandson Anton Wong and the family of Howard Thurman to reproduce copies of four letters from Dr. Thurman to James Earl Massey.

I offer a special note of gratitude to Jennifer Gunter King and Jane Parr at the Howard Thurman & Sue Bailey Thurman Collections,

Howard Gotleb Archival Research Center, Boston University for their support in providing me with an earlier Massey manuscript.

And special thanks to my long-term friends Edward Foggs, Michael Smith, Aldean Miles, Robin Bell, and Cecilia Williams; and to my family Karen, Rachel, Jonathan, and Dane—all who have been known to find solace in the words of Howard Thurman and the person and words of James Earl Massey.

Curtiss Paul DeYoung

SECTION ONE

Editorial Prologue—Curtiss Paul DeYoung

James Earl Massey was a noted preacher, pastor, professor, and author. He was born and raised in Detroit, Michigan, where he was the senior pastor of the Metropolitan Church of God for many years. He also served as Seminary Dean, Dean of Chapel and Professor at Anderson University in Anderson, Indiana, and the Principal and Faculty member at Jamaica School of Theology, Kingston, Jamaica. His tenure as the Dean of Chapel at Tuskegee University in Alabama was a career high point. During his lifetime, Massey authored eighteen books, many book chapters, and numerous journal and magazine articles. His five books on preaching continue to be celebrated, and he was known as the Prince of Preachers. He also published books on biblical studies, prayer, worship, church history, and spiritual disciplines. In the 1970s, James Earl Massey completed a book manuscript on his mentor, the noted mystic activist[1] and theologian Howard Thurman. It was never published. That book is the centerpiece of this volume, finally available for the first time to the general public.

In his autobiography, *Aspects of My Pilgrimage*, Massey wrote, "As I have come to understand it, the 'Not yet!' element at work

1. See Alton Pollard, III, *Mysticism and Social Change: The Social Witness of Howard Thurman* (New York: Peter Lang, 1992), 1, for use of "mystic activist" as a descriptor for Howard Thurman.

in our life is part of the discreteness in God's plan to shape us in circumstances, discipline us by containment, enhance us by allowing choice, and lure us forward through anticipation."[2] Massey had every intention of publishing his biography and analysis of Howard Thurman. Despite his prolific publishing record, his Thurman book seemed to have had a divine "Not yet!" holding it back from publication. In this volume, we explore the relationship between James Earl Massey and Howard Thurman, discuss the reasons that the book never made it into print, and present to readers the now-published book itself.

The Relationship between James Earl Massey and Howard Thurman

In early 1931, Howard Thurman preached in Detroit, Michigan, "in what had become an annual appearance in a Lenten series during Holy Week—Detroit by this time was home to an active and ardent Howard Thurman fan club."[3] Residing in Detroit was an infant named James Earl Massey. Eighteen years later in 1949, James Earl Massey and Howard Thurman would meet for the first time in that same Detroit Lenten series. Massey was nineteen years old and Thurman was forty-nine years old. Massey described how they met. "I first heard Dr. Howard Thurman preach in Detroit in the Spring of 1949. He had come to preach for three days during the Annual Noon-Day Lenten Services sponsored by the Metropolitan Detroit Council of Churches. The noon-hour services were held at Central Methodist Church downtown, quite a distance from my classes at the University of Detroit, but I decided that I should not miss seeing and hearing that renowned Black pulpit master." He convinced his fiancée Gwendolyn Kilpatrick to miss her classes at Wayne State University and join him at the service where Thurman was preaching.

Massey recalled, "The contents of the three sermons delivered by Dr. Thurman during those three days at Central Methodist Church

---

2. James Earl Massey, *Aspects of my Pilgrimage: An Autobiography* (Anderson: Anderson University Press, 2002), 448.

3. Peter Eisenstadt, *Against the Hounds of Hell: A Life of Howard Thurman* (Charlottesville: University of Virginia Press, 2021), 133.

are still vivid in my memory. I was moved by his preaching, very deeply moved, partly because what he said was so insightful, partly because hearing it all validated my own spiritual quest and findings in a way that no other preacher's words or pulpit approach had ever done, and partly because of the realization of divine presence I experienced in connection with his witness. As I listened, understood his witness, and experienced God in my spirit, I sensed then and there that Dr. Howard Thurman and I were inwardly kin."[4] At the end of the three-day series, Massey waited in line to meet, greet, and thank Thurman for the way he ministered to the young Massey. Over the years they would develop a very close kinship. Dr. Massey once told me that Howard Thurman was the person he felt most at one with.

In a letter to Howard Thurman in 1971, Massey recounts that first meeting in 1949. "As I left the sanctuary of the church that day I knew that I had found one whose insights spoke essentially to me. I knew that I had met a man whose range of concerns as a preacher would continue to bless my own pilgrimage. Afterward, I tried to hear you whenever you were scheduled to preach in Detroit, or at any point within driving distance of the city." He further recounts the impact of the encounter. "I had found another mentor for my life. I sensed in your presence and in your words something with which I had long been acquainted from my boyhood years—a presence, a feel, an awareness of exposure to the Spirit of God. . . . Your ministry has continued to be so for me across the years that I have been privileged to read your writings, hear you preach, and to know you at closer range."[5]

In 1956, Howard Thurman first received a letter penned by James Earl Massey to him. Massey writes: "This is not my first letter to you

---

4. Massey, *Aspects of My Pilgrimage*, 64-65.

5. Massey, James Earl. Letter to Howard Thurman. 5 November 1971. *James Earl Massey Papers*. Anderson University and Church of God Archives, Nicholson Library, Anderson, IN; see also "From James Earl Massey, 5 November 1971," in Walter Earl Fluker, ed., *The Papers of Howard Washington Thurman: Volume 5, The Wider Ministry January 1963-April 1981* (Columbia: University of South Carolina Press, 2019), 224-225. During Lent of 1971, Massey was the speaker for this same Detroit Lenten series where they first met. It was as if he had come full circle. See Massey, James Earl. Letter to Howard Thurman. 14 April 1971. *James Earl Massey Papers*. Anderson University and Church of God Archives, Nicholson Library, Anderson, IN.

but the first from me to you that you have had the occasion to read. I turned over in my mind, for many years, the desire to write to you and tell you what a blessing you have been through your writing and speaking. While in Europe in 1952, as a soldier, I wrote to you while you were still in California at the Church for the Fellowship of All Peoples—but alas: you didn't get the letter because I sent it to Los Angeles when it should have been sent to San Francisco! However, here is another occasion. . . . Perhaps I will someday be privileged to have you speak to our interracial congregation here. . . . During my vacation this summer, I intend to stop in Boston, if possible, and perhaps meet you really along with your family."[6] Thurman replied with a handwritten note on April 27, 1956: "How kind of you to take the time to write me . . . I will be preaching here . . . all during the month of June—it will be a pleasure to see you if you are in the city."[7]

There is no definitive record of the Thurman-Massey relationship. Massey wrote of his interactions with Thurman occasionally. More often when writing of Thurman, he spoke of his theology, preaching, and ministry. My summary here draws from Massey's writings, but also from personal recollections he and his wife, Gwendolyn Inez Kilpatrick Massey, shared with me in conversation. But the primary treasure trove of information comes from a collection of seventy-five or so letters between them from 1956 to 1978. James Massey saved letters he received from Howard Thurman and saved copies of letters he had sent to Thurman. So there is a rich reservoir of communication between them from which to assess their relationship.[8] Their correspondence exhibits a warmth of friendship, mentor-mentee engagement, and ministerial collegiality.

---

6. Massey, James Earl. Letter to Howard Thurman. 17 April 1956. *James Earl Massey Papers.* Anderson University and Church of God Archives, Nicholson Library, Anderson, IN; see also "From James Earl Massey, 17 April 1956," in Walter Earl Fluker, ed., *The Papers of Howard Washington Thurman: Volume 4, The Soundless Passion of a Single Mind June 1949-December 1962* (Columbia: University of South Carolina Press, 2017), 154-157.

7. Thurman, Howard. Letter to James Earl Massey. 27 April 1956. *James Earl Massey Papers.* Anderson University and Church of God Archives, Nicholson Library, Anderson, IN.

8. These letters are preserved at the *James Earl Massey Papers*, Anderson University and Church of God Archives, Nicholson Library, Anderson, IN.

One way to understand their connection is to note the many ways their lives and career journeys aligned. They were both raised in the Black Church but were pastors of congregations that aspired to and became multiracial. They both spent a significant portion of their careers in academia as Deans of Chapel, professors, and they served these institutions in many other ways. It is also important to note that they both were employed at Historically Black Colleges and Universities (HBCUs) and predominantly white institutions (PWIs). Both were engaged in the Civil Rights Movement and other avenues for seeking racial justice and reconciliation. These areas of alignment are also evident in what Massey chose to include in the biographical portion of his book on Thurman. He spends a significant amount of time describing the pastoral placements, the Dean of Chapel appointments, and the professorial roles of Thurman. Let me share some of these connections. I do so in a cursory manner when it comes to Howard Thurman, as Massey provides the details of his career in his biographical portrait in the next section.

When Howard Thurman graduated from seminary, he became the pastor at Mount Zion Baptist Church in Oberlin, Ohio.[9] This was a Black congregation whose worshipping attendance became multiracial when Thurman was in the pulpit. He did some further theological study at Oberlin College's Graduate School of Theology. Later, James Massey was an alumnus of Oberlin's School of Theology. According to Massey, the school had a "proverbial and enviable record as a place of racial openness since its earliest years."[10] Thurman's season in Oberlin, Ohio, was an important life and theological link for Massey.

Howard Thurman is known for leading the first intentionally multiracial and interfaith congregation in the United States, when in 1944 he decided to join Albert G. Fisk as the co-pastor of The Church for the Fellowship of All Peoples in San Francisco, California. James Massey was raised in the Church of God (Anderson, IN), which has

---

9. Massey shared in a letter to Thurman that he had preached at Mount Zion Baptist Church in 1965, "The memory of your work is still fresh there." Massey, James Earl. Letter to Howard Thurman. 7 January 1965. *James Earl Massey Papers*. Anderson University and Church of God Archives, Nicholson Library, Anderson, IN.

10. Massey, *Aspects of My Pilgrimage*, 195.

a foundational theological commitment to unity. For Massey, unity was best lived out in the local congregation. His pastorate at Metropolitan Church of God in Detroit aspired to what Thurman had accomplished at Fellowship Church. Massey described this effort: "Metropolitan Church of God, as I envisioned its scope and sought to shape its life and direction, was to be an interracial and cross-cultural fellowship. . . . Our setting in the Detroit metropolitan area not only allowed for an interracial and cross-cultural congregation, it demanded nothing less. . . . I was intent to develop a congregation whose members would not be fettered by any denominational or racial prejudices."[11] Massey was drawn to a relationship with Thurman due to this similar sense of calling. In his very first letter to Thurman he wrote, "Perhaps I will someday be privileged to have you speak to our interracial congregation."[12]

The Thurman-Massey alignment also exhibited itself in their significant involvement in higher education. Following his pastorate in Oberlin, Thurman returned to his alma mater Morehouse College, and also Spelman College, as a professor. Next he went to Howard University School of Religion as a theology professor and would eventually be named the Dean of Chapel for the entire university in 1936—"the first African American minister to be given that title."[13] Thurman shared in his autobiography that "the designation of chapel dean had been made only twice before on any American university campus, and for a long period thereafter there were only three such appointments in American education—at the University of Chicago, at Princeton University, and at Howard."[14] He would end his academic career as the Dean of Chapel at Boston University, making him the first African American to serve as Dean of Chapel at a predominately white university.

James Earl Massey's academic career began as the Principal at the Jamaica School of Theology in Kingston, Jamaica—where he served during a leave of absence from Metropolitan Church of God in Detroit. While in Jamaica, he received an invitation to be

11. Massey, *Aspects of My Pilgrimage*, 147, 167.

12. Massey, Letter to Howard Thurman. 17 April 1956. *JEM Papers*.

13. Eisenstadt, *Against the Hounds of Hell*, 8, 159.

14. Howard Thurman, *With Head and Heart: The Autobiography of Howard Thurman* (New York: Harcourt Brace Jovanovich, 1979), 88.

the Dean of Chapel at Anderson College (later renamed Anderson University) in Anderson, Indiana. Upon departing from Jamaica he would accept that offer, while also remaining as the senior pastor of Metropolitan Church of God in Detroit. During his time of discernment, he wrote Thurman who was then Dean of Chapel at Boston University: "I believe that it will be of particular interest to you that I, a Negro, have been invited by Anderson College (Anderson, Indiana), one of our Church of God colleges, to consider becoming dean of its chapel and coordinator of religious life. . . . Anderson College is an institution with over 1300 students, with less than 25 Negroes. . . . I write to you to let you know how your own ministry has given me inspiration across the years. I also write because I am interested in receiving your guidance on how to initiate such a program."[15]

Thurman replied and offered his "felicitations on your prospective appointment." Thurman proceeded to provide some suggestions. "My chief purpose was to develop, in connection with Marsh Chapel, a worship center which cut across all sectarian and class, race and creedal lines. It would seem to me that one of the functions of a Dean of Chapel in a denominational college would be to deepen the roots of the college community in the genius of the particular denomination and at the same time, to open windows into which the winds of God could blow from other regions beyond. . . . one should be free to experiment with worship forms and patterns and to provide a spiritual growing edge. . . . Above all else, it is important that your pulpit be a free pulpit which is a fearful responsibility upon the preacher."[16]

Howard Thurman also taught courses at Boston University as the Professor of Spiritual Disciplines and Resources. Massey noted in his letter regarding the invitation from Anderson College that "an added feature of the intended work is the teaching of classes whose subject matter fall under the category of religious life. Since this area is largely a matter of pioneering, I would appreciate suggestions you might offer in this regard also. I have read your *Disciplines of the*

15. Massey. Letter to Howard Thurman, 7 January 1965. *JEM Papers*.

16. Thurman, Howard. Letter to James Earl Massey. 18 January 1965. *James Earl Massey Papers*. Anderson University and Church of God Archives, Nicholson Library, Anderson, IN.

Spirit and observe that much of the materials are from your teaching while at Boston University."[17]

Massey noted in his autobiography that he taught a course at Anderson College titled, "Christian Disciplines and Resources." He stated further that "I was influenced in that choice by the success of Howard Thurman's pioneering course at Boston University on 'Spiritual Disciplines and Resources.' Some of the results of his course were published in his book *Disciplines of the Spirit* (Harper & Row, 1963). Out of my preparation and teaching I captured several aspects in my book *The Hidden Disciplines* (Warner Press, 1972)."[18]

After the death of Howard Thurman in 1981, James Massey would continue his academic journey as the Dean of Chapel at Tuskegee Institute (1984-1989; 1997-1998) and as the Dean of the School of Theology at Anderson University (1989-1995). Massey felt a special connection to Thurman while at Tuskegee. Thurman had preached a "trial sermon for campus ministry" there in 1929.[19] Thurman noted, "There I met George Washington Carver. To the end of my years I will carry in memory his face as he sat in his special pew in chapel, looking intently into mine as I preached the morning's sermon."[20] Massey wrote that "holding a post at Tuskegee . . . as my wife put it, 'had my name on it.'"[21] He wrote Sue Bailey Thurman, Howard Thurman's wife, that "I told Gwendolyn that Dr. T (Howard Thurman) had preached in the Institute Chapel many times, and that back in 1929 Dr. Robert Russa Moton had asked him to take the chaplaincy, but he had to decline because of his commitment to teach and preach at Morehouse and Spelman that fall. . . . In a sense, my deanship here has allowed him to minister anew, for apart from Dr. T's example and encouragement I might well not have moved in this direction of thought and work some years ago. But I did: and I have been so meaningfully engaged and joyously rewarded. Thanks for making tracks with him to the

---

17. Massey, James Earl. Letter to Howard Thurman. 7 January 1965. *JEM Papers*.
18. Massey, *Aspects of My Pilgrimage*, 284.
19. Eisenstadt, *Against the Hounds of Hell*, 118.
20. Thurman, *With Head and Heart*, 77-78.
21. Massey, *Aspects of My Pilgrimage*, 401.

water's edge."[22] Sue Thurman wrote to James and Gwendolyn Massey: "Dear friends, I can only regret that Howard is not here in person to greet and congratulate you on your installation day, as Dean of the Institute Chapel, September 9th. He would most likely be calling you early that Sunday morning (if he were not able to be present) telling you of his joy and expectation in this your high moment of fulfillment. There would be gladness, expressed in deep laughter and then he would wrap you in a prayer. But you must sense it all anyway even as I see it."[23]

Massey and Thurman shared the experience of serving at both HBCUs and predominantly white universities. We will see in Massey's description of Thurman's time at Morehouse, Spelman, and Howard the importance of HBCUs to Thurman. Massey writes of accepting the invitation to Tuskegee, "In going there I was moving intentionally into a major center of Black education and the Black American heritage in a new way. I sensed it was important for me to do so at just that time. More importantly, Gwendolyn and I felt assured that God was being honored in our going there to serve. The following years strongly confirmed the wisdom and timeliness of our choice."[24]

Both Thurman and Massey faced the racial challenges of being Black at predominantly white institutions. In his biography of Thurman, Paul Harvey notes regarding Boston University, "To accomplish what he had, as a prominent Black mystic and cosmopolitan at an overwhelmingly white and historically Methodist institution, was remarkable."[25] Peter Eisenstadt, associate editor of the Thurman Papers Project and biographer, offers a different perspective on Thurman's experience at Boston University and the issue of

---

22. Massey, James Earl. Letter to Sue Bailey Thurman. 17 October 1984. *James Earl Massey Papers*. Anderson University and Church of God Archives, Nicholson Library, Anderson, IN.

23. Thurman, Sue Bailey. Letter to James Earl and Gwendolyn Massey. Undated. *James Earl Massey Papers*. Anderson University and Church of God Archives, Nicholson Library, Anderson, IN. Written prior to the September 9, 1984, installation of James Earl Massey at Tuskegee Institute.

24. Massey, *Aspects of My Pilgrimage*, 359.

25. Paul Harvey, *Howard Thurman & The Disinherited: A Religious Biography* (Grand Rapids: William B. Eerdmans Publishing Company, 2020), 193.

racism: "If Thurman's mysticism, or disdain for the outer forms of religion and particularly those of Protestant Christianity, was one of the causes of tension during his years at Boston University, so too were personality clashes, fights with administration hierarchy, the great pull of demands on his time and attention, and the plight of a very proud Black man working exclusively with white colleagues, knowing or feeling the novelty of his appointment meant that he would be judged as much by the color of his skin as by his accomplishments or failures, and his perpetual uncertainty as to when and whether principled objections to his proposals carried a hidden tone of racial bias. Of all of Thurman's jobs, the one he liked least was Boston University."[26]

James Massey also experienced challenges in the white academic and church spaces where he provided leadership. "There were times when my bi-cultural upbringing and approach made me appear suspect when I was not in agreement regarding some issue involving race. There were occasions and settings when my being Black seemed to set me in a place apart, causing discomfort for some others, despite the fact that I fully belonged where I was."[27] Both Massey and Thurman were diplomatic in their public approach, more often speaking of racism in its systemic and historic forms, rather than sharing the personal affronts they had experienced. Having had such a long mentorship with Dr. Massey, he would at times share more bluntly with me.

In 2019, about a year after James Massey's death, his wife Gwendolyn shared with me in a conversation the importance of her husband's relationship with Howard Thurman for his own engagement with his Blackness. She recalled the first commencement he participated in at Tuskegee Institute. She saw him standing with some of the school's leaders and they had placed their hands on his shoulders. He had a look on his face as though he had found his home. Mrs. Massey later shared with her husband her assumptions based on what she had observed. He replied that she saw it accurately. Gwendolyn Massey felt that James Massey struggled with feeling at home in his Blackness having been in so many white contexts wondering if he was just a token. At the HBCU Tuskegee Institute,

---

26. Eisenstadt, *Against the Hounds of Hell*, 306-307.
27. Massey, *Aspects of My Pilgrimage*, 313.

he received the affirmation he needed and gained confidence that remained with him the rest of his life. She believed that prior to Tuskegee, Howard Thurman was the anchor that provided him with that sense of being at home in his Blackness. After Tuskegee, she said James Earl Massey finally wore the crown on his head he had been waiting to wear (borrowing a reference from Thurman).[28]

Thurman had spent years determined "to be at once Black (and) fully human."[29] Jesse Jackson, Sr. noted that Howard Thurman was "Black, but he did not wear his Blackness as a garment. He did not have to work at being Black. He was Black without effort; and so, he focused beyond ethnicity on that which is ethical."[30] Jackson's description of Thurman came to also be apt for Massey, thanks to Thurman's mentorship and later the enrichment of the Tuskegee context.

Thurman and Massey were certainly aligned in their commitment to the Civil Rights Movement and the work of racial justice and reconciliation. Howard Thurman served as a mentor to many of the faith-inspired leaders at the forefront of the Civil Rights Movement. Thurman was a Morehouse classmate and friend to Martin Luther King, Jr.'s, father[31] and recounts his relationship with King Jr. in his autobiography.[32] James Massey, also a friend of Martin Luther King, Jr., was engaged in the Civil Rights Movement from the context of his Detroit congregation. He writes: "The plethora of tragic happenings in Detroit and across America during the late 1960s affected me deeply, and quickened my concern to be more effective in the public arena as a moral and spiritual leader. The times demanded relevant spiritual activism and I felt compelled to be more strategically involved."[33]

The relationship between James Earl Massey and Howard Thurman can be understood through their aligned public and career

---

28. Howard Thurman, *Meditations for Apostles of Sensitiveness* (Mills College, CA: The Eucalyptus Press, 1947), 1. "A crown is placed over our heads that for the rest of our lives we are trying to grow tall enough to wear."

29. Eisenstadt, *Against the Hounds of Hell*, 367.

30. Eisenstadt, *Against the Hounds of Hell*, 367.

31. Eisenstadt, *Against the Hounds of Hell*, 158; Thurman, *With Head and Heart*, 254.

32. Thurman, *With Head and Heart*, 222-224, 254-255.

33. Massey, *Aspects of My Pilgrimage*, 244-245.

engagements. I could also share in a similar fashion the ways the content of their writings and their preaching intersected. The influence of Thurman on Massey as mentor and model is undeniable. Their shared passions and concerns mirror each other. The collection of their correspondence preserved by James Massey and now housed at the James Earl Massey Papers at Anderson University and Church of God Archives, Nicholson Library, Anderson, IN, offers a deeper and more personal glimpse into their relationship. The letters from 1956 to 1978 reveal a growing closeness.

The letters in the 1950s and 1960s used formal greetings like "Dr. Thurman"[34] and "Rev. Massey."[35] By the 1970s, Massey was greeting Thurman as "Dr. T."[36] and signing his letters "Your Son" or "Your Son James."[37] Thurman addressed Massey as "James," "James Earl," "Son James," or just "Massey."[38] As another sign of Thurman's affection for Massey, several of his letters included his trademark hand sketched penguin.[39] Massey wrote, "At the bottom of the letter, and to the left side of his signature, (a) tell-tale sign of an authentic letter from Howard Thurman (was) his hand-drawn pen and ink sketch of a penguin!"[40] Thurman had taken up the practice of sketching and painting penguins. In his autobiography, Thurman

---

34. Massey. Letter to Howard Thurman. 17 April 1956. *JEM Papers*. Massey's first letter to Thurman.

35. Thurman. Letter to James Earl Massey. 27 April 1956. *JEM Papers*. Thurman's first letter to Massey.

36. Massey, James Earl. Letter to Howard Thurman. 25 May 1973. *James Earl Massey Papers*. Anderson University and Church of God Archives, Nicholson Library, Anderson, IN. The greeting "Dr. T." is first seen. Also, Thurman hand signs a letter with "Dr. T." Thurman, Howard. Letter to James Earl Massey. 24 August 1974. *James Earl Massey Papers*. Anderson University and Church of God Archives, Nicholson Library, Anderson, IN.

37. Massey, James Earl. Letter to Howard Thurman. 5 November 1971. *JEM Papers*. Massey first uses "Your Son."

38. Thurman, Howard. Letter to James Earl Massey. 16 December 1970. *James Earl Massey Papers*. Anderson University and Church of God Archives, Nicholson Library, Anderson, IN. Thurman begins using informal greetings.

39. Thurman. Letter to James Earl Massey. 16 December 1970. *JEM Papers*. The first time a penguin appeared on a letter to Massey.

40. Massey, *Aspects of My Pilgrimage*, 270.

stated that "I paint the Penguin's View of Himself! When my friends say, 'That doesn't look like a penguin to me,' my answer is 'Maybe not. But it does to the penguin.'"[41]

In the letters written in the 1970s, they both express deep appreciation and admiration for each other. Some examples from Massey beyond what has already been noted earlier:

- Massey refers to two weeks spent in a seminar Thurman led at Virginia University as "the most important and meaningful weeks that I have ever lived. I want to say again that I am so indebted to you for your ministry and the marks you have left along the way so that I have been able to see my way as a younger man intent on living by truth. You have encouraged me across many weary years of searching and probing, praying and hoping. You have done so by example, your writings, your sermons on record, and your presence when it was possible for us to meet."[42]
- "I shall spend the Summer at Pacific School of Religion—and be near to assist you in any way needful, as well as learn more by 'sitting at your feet.'"[43]

Some examples from Thurman:

- "First of all, permit me to say how excited I was to see you and the apple of your eye at Germantown."[44]
- "It was good to visit with you. . . . I pray God that the demands upon your life are not greater than your root system can sustain."[45]

---

41 Thurman, *With Head and Heart*, 241.

42. Massey, James Earl. Letter to Howard Thurman. 9 September 1970. *James Earl Massey Papers*. Anderson University and Church of God Archives, Nicholson Library, Anderson, IN.

43. Massey, James Earl. Letter to Howard Thurman. 20 March 1972. *James Earl Massey Papers*. Anderson University and Church of God Archives, Nicholson Library, Anderson, IN.

44. Thurman, Howard. Letter to James Earl Massey. 16 December 1970. *JEM Papers*.

45. Thurman, Howard. Letter to James Earl Massey. 30 July 1972. *James Earl Massey Papers*. Anderson University and Church of God Archives, Nicholson Library, Anderson, IN.

- "I think God has blessed you decisively by giving you a good mind, reasonably holy enthusiasm, and a wife who can keep you confined to a manageable unit."[46]
- "It was utterly refreshing to see you and your girlfriend while I was in Indianapolis. . . . Let me know your plans for coming this way. Mrs. Thurman joins me in affectionate salutations to you and Gwendolyn."[47]
- "A little line because you are moving around in my heart all day. It is a good omen. . . . What a gift your spirit and mind are to so many of us. That I walk with you in prayer is no light utterance of a careless heart. Sue often speaks of your wife. I do not know what happened between them but she was touched deeply by something."[48]
- "Just a note to thank you for the article. It is a very sensitive and effective piece. You are utterly amazing to me. Please know how much I look forward to your sermons."[49]
- "You are a solid preacher. The 'Finger of God' certainly points you the way. I am grateful to God for you. . . . Much love to you and Mrs. Massey from the two of us."[50]

In June of 1971, Howard Thurman was invited to submit a letter of appreciation to be read at a celebration event for James Massey's twenty-fifth anniversary of ordination to Christian ministry hosted

---

46. Thurman, Howard. Letter to James Earl Massey. 1 January 1975. *James Earl Massey Papers*. Anderson University and Church of God Archives, Nicholson Library, Anderson, IN.

47. Thurman, Howard. Letter to James Earl Massey. 26 November 1975. *James Earl Massey Papers*. Anderson University and Church of God Archives, Nicholson Library, Anderson, IN.

48. Thurman, Howard. Letter to James Earl Massey. 21 August 1977. *James Earl Massey Papers*. Anderson University and Church of God Archives, Nicholson Library, Anderson, IN.

49. Thurman, Howard. Letter to James Earl Massey. 21 May 1978. *James Earl Massey Papers*. Anderson University and Church of God Archives, Nicholson Library, Anderson, IN.

50. Thurman, Howard. Letter to James Earl Massey. 23 June 1978. *James Earl Massey Papers*. Anderson University and Church of God Archives, Nicholson Library, Anderson, IN.

by Metropolitan Church of God in Detroit. It is a powerful affirmation of Thurman's love for Massey as a son. He writes, "There will be no word from anyone who stands in relation to you as I do. Under ordinary circumstances our paths would not have crossed and there would have been no moment of encounter to mark our kinship. But such is the mystery of Grace that our paths have crossed, and to the delight of our spirits it is as if we had been companions of the Way from the beginning. . . . On this occasion, therefore, I salute you as a blood brother of the mind AND of the spirit. If it had been my portion to have had a son and, as a part of the discreetness of life I had been privileged to custom-make him, he would be a young man like you. I say no more; no more is necessary to say."[51]

Why the Book was Never Published

In the 1970s when James Earl Massey was in his forties and Howard Thurman in his seventies, Massey penned a biography of Thurman that included an interpretation and assessment of his contributions.[52] In a letter Massey sent to Thurman in September 1970 he informed his mentor of the project, "You will be interested to know that I am fast at work on my intended book dealing with your theology. (I am not moving so fast without a carefully laid plan, however, and I have been at work on research across several years.) I promise to send a chapter or two at a time, asking that you assess the data and the treatment as you alone would be able to do."[53] As stated, Massey began to send chapters to Thurman that Fall. With the first chapter sent he wrote, "I am working away on the MS. My basic research started years ago. I believe that you will be pleased with what is

51. Thurman, Howard. Letter to James Earl Massey. 28 June 1971. *James Earl Massey Papers*. Anderson University and Church of God Archives, Nicholson Library, Anderson, IN. See Massey, *Aspects of My Pilgrimage*, 268-270.

52. For an insightful overview of Thurman's life and ministry during the 1970s when he and Massey were discussing Massey's proposed book, see Eisenstadt, *Against the Hounds of Hell*, 363-394.

53. Massey, James Earl. Letter to Howard Thurman. 9 September 1970. *JEM Papers*.

being shaped in your honor."[54] In December 1970, Thurman wrote of his intention to invite Massey to visit him so they "could talk everything through."[55]

In February 1971, Massey shared more details about his emerging manuscript. "My proposed title is Howard Thurman: His Pilgrimage and Theology . . . I have planned seven (7) chapters in all. . . . Chapter VII is planned as a chapter on your responses to my interpretation of your theology. We can sit and share some discussion, especially along the lines of some questions I will pose beforehand. I will tape the interview(s) and afterword edit them with your corrections before making them a part of the book."[56] They met in May 1971 for Massey to pose a set of questions to Thurman and engage in a broader conversation. That occurred and the results are found in Section Two in Chapter Eight, "Thurman and Massey in Conversation."

Massey continued to send chapters to his mentor. Thurman wrote Massey in July 1972 that he and his wife, Sue Bailey Thurman, were both reading the manuscript. He admits that despite getting the chapters previously, this was his first close read. "Mrs. Thurman is reading the MSS—I am taking it with me on the train & will look over it carefully and thoughtfully for the first time. I will write you a full & complete reaction with whatever must be addressed or taken away to make it both factual & truthful. If the acceptance comes meanwhile, hold everything until you hear from me after August 15th."[57]

Howard Thurman replied as promised. He began with some general comments. "I have read and re-read the manuscript. As I indicated to you in a previous note, I am embarrassed because I did not read, except very casually, the installments as you sent them alone. I

---

54. Massey, James Earl. Letter to Howard Thurman. 6 October 1970. *James Earl Massey Papers*. Anderson University and Church of God Archives, Nicholson Library, Anderson, IN.

55. Thurman, Howard. Letter to James Earl Massey. 16 December 1970. *JEM Papers*.

56. Massey, James Earl. Letter to Howard Thurman. 23 February 1971. *James Earl Massey Papers*. Anderson University and Church of God Archives, Nicholson Library, Anderson, IN.

57. Thurman, Howard. Letter to James Earl Massey. 30 July 1972. *JEM Papers*.

have a peculiar kind of self-consciousness that makes it very difficult for me to act critically where materials concerning me are written. I have made some two pages of notes having to do with corrections of fact and details of that sort. But all of this aside from my main and central feeling concerning the manuscript." Then he expressed his feeling that the manuscript needed greater focus. Massey needed to decide whether to do an assessment of Thurman's theology, preaching, and philosophy of religion; or to pen a biographical study. Thurman believed that Massey was better suited to do the assessment than the biography. So he suggested that Massey "develop the logic of the concepts that are present therein, using flashbacks into my past that may reveal the germination of the positions arrived at in my thought. Any materials which I have and any amount of time that you will need for clarification will be at your disposal. You are utterly capable of doing this. In my judgment you would make a major contribution to religious thought as expressed in the thinking of a man who is the grandson of a slave."[58]

A month later Massey replied, "I have read and reread your letter which gives your reactions to my manuscript dealing with your life and theology. I await the return of the manuscript, together with your pages of notes giving corrections of fact and details from your point of view. When I have received these materials, I will busy myself in making the necessary changes. Your suggestion about developing the technique of 'flash back' as a background against which your theology can be projected and better understood, is a challenging one. Your judgement that I am capable of performing this skillful maneuver encourages me to attempt it. At least, I will try, unless I see that I will make a mess of it."[59]

Thurman replied in December 1972, "I have delayed months in writing to you about the manuscript because what is needed is a detailed discussion. I have some two pages of factual correction, but that is inconsequential in the light of what seems to me to be

---

58. Thurman, Howard. Letter to James Earl Massey. 23 August 1972. *James Earl Massey Papers*. Anderson University and Church of God Archives, Nicholson Library, Anderson, IN.

59. Massey, James Earl. Letter to Howard Thurman. 28 September 1972. *James Earl Massey Papers*. Anderson University and Church of God Archives, Nicholson Library, Anderson, IN.

the best way to carry out the original design. What I have in mind is a very difficult undertaking but one which I am confident you can do." Thurman followed with an outline of what he had in mind as an assessment of his thought. "I realize that this is a far more difficult undertaking than one which you envisioned originally, but it is the only kind of volume covering material that is not already available."[60] Some months later, perhaps concerned that Massey was feeling challenged, Thurman sent a handwritten note, "Dear Massey, It has been a long long time since I have heard anything."[61]

A few weeks later, Massey responded, "Dear Dr. T, I have at hand your recent letter to me which did many things to my consciousness. For one thing, it stirred me to repentance—for waiting so long to write. For another thing, it stirred me to retaliate—but only mildly, since I was waiting on your two pages of factual corrections before I proceeded to complete the revision on which I have been at work. [And] still another thing, the letter deepened my love for you, realizing anew our common tie and the depth level on which our association continues to move. . . . Your suggestions on revision did involve me in a difficult undertaking. I am still in the midst of making the suggested changes in format. I suspect, however, that my greatest difficulty is in using the 'flash-back' technique. . . . At any rate, the reworking has been taking place and the final revision now awaits your sheets of corrections and a time of final discussion with you, presumably in San Francisco."[62] Massey closed his letter by sharing that his delay was also caused by some health issues.

Thurman responded immediately, "Before I see you in July, I will go through the manuscript again. Meanwhile, I'm anxious to see how the present form of the new manuscript takes shape. I realize it is much easier to have ideas concerning how rather than having

---

60. Thurman, Howard. Letter to James Earl Massey. 29 December 1972. *James Earl Massey Papers*. Anderson University and Church of God Archives, Nicholson Library, Anderson, IN.

61. Thurman, Howard. Letter to James Earl Massey. 6 May 1973. *James Earl Massey Papers*. Anderson University and Church of God Archives, Nicholson Library, Anderson, IN.

62. Massey, James Earl. Letter to Howard Thurman. 25 May 1973. *JEM Papers*.

the responsibility to do."[63] A few months later Massey informed Thurman that due to more health issues and surgery, he had made "very little progress on the manuscript changes. . . . How I wish that I were now done with the manuscript, ready to place it for handling in the lap of the publisher—having pleased your knowing eyes! This delay continues to disturb me, but I can wait for the Lord to renew my strength."[64]

In April 1974 Massey reported, "The book manuscript dealing with your life and pilgrimage has been completed.[65]. . . The enclosed Table of Contents shows the new pagination and reflects the preaching emphasis in the manuscript, namely the emphasis upon you as preacher." Massey had changed the title of the book from "Howard Thurman: His Pilgrimage and Theology" to "Howard Thurman: Preacher." Massey wrote that "your theology needs to be understood against the background of your life, which demanded restating a large part of what is to be found in your previous autobiographical works and the biography by Elizabeth Yates.[66] Although I would like to believe that those who would read this manuscript when it is published already know your life, I have discovered that many with whom I have been conversing are very much unaware of your pilgrimage—although they honor your ministry. For this reason, I have had to retain a lengthy focus on the background and the process by which God shaped your years. . . . The present revision, which is the fourth since I started, reflects my most mature expression in both writing style, concern for popular treatment, and theological insight into your work. I have followed your suggestions carefully, but I must confess that at some points in revising the manuscript I have

---

63. Thurman, Howard. Letter to James Earl Massey. 6 June 1973. *James Earl Massey Papers*. Anderson University and Church of God Archives, Nicholson Library, Anderson, IN.

64. Massey, James Earl. Letter to Howard Thurman. 20 September 1973. *James Earl Massey Papers*. Anderson University and Church of God Archives, Nicholson Library, Anderson, IN.

65. Massey, James Earl. Letter to Howard Thurman. 2 April 1974. *James Earl Massey Papers*. Anderson University and Church of God Archives, Nicholson Library, Anderson, IN.

66. Elizabeth Yates, *Howard Thurman: Portrait of a Practical Dreamer* (New York: The John Day Company, 1964).

chosen to leave some aspects of treatment as they were originally conceived."[67] It had been four years in the making and this was the fourth revision in response to Thurman's critiques.

In late August, Thurman wrote to Massey, "Dear James, I have postponed writing this letter for many weeks because I am unhappy about it. I have read and studied your entire manuscript. I asked the person who knows me best in the world, Mrs. Thurman, to read it carefully and to give me her reaction as well. My conclusion is that the manuscript is not satisfactory. I recognize the fact that you have put in a great deal of work and effort but the only way that I know is to express my authentic judgment concerning it." Echoing his earlier concerns, Thurman felt that the biographical portion lacked depth. As for the portion of the book that assessed Thurman's theology, he wrote: "In tracing the development the manuscript is sensitive and insightful. The great weakness is that it abounds in a series of quotations from my own books. The result is that what we have is an anthology of my religious material rather than an interpretation of their significance as the material passes through your creative mind and spirit and with what impact."[68]

Paul Harvey comments regarding Thurman's words to Massey, "As always, Thurman wanted his disciples to reflect more of their own inward journey than on repeating the words of others, even of the spiritual master."[69] Thurman wrote mentee and theologian Luther Smith in 1974 saying that Elizabeth Yates' biography did "not go into depth except when she is quoting." He further noted, a good biography "would have to be both factual and creative."[70]

Howard Thurman did not share with Massey the assessment of his wife regarding Massey's manuscript. But her handwritten notes about the manuscript have survived in the Howard Thurman & Sue Bailey Thurman Collections, Howard Gotleb Archival Research Center, Boston University. Sue Bailey Thurman wrote to her husband

---

67. Massey, James Earl. Letter to Howard Thurman. 16 April 1974. *James Earl Massey Papers*. Anderson University and Church of God Archives, Nicholson Library, Anderson, IN.

68. Thurman, Howard. Letter to James Earl Massey. 24 August 1974. *JEM Papers*.

69. Harvey, *Howard Thurman & The Disinherited*,183.

70. Eisenstadt, *Against the Hounds of Hell*, 379.

Howard, regarding Massey's manuscript: "I think if you take plenty of time . . . you could help this well meaning young man produce a final copy ready, if accepted, for print." She continued saying that Massey "was not a keenly observant writer and therefore depended on your relating the story of your life, for the meat of his interpretation." She noted certain points of disagreement with Massey's assessment or chronological placements. She was most disturbed by Massey centering Rufus Jones as his primary mentor in mysticism. She stated, "You were 40 leagues deep in mysticism long before you met . . . Rufus Jones. . . . If Massey would just stay with the facts, facts, facts of your life—then the truth, so long denied in your biographies, etc.—will emerge with blinding light! . . . It can still be a fine book and he does well when it comes to interpreting you as a preacher!"[71]

Howard Thuman closed his letter to Massey, "My suggestion is that you start all over again and plan your time so that we might work together on this biographical interpretation of my life. None of the work you have done is wasted. As you know if I did not believe in the quality of your mind the depth of your religious insight and your personal feeling for me, I would never have been involved. There is a tie that binds us together. If you still want to do this then let us make the kind of provision in time and opportunity needful." Wanting to ensure that his kinship with Massey remained, Thurman wrote, "Please, Jim, take this in the spirit in which I am writing it and know that it is as honest as I know how to be. My best to you. Dr. T." This is the only time I have observed in his correspondence that he called Massey, "Jim," and he uses Massey's term of affection "Dr. T," as his handwritten signature for the lengthy typed letter.[72]

After I read this letter for the first time, I wondered how their relationship survived it. James Massey had been writing this book for four years, even longer if earlier research is included. This was the fourth revision he had made. And now Thurman suggests that he start all over again. The next letter from Massey was four months

---

71. Sue Bailey Thurman, "Comments on Unpublished Biographical Draft of James Earl Massey" (ca. 1974). Folder 7, Box 17, Howard Thurman Collection, Howard Gotlieb Archival Research Center, Boston University.

72. Thurman, Howard. Letter to James Earl Massey. 24 August 1974. *JEM Papers*.

later and does not directly reference Thurman's letter. I must assume that they spoke by phone or in person about it. In this December 1974 letter, Massey suggested dates for "extended discussion periods in San Francisco." He also noted that he had "been studying additional models by which to recast the manuscript." He wrote, "I have examined critically Erickson's study of Gandhi but find it more psychologically oriented than would suit our purpose. Another study by Woelfel on the theology of Bonhoeffer's theology seems a bit more in line with our concern; I have also gotten much insight from de La Grange's book on Gustav Mahler. Perhaps during our visit together we can finalize the business of the model to be followed." He also noted that he had a sabbatical coming up with "the possibility of spending a portion of the sabbatical leave doing further study among your tapes. At any rate, the sabbatical will grant me sufficient detachment for restructuring of the manuscript for publication."[73] Thurman replied, "I like the idea of our having time together at staggered intervals. How it can be worked out is not clear."[74]

The next letter in the correspondence is nearly a year later. Massey was writing with birthday greetings to Thurman and referenced hearing Thurman speak: "It was just the right time, yet again, for hearing you treat anew some aspects of your life, unfolding them in still fuller fashion and further feeding my store of materials and understanding out of which my writing about you is being shaped. I shall not stop in my quest to write that which is worthy of your life and thought! Your pilgrimage and meaning demand the highest treatment possible on my part! . . . I will need a few more extended interviews with you and more time for analysis and critical reflection. God will grant us the time and the place, I am hopeful that a foundation will pick up the cost. I am applying for a grant to come West again for the summer and fall of 1976."[75] This is the last letter

---

73. Massey, James Earl. Letter to Howard Thurman. 19 December 1974. *James Earl Massey Papers*. Anderson University and Church of God Archives, Nicholson Library, Anderson, IN.

74. Thurman, Howard. Letter to James Earl Massey. 1 January 1975. *JEM Papers*.

75. Massey, James Earl. Letter to Howard Thurman. 14 November 1975. *James Earl Massey Papers*. Anderson University and Church of God Archives, Nicholson Library, Anderson, IN.

where the book project is mentioned. In a letter to Sue Bailey Thurman in 1985, four years after her husband's death, Massey wrote, "This is just a brief note to tell you 'Good Day!' and to share with you some of the latest results from my continuing research on your husband's life and work."[76] This may or may not be a reference to his unpublished manuscript. Even without publication, Massey was "the author of some of the earliest serious scholarly considerations of Thurman as a religious thinker."[77] He continued to be a scholar of Thurman until his death.[78]

Howard Thurman never did fully approve of James Earl Massey's rendition of his life and assessment of his theology. Thurman also was not much of a fan of Elizabeth Yates' biography.[79] Peter Eisenstadt states, "Before future biographers had their chance, Thurman wrote his own life story."[80] Howard Thurman wrote his own autobiography, *With Head and Heart* (1979). Massey had told Thurman that their work together on Massey's manuscript would "help you trace out lines of relationship in your developed thought as you prepare your autobiography. Perhaps in this way I will be of some help to you as well as to our readers."[81]

In an inadvertent way, Massey may have helped Howard Thurman. Sue Bailey Thurman's four-page handwritten note to her husband about Massey's manuscript was more than just an assessment of Massey's work. The note about Massey's manuscript served as a launching pad for her to discuss concerns with how her husband

---

76. Massey, James Earl. Letter to Sue Bailey Thurman. 12 February 1985. *James Earl Massey Papers*. Anderson University and Church of God Archives, Nicholson Library, Anderson, IN.

77. Eisenstadt, *Against the Hounds of Hell*, 293.

78. James Earl Massey, "The Church, Preaching, and Christian Music," in David S. Dockery, James Earl Massey, and Robert Smith, Jr., eds. *Worship, Tradition, and Engagement: Essays in Honor of Timothy George* (Eugene: Picknick Publications, 2018), 307-317. Published the year of Massey's death. It offers some thoughts on Thurman and music.

79. Harvey, *Howard Thurman & The Disinherited*, 234, "A biography that even Thurman admitted was not quite up to the task."

80. Eisenstadt, *Against the Hounds of Hell*, 379.

81. Massey, James Earl. Letter to Howard Thurman. 5 November 1971. *JEM Papers*.

seemed to dismiss her contributions to who he was. Paul Harvey comments, "Sue expressed some exasperation at her husband for implicitly, and perhaps unconsciously, subsuming Sue as a separate person into accounts of his own life he gave to interviewers and biographers."[82]

Sue Bailey Thurman wrote, "I have entirely given up on your references to me in telling your story by written or spoken word. That I start out in the narrative as a statistic—a non-person, simply says that you have not been able to deal with my 42 years joined to you. . . . It would do you good to state my contributions and meaning to your work, at least, for Massey, not necessarily to be included in the book, but as a good exercise for you until you can speak of me in some terms that would show a bit of affection in the matter of Being. . . . I think it is called 'preferred identity.' Where you have someone become a part of you in your ways that cannot separate out the things they do with you, or their thought, word, effort that has become so much yours—your products and possession, that the other person ceases to exist and becomes a non-person. Think about this and lets have it all come out in the light of the sun before the end of the age."[83]

Since Massey's book on Thurman was based significantly on his conversations with Howard Thurman, then the lack of credit given to Sue is a result of her husband not giving her credit. Howard Thurman was a human being, and a man that reflected male sentiments of the time. But as we will see in Massey's book, he was mentored by strong women—his mother, his grandmother, and Mary McLeod Bethune. And clearly, he was married to a strong woman.

Howard Thurman must have heard his wife's concerns. Maybe he even welcomed the moment of truth telling. By the time he wrote his autobiography he stated: "Sue brought into our coming together a rare beauty of person, clear and analytical mind, a sensitive imagination, and a fresh enthusiasm of heart that only love could inspire. In a manner that after forty-seven years remains a mystery, she related to me as a person, as a man, giving to me at my center a life of heart that made the whole world new. In the realm of ideas and dreams, she continues to be an active 'tennis player.' We play the court, bouncing the balls back and forth until there emerges

82. Harvey, *Howard Thurman & The Disinherited*, 45-46.

83. Sue Bailey Thurman, "Comments on Unpublished Biographical Draft of James Earl Massey."

an unanimity both of mind and of plan."[84] The Massey manuscript became a talking point for Sue to help her husband Howard Thurman realize that the person he had become was deeply intertwined with his wife Sue Bailey Thurman. So rather than this episode shining poorly on Thurman, it demonstrates his ability to hear women and make self and life corrections that aligned with his own belief in the unity and equality of all humanity.

Toward the end of the 1970s, it seems that James Earl Massey took a break from the project while Thurman aged and eventually died in 1981. After Thurman's death and Massey's selection to be the Dean of Chapel at Tuskegee University in 1984, Gwendolyn Massey shared with me that her husband told her that he put the book aside.

James Massey often told me and others that he had written a book about Howard Thurman that he planned to publish. I am not sure if he ever approached publishers following Thurman's death.[85] In his later years, he would tell me that he was waiting for the five-volume *The Papers of Howard Washington Thurman* project to be complete and published so he could add relevant citations. Massey served on the advisory board of the Howard Thurman Papers Project.[86] The editor-in-chief Walter Earl Fluker wrote regarding those supporting the Thurman Papers Project, "Most memorable is the late James Earl Massey, who, until his death in 2018, would call regularly and inquire about the work, and most importantly, the state of my soul."[87] Two of Massey's personal letters to Howard Thurman were included in published volumes.

In 2005, Dr. Massey asked me to serve as his literary executor upon his death.[88] In our conversations since that time he often

---

84. Thurman, *With Head and Heart*, 84.

85. During the 1970s season of writing, Massey approached Harper & Row, Eerdmans, and Abingdon regarding publications. Those letters of inquiry are found in the *James Earl Massey Papers*, Anderson University and Church of God Archives, Nicholson Library, Anderson, IN.

86. www.thurmanpapersproject.org

87. Walter Earl Fluker, Preface," in Walter Earl Fluker, ed. *The Unfinished Search for Common Ground: Reimagining Howard Thurman's Life and Work* (Maryknoll: Orbis Books, 2023), xvii.

88. Letter from James Earl Massey to Curtiss Paul DeYoung, November 5, 2005. In possession of the editor.

referred to my role. He even stated this as one of the reasons why he wanted me to work as an editor on what would be his last book *Views from the Mountain*.[89] He felt that my experience with publishers and as a writer, and my knowledge of his writing, equipped me for the role. In our many conversations through the years, he would often speak of his relationship with Howard Thurman and the unpublished book.

A few days after James Earl Massey's death, I entered his office called "The Outback"[90] at his home in Greensboro, Alabama. I hoped to discover his Howard Thurman book manuscript. In a phone call a few months before his death, I was asking again about his Thurman book (I would often ask about it). He sometimes spoke cryptically. He said on the phone, "I suppose it is time for me to give you the Thurman correspondence." This was his way of saying that he would not live to complete the Thurman book and he needed to pass that project to me. This was the first time I had heard that he also had a folder of correspondence between him and Howard Thurman. In The Outback on that hot Alabama day (over 100 degrees) I saw a box marked Howard Thurman. In that box I found a folder of his letters with Howard Thurman and a manuscript that appeared to be his book on Thurman—all now at the *James Earl Massey Papers*, Anderson University and Church of God Archives, Nicholson Library, Anderson, IN. The other Thurman item in his office that I saw for the first time was his painting of Howard Thurman, which serves as the cover of this book. I was not aware that portrait painting was among his gifts (he had also painted a portrait of Martin Luther King, Jr., that was hanging on his wall).

After James Earl Massey's death in 2018, the Alabama probate process slowed any consideration of immediately publishing the book. As time passed by, Mrs. Massey decided that the Thurman biography should not be published. From her vantage point, death had also silenced her husband's publishing voice. Then at her death in 2024, there was yet another Alabama probate process. Only now

---

89. James Earl Massey, *Views from the Mountain: Select Writings of James Earl Massey*, eds. Barry L. Callen & Curtiss Paul DeYoung (Glendora, CA: Aldersgate Press, 2018).

90. Massey, *Aspects of My Pilgrimage*, 444-445. He describes "The Outback."

with the support of the Massey family and the permission of the Anderson University Archives has the "not yet" become, now is the time!

The Uniqueness of the Massey Book

Eight years after the death of James Earl Massey, we bring his book to print. The final title that Massey gave to his book, listed in his last personal bibliography before his death in 2018, was *Howard Thurman: A Luminous Life*. I am using a version of that title for the entire volume. The latest manuscript that Dr. Massey had in his files was dated 1977 and titled *Howard Thurman: Preacher*. This 1977 version of his book manuscript, believed to be the most recent, is the one used for the development of this published book and is in the James Earl Massey Papers at Anderson University. As noted earlier, he originally titled his book: *Howard Thurman: His Pilgrimage and Theology*. A draft of this earlier version dated 1972 is in the Howard Thurman & Sue Bailey Thurman Collections, Howard Gotleb Archival Research Center, Boston University.

Since the manuscript of Massey's book on Thurman was written in the 1970s, the biographical section does not cite Thurman's autobiography, *With Head and Heart: The Autobiography of Howard Thurman* (1979), which was written after Massey's 1977 manuscript. It also does not speak of Thurman's death in 1981. Massey wrote about this in his own autobiography. New biographies of Howard Thurman have been written. Two of particular note, published in this decade, are the beautifully written *Howard Thurman & The Disinherited: A Religious Biography* (2020) by Paul Harvey and the seminal work *Against the Hounds of Hell: A Biography of Howard Thurman* (2021) by Peter Eisenstadt. Also the five-volume *Papers of Howard Washington Thurman* (2009-2019) offers an amazing chronological study of Thurman through his writings and correspondence.

There were few biographical treatments of Howard Thurman's life and thought available in the 1970s. There was only one book length biography of Thurman by Elizabeth Yates, *Howard Thurman: Portrait of a Practical Dreamer* (1964). Massey occasionally quoted Yates in his biography. Paul Harvey notes that Yates' biography is "a work that reads more or less like a transcription of Thurman's oral history of himself."[91] Massey was writing his book while Thurman was alive, and he was in collaboration with Thurman through many extensive personal conversations.[92] There were quotes in the manuscript without citation—likely from these conversations with Thurman. Massey's book was written from the vantage point of a mentee, admirer, and someone very close to Howard Thurman. This is not a critical biography. Yet Massey was one of the first to evaluate Thurman's theology and mysticism. He is a pioneer in scholarship on Thurman.

I kept the manuscript mostly in its original form. In many ways it is a period piece. I retained the present tense, since it was written while Thurman was alive. As Massey did with his own later writings, I have updated language to be gender inclusive and use current cultural/racial identifiers. (I have not changed any quotes from Thurman to reflect current sensibilities. They have been left in original form.) I have done light copy-editing. Occasionally I enhance Massey's biography with citations from Thurman's autobiography *With Head and Heart*, the five-volume Howard Thurman Papers Project, and the biographies by Peter Eisenstadt and Paul Harvey.[93]

I corrected a few factual mistakes I discovered in the manuscript. Earlier it was noted that Thurman had written two pages of corrections. It appears that those corrections were never sent to Massey. I read through a copy of the 1972 version of the manuscript from the Boston University Archives. On the manuscript Thurman made handwritten notes and corrections. None of these show up as corrections in Massey's 1977 manuscript. So I made those corrections. During the 1970s, there were no other biographies to compare his manuscript with, except for Yates' (which also contains some errors in its published form). Massey was completely dependent on Thurman for any factual or chronological corrections.

Massey wrote about Thurman through his own experiential lens as a pastor, Dean of Chapel, academic, and mystic. It seems that it was Massey's intent to use the biographical chapters as a foundation

---

91. Harvey, *Howard Thurman & The Disinherited*, 234.

92. Three audio tapes of conversations between Massey and Thurman are at the James Earl Massey Papers at Anderson University.

93. To differentiate from Massey's original citations in Section Two, I cite using this notation: **ED:**

for his analysis of Thurman's preaching and theology. This biographical portion contains very limited references to Thurman's family life, daily career activity, and the like. Thurman's work as a pastor and Dean of Chapel are presented with great programmatic detail. Massey does feature some aspects of Thurman's childhood, combined with a chapter on his study on mysticism with Rufus Jones, to set up his analysis of Thurman's mysticism.

One of Howard Thurman's critiques of Massey's analysis of his theology was that it read like an anthology of quotes from his many books. I would agree that Chapter Six does include extensive quoting. Thurman wanted Massey to engage in his own commentary on Thurman's perspectives. Had Massey finished his book in the years after Thurman's death, I am sure there would be more analysis through engagement with other Thurman scholars. At the time, Massey only had Thurman's actual work. Massey was mostly alone as a Thurman scholar. But we should not discount what Massey has done. He has categorized Thurman's theological musings from across his many books. So while at times one is reading extensive quoting, if we pay close attention to what Massey selected, we gain insights into Thurman's thought. And what powerfully insightful thought it was! Massey's own intellect enabled him to engage with Thurman, fully understanding his philosophically deep and contemplative perspectives. Across the analysis in Chapters Five, Six, and Seven, we experience Thurman as theologian, philosopher, preacher, mystic, and social commentator.

Chapter One describes Thurman's childhood in Daytona Beach, Florida; undergraduate years at Morehouse College in Atlanta; seminary education at Rochester Theological Seminary in New York state; and a pastorate in Oberlin, Ohio—during this time period his first wife Kate Kelly died. Chapter Two shares insights into Thurman's apprenticeship in mysticism under the tutelage of noted Quaker mystic Rufus M. Jones. Chapter Three recounts Thurman's academic leadership at Morehouse and Spelman Colleges and as the Dean of Chapel at Howard University; his life transforming visit to India and meeting Mohandas Gandhi; and marriage to his second wife and life partner Sue Bailey. Chapter Four notes the ways Thurman's life and ministry flourished in the prime of his life. He co-launched the first intentionally multiracial congregation in the United States—The Church for the Fellowship of All Peoples in San Francisco. His final vocational endeavor was as the Dean of Chapel at Boston University. This ends the biographical portion of the book.

Chapter Five serves as an opportunity for Massey to assess Howard Thurman as a preacher. Given Massey's status as a professor of preaching and noted preacher in his own right, this is a particularly valued reflection. In Chapter Six, Massey explores Thurman's theology. This begins with his foundational beliefs and his Christology. For Massey, the writings of Thurman offer an abundance of spiritual riches. So in Chapter Six there is too much to assess, therefore there is extensive quoting of Howard Thurman as noted. But yet, what is presented is very valuable. The reader should take their time in order to comprehend Thurman's insights—soaking in the spiritual depths. This chapter is one place where Massey offers some critique of Howard Thurman as it relates to his Christology. Chapter Seven focuses on Thurman's practical mysticism and interreligious perspective. In Chapters Six and Seven, we observe that Massey and Thurman are alike in mind, very deep, equally dense, yet powerfully insightful.

Chapter Eight is a conversation between Massey and Thurman. In preparation for his book, Massey sat down with Howard Thurman in 1971 and taped an interview. The final form is the result of them editing this together. The content here is unique and profound. It offers a rare glimpse into Thurman's relationship with his mentor Mary McLeod Bethune. Chapter Nine is a collection of Massey's reflections on Thurman in the years following his death that were not included in the original manuscript.

The Book Editor and James Earl Massey

I knew Dr. Massey for over forty years (1976-2018) as his student and mentee. As noted earlier, in 2005 he asked me to serve in a literary executor role due to my in-depth knowledge of his writings. I am also well versed in Howard Thurman. I met the Rev. Dr. James Earl Massey in 1976 when I arrived as an eighteen-year-old first-year student on the campus of Anderson College in Anderson, Indiana. He was the forty-six-year-old Dean of Chapel and Professor of Biblical Studies. I first sought him out for conversation when I learned he was a friend of Martin Luther King, Jr. I read King's books and listened to vinyl LP albums of his sermons during my high school years. It was not long until I was enamored by Massey himself.

I had heard Massey preach at our national church conventions. He and I were raised and ordained in the same denomination—Church of God (Anderson, IN). I discovered later that my mother knew of James Massey in her teens. My grandfather was also a Church of God minister. While serving as a pastor in Michigan, he would take his family to attend a local Church of God camp meeting in Burlington, Michigan, that served African American Church of God congregations. James Massey, also a teenager, would periodically play the piano for the worship services where my mother was one of two white youth in the camp meeting choir.

James Earl Massey was gifted in preaching, music, art, linguistics, teaching, writing, pastoring, scholarship, and on. Yet being born gifted does not automatically make you a grace-filled person. Massey was both gifted and grace filled. As a grace-filled person there was a dignity and reverence that always accompanied the presence of Massey and made those around him act in ways that honored him. For example, according to Massey, out of respect for his holiness beliefs, Martin Luther King, Jr., would never smoke a cigarette in front of him.

Over the years, Massey and his wife Gwendolyn extended to me much grace that shaped my life. A few years after college graduation, I was living and working in New York City and serving at Congregational Church of God in Harlem. On a visit to New York City, Massey asked me when I was coming to seminary. Of course, I immediately enrolled at Anderson School of Theology where he had become a faculty member. The following year—after taking as many Massey courses as I could fit into my schedule—I transferred to Howard University School of Divinity. The presence of James Earl Massey preceded me. Howard University's Dean of Chapel and preaching professor Evans Crawford, a close friend of Massey, said to one of my colleagues that "DeYoung came preaching," which said much more about Massey's renown as a professor of preaching than it did about my skills at the time. My wife Karen and I met with Dr. Massey a few months prior to our wedding in 1984, and he prayerfully blessed us with a vision of a time when interracial marriages would not be unusual or undesired. On July 7, 1985, Massey preached my ordination. He was the primary mentor in my life and ministry as I pursued pastoring, academia, and activism.

The most important mentor in shaping the Godly grace-filled James Earl Massey was Howard Thurman. Through the years, Howard Thurman was a ministry father mentor for James Earl Massey in the same way Massey was a mentor and ministry father for me. Once I was lamenting that I had never met Howard Thurman. A fellow Massey mentee responded, "If you know Massey you knew Thurman."

Now we read Massey's biography and reflections on his mentor Howard Thurman so that we might know the Thurman who Massey knew.

Photos

James Earl Massey with Howard Thurman

James Earl Massey with Curtiss Paul DeYoung

Correspondence

September 9, 1970

Dr Howard Thurman
Howard Thurman Educational Trust Office
2018 Stockton Street
San Francisco, California

Dear Dr Thurman:

I am still basking in the sunlight of the recent Seminar you conducted for us at Virginia Union University a few weeks ago. I do no violence to the truth when I report that the two weeks spent there under your leadership rank as two of the most important and meaningful weeks that I have ever lived. I want to say again that I am so indebted to you for your ministry and the marks you have left along the way so that I have been able to see my way as a younger man intent on living by truth. You have encouraged me across many weary years of searching and probing, praying and hoping. You have done so by your example, your writings, your sermons on record, and your presence when it was possible for us to meet. Again I say, Thank you!

You are scheduled to preach in Philadelphia on the first Sunday in November, I believe. My wife Gwendolyn and I are planning to be present in the service that day, if God permits. If your schedule will allow, I would like to invite you to return with us to Anderson, Indiana, and preach to our campus community in our chapel service on Tuesday morning, November 3rd, at 9 a.m. I know that you prefer to travel by train and I am confident that you could make connections between Philadelphia and Indianapolis, which is just about thirty-five miles from Anderson. It would be such a benefit to have you on the campus for that day, or any portion of it.

You will be interested to know that I am fast at work on my intended book dealing with your theology. (I am not moving so fast without a carefully laid plan, however, and I have been at work on research across several years.) I promise to send a chapter or two to you at a time, asking that you assess the data and the treatment as you alone would be able to do. By the way, there is a place on my office wall that I have left vacant for your picture, signed in your distinctive handwriting, of course. I will place it right beside the beautifully printed passage from your journal which you titled "On Viewing the Coast of Africa."

James Earl Massey
Campus Minister

JEM/jm

A letter from James Earl Massey to Howard Thurman, September 9, 1970

Letter from James Earl Massey to Howard Thurman, September 9, 1970

Dear Dr Thurman:

I am still basking in the sunlight of the recent Seminar you conducted for us at Virginia Union University a few weeks ago. I do no violence to the truth when I report that the two weeks spent there under your leadership rank as two of the most important and meaningful weeks that I have ever lived. I want to say again that I am so indebted to you for your ministry and the marks you have left along the way so that I have been able to see my way as a younger man intent on living by truth. You have encouraged me across many weary years of searching and probing, praying and hoping. You have done so by your example, your writings, your sermons on record, and your presence when it was possible for us to meet. Again I say, Thank you!

You are scheduled to preach in Philadelphia on the 1st Sunday in November, I believe. My wife Gwendolyn and I are planning to be present in the service that day, if God permits. If your schedule will allow, I would like to invite you to return with us to Anderson, Indiana, and preach to our campus community in our chapel service on Tuesday morning, November 3rd, at 9 a.m. I know that you prefer to travel by train, and I am confident that you could make connections between Philadelphia and Indianapolis, which is just about thirty-five miles from Anderson. It would be such a benefit to have you on the campus for that day or any portion of it.

You will be interested to know that I am fast at work on my intended book dealing with your theology. (I am not moving so fast without a carefully laid plan, however, and I have been at work on research across several years.) I promise to send a chapter or two to you at a time, asking that you assess the data and the treatment as you alone would be able to do. By the way, there is a place on my office wall that I have left vacant for your picture, signed in your distinctive handwriting, of course. I will place it right beside the beautifully printed passage from your journal which you titled "On Viewing the Coast of Africa."

James Earl Massey
Campus Minister

Howard Thurman

DEAN EMERITUS
MARSH CHAPEL
BOSTON UNIVERSITY

June 28, 1971

2020 STOCKTON STREET
SAN FRANCISCO 94133

To James Massey, my friend:

A letter such as this should be written with my fountain pen or my pencil. I refrain from using either, because I do not wish to add to the normal rhythm of your frustrations by creating for you a psychological impasse resulting from your inability to read what I have written.

I am profoundly pleasured to send this authentic word of appreciation and felicitation for and of the fact that this marks the 25th year of your Ordination as a minister of the Church. During this period of celebration, you will hear many things said about you and will receive many congratulations; but there will be no word from anyone who stands in relation to you as I do. Under ordinary circumstances our paths would not have crossed and there would have been no moment of encounter to mark our kinship. But such is the mystery of Grace that our paths have crossed, and to the delight of our spirits it is as if we had been companions of the Way from the beginning. You have the neatness of mind that is only matched by your neatness in dress. There is a neatness of mind that is stark, austere, antiseptic, and boring. Yours, however, is a neatness that is paradoxically exuberant, lush, creative. You could belong to any period in any age in any faith, but it happens that you belong to this period, this age, and to your particular religious faith. It is this timeless dimension of mind which I am characterizing by the word 'neatness' that is a part of the content of my thanksgiving to God that your life has touched mine and mine has touched yours.

On this occasion, therefore, I salute you as a blood brother of the mind AND of the spirit. If it had been my portion to have had a son and, as a part of the discreetness of life I had been privileged to custom-make him, he would be a young man like you. I say no more; no more is necessary to say.

May God secure you in all levels of your needings and grant to you in full measure all that is needful for your peace in the years left for your fulfillings.

Sincerely,

Howard Thurman

Howard Thurman

A letter from Howard Thurman to James Earl Massey, June 28, 1971

Letter from Howard Thurman to James Earl Massey, June 28, 1971

To James Massey, my friend:

A letter such as this should be written with my fountain pen or my pencil. I refrain from using either, because I do not wish to add to the normal rhythm of your frustrations by creating for you a psychological impasse resulting from your inability to read what I have written.

I am profoundly pleasured to send this authentic word of appreciation and felicitation for and of the fact that this marks the 25th year of your Ordination as a minister of the Church. During this period of celebration, you will hear many things said about you and will receive many congratulations; but there will be no word from anyone who stands in relation to you as I do. Under ordinary circumstances our paths would not have crossed and there would have been no moment of encounter to mark our kinship. But such is the mystery of Grace that our paths have crossed, and to the delight of our spirits it is as if we had been companions of the Way from the beginning. You have the neatness of mind that is only matched by your neatness in dress. There is a neatness of mind that is stark, austere, antiseptic, and boring. Yours, however, is a neatness that is paradoxically exuberant, lush, creative. You could belong to any period in any age in any faith, but it happens that you belong to this period, this age, and to your particular religious faith. It is this timeless dimension of mind which I am characterizing by the word 'neatness' that is a part of the content of my thanksgiving to God that your life has touched mine and mine has touched yours.

On this occasion, therefore, I salute you as a blood brother of the mind AND of the spirit. If it had been my portion to have had a son and, as a part of the discreetness of life I had been privileged to custom-make him, he would be a young man like you. I say no more; no more is necessary to say.

May God secure you in all levels of your needings and grant to you in full measure all that is needful for your peace in the years left for your fulfillings.

Sincerely,

Howard Thurman

Anderson College · Anderson, Indiana 46011
OFFICE OF THE CAMPUS MINISTER

November 5, 1971

DR. HOWARD THURMAN
HOWARD THURMAN EDUCATIONAL TRUST OFFICE
2018 Stockton Street
San Francisco, California 94133

Dear Dr. Thurman:

This is the month of your birthday. It is also the month of Thanksgiving Day. I am eager to be one of the first, if not the first, to extend greetings to you as you prepare to celebrate the meaning of your life. I am also anxious to express myself in a statement of thanksgiving and regard for you as one who has blessed my life immeasurably.

Dr. Thurman, I first met you in the Spring of 1949. You were in Detroit, Michigan, as one of the speakers for the Annual Lenten Services sponsored by the Metropolitan Detroit Council of Churches. It had been my custom to attend the noon-hour services there, so I went to hear you preach for three days. The crowd was not large on the first day when you ministered, as I recall, but as you began the sermon and developed it the sanctuary of Central Methodist Church seemed strangely full. It was a real listening and worship experience for me. My reactions to the sermon are still vivid in my memory. I was moved, very deeply moved, by the drama of the truth you uttered. The spirit of questing was evident throughout the service, and the experience of Presence was so engaging that I just had to attend the next two services and hear you preach again.

Dr. Thurman, you did not preach as others whom I had heard. There was an "insideness" to your words. There was a magnetism and an exhilaration in your expression. You were creative, arresting, and the subject-matter was appealing in its own right, while your style was at one with the subject-matter. I was both fascinated and fed.

I went forward to meet you when the service ended. I thanked you for your ministry. As I left the sanctuary of the church that day I knew that I had found one whose insights spoke essentially to me. I knew that I had met a man whose range of concerns as a preacher would continue to bless my own pilgrimage. Afterward, I tried to hear you whenever you were scheduled to preach in Detroit, or at any point within driving distance of the city. I had found another mentor for my life. I sensed in your presence and in your words something with which I had long been acquainted from my boyhood years -- a presence, a feel, an awareness of exposure to the Spirit of God. Dr. Thurman, you had preached with a contagious spirit

A letter from James Earl Massey to Howard Thurman, November 5, 1971 of worship, and your deed was an unmistakable aid to my worship. Your ministry has continued to be so for me across the years that I have been privileged to read your writings, hear you preach, and to know you at closer range.

I thank you for being who you are, and for being what you are in the will of God. Be encouraged as you live within the golden years of life. Be joyful as you meet new events in time. Be assured as you make new steps with each new day in this world.

"Be strong, and let your heart take courage, all you who wait for the Lord!" (Ps. 31:24)

Sincerely,

James Earl Massey

James Earl Massey
CAMPUS MINISTER

JEM/mrb

A letter from James Earl Massey to Howard Thurman, November 5, 1971 (cont.)

Letter from James Earl Massey to Howard Thurman, November 5, 1971

Dear Dr. Thurman:

This is the month of your birthday. It is also the month of Thanksgiving Day. I am eager to be one of the first, if not the first, to extend greetings to you as you prepare to celebrate the meaning of your life. I am also anxious to express myself in a statement of thanksgiving and regard for you as one who has blessed my life immeasurably.

Dr. Thurman, I first met you in the Spring of 1949. You were in Detroit, Michigan, as one of the speakers for the Annual Lenten Services sponsored by the Metropolitan Detroit Council of Churches. It had been my custom to attend the noon-hour services there, so I went to hear you preach for three days. The crowd was not large on the first day when you ministered, as I recall, but as you began the sermon and developed it the sanctuary of Central Methodist Church seemed strangely full. It was a real listening and worship experience for me. My reactions to the sermon are still vivid in my memory. I was moved, very deeply moved, buy the drama of the truth you uttered. The spirit of questing was evident throughout the service, and the experience of the Presence was so engaging that I just <u>had</u> to attend the next two services and hear you preach again.

Dr. Thurman, you did not preach as others whom I had heard. There was an "insideness" to your words. There was a magnetism and an exhilaration in your expression. You were creative, arresting, and the subject-matter was appealing in its own right, while your style was at one with the subject-matter. I was both fascinated and fed.

I went forward to meet you when the service ended. I thanked you for your ministry. As I left the sanctuary of the church that day I knew that I had found one whose insights spoke essentially to me. I knew that I had met a man whose range of concerns as a preacher would continue to bless my own pilgrimage. Afterward, I tried to hear you whenever you were scheduled to preach in Detroit, or at any point within driving distance of the city. I had found another mentor for my life. I sensed in your presence and in your words something with which I had long been acquainted from my boyhood years—a presence, a feel, an awareness of exposure to the Spirit of God. Dr. Thurman, you had preached with a contagious spirit of worship, and your deed was an unmistakable aid to my worship. Your ministry has continued to be so for me across the years that I have been privileged to read your writings, hear you preach, and to know you at closer range.

I thank you for being who you are, and for being what you are in the will of God. Be encouraged as you live within the golden years of life. Be joyful as you meet new events in time. Be assured as you make new steps with each new day in this world.

"Be strong, and let your heart take courage, all you who wait for the Lord!" (Ps. 31:24)

Sincerely,

James Earl Massey
CAMPUS MINISTER

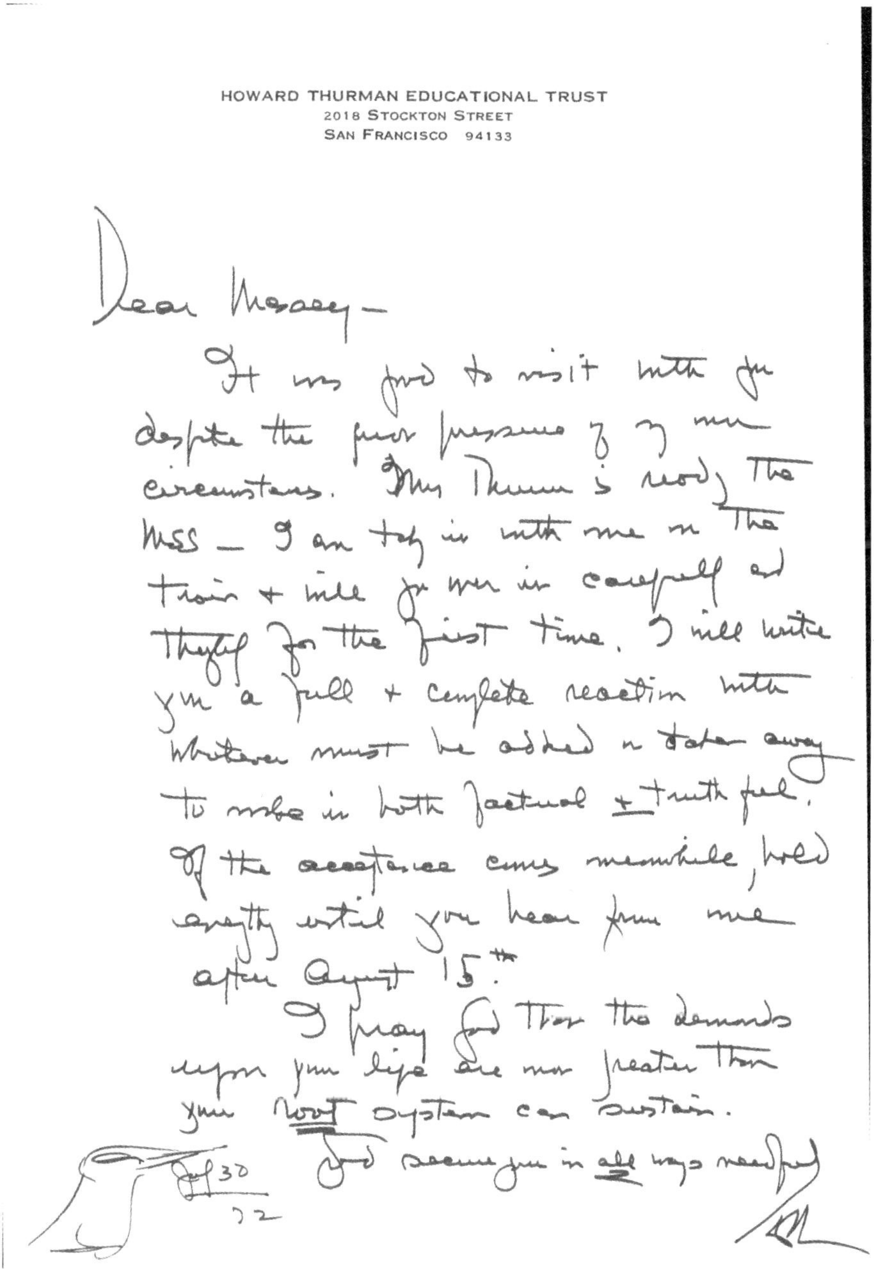
HOWARD THURMAN EDUCATIONAL TRUST
2018 STOCKTON STREET
SAN FRANCISCO 94133

Dear Massey—

It was good to visit with you despite the [illegible] pressures of my own circumstances. Mrs Thurman is reading the MSS — I am taking it with me on the train & will go over it carefully and thoroughly for the first time. I will write you a full & complete reaction with whatever must be added or taken away to make it both factual & truthful. If the acceptance comes meanwhile, hold everything until you hear from me after August 15th.

I pray God that the demands upon your life are not greater than your root system can sustain.

God secure you in all ways needful

Jul 30 72

A hand-written letter from Howard Thurman to James Earl Massey, July 30, 1972.

Letter from Howard Thurman to James Earl Massey, July 30, 1972

Dear Massey –

It was good to visit with you despite the great pressures of my new circumstances.

Mrs. Thurman is reading the MSS—I am taking it with me on the train & will go over it carefully and thoughtfully for the first time. I will write you a full & complete reaction with whatever must be addressed or taken away to make it both factual & truthful. If the acceptance comes meanwhile, hold everything until you hear from me after August 15th.

I pray God that the demands upon your life are not greater than your root system can sustain.

God secure you in all ways needful. HT

Anderson School of Theology

Anderson College, Anderson, Indiana 46011
Telephone: 317-644-0951

November 14, 1975

President
Robert H. Reardon
Dean
Barry L. Callen
Associate Dean
John W.V. Smith
Admissions
Hollis Pistole
Registrar
Lucille Shawn
Librarian
Delena Goodman

Old Testament
George Kufeldt
Gustav Jeeninga
New Testament
Boyce W. Blackwelder
Christian Doctrine
Barry L. Callen
Gene W. Newberry
Church History
John W.V. Smith
Church Ministries
James E. Massey
T. Franklin Miller
Hollis Pistole
Fredrick H. Shively
Pastoral Care
John M. Vayhinger
Christian Education
Jerry C. Grubbs

Dr Howard Thurman
2020 Stockton Street
San Francisco, California 94133

Dear Dr Thurman:

The time for birthday greetings has come again, and I am eager to submit my statement of appreciation to God and to you for what your life has meant and continues to mean for my pathway in the will of God. Happy Birthday!

The recent trip you made to Indianapolis was at just the right time, and I mean this in so many ways. It was just the right time for the church in which you ministered. It was just the right time for so many of those present to hear you and gain proper introduction to your meaningful thought. It was just the right time in terms of my Fall schedule, which found me in Anderson after a lecture trip which carried me to Pasadena, California, and Ashland, Ohio, just before you came. It was just the right time also for my wife's schedule, since she was free at least two nights from her set of responsibilities on various civic and county boards.

It was just the right time, yet again, for hearing you treat anew some aspects of your life, unfolding them in still fuller fashion and further feeding my store of materials and understanding out of which my writing about you is being shaped. I shall not stop in my quest to write that which is worthy of your life and thought! Your pilgrimage and meaning demand the highest treatment possible on my part!

I have continued to write, as expected. One new book will be published next April, as the enclosed letter-copy reveals. In connection with our project I will need a copy of the correspondence between you and Dr. Alfred Fisk. I will need a few more extended interviews with you, and more time for analysis and critical reflection. God will grant us the time and the place, while I am hopeful that a foundation will pick up the cost. I am applying for a grant to come West again for the Summer and Fall of 1976.

Greet Mrs Thurman for me. I send the warm regards of my wife Gwendolyn. Thanks again for blessing Indiana with your presence.

Sincerely,

James Earl

James Earl Massey

JEM/jem

A letter from James Earl Massey to Howard Thurman, November 14, 1975

Letter from James Earl Massey to Howard Thurman, November 14, 1975

Dear Dr Thurman:

The time for birthday greetings has come again, and I am eager to submit my statement of appreciation to God and to you for what your life has meant and continues to mean for my pathway in the will of God. Happy Birthday!

The recent trip you made to Indianapolis was at just the right time, and I mean this in so many ways. It was just the right time for the church in which you ministered. It was just the right time for so many of those present to hear you and gain proper introduction to your meaningful thought. It was just the right time in terms of my Fall schedule, which found me in Anderson after a lecture trip which carried me to Pasadena, California, and Ashland, Ohio, just before you came. It was just the right time also for my wife's schedule, since she was free at least two nights from her set of responsibilities on various civic and county boards.

It was just the right time, yet again, for hearing you treat anew some aspects of your life, unfolding them in still fuller fashion and further feeding my store of materials and understanding out of which my writing about you is being shaped. I shall not stop in my quest to write that which is worthy of your life and thought! Your pilgrimage and meaning demand the highest treatment possible on my part!

I have continued to write, as expected. One new book will be published next April, as the enclosed letter-copy reveals. In connection with <u>our</u> project I will need a copy of the correspondence between you and Dr. Alfred Fisk. I will need a few more extended interviews with you, and more time for analysis and critical reflection. God will grant us the time and the place, while I am hopeful that a foundation will pick up the cost. I am applying for a grant to come West again for the Summer and Fall of 1976.

Greet Mrs Thurman for me. I send the warm regards of my wife Gwendolyn. Thanks again for blessing Indiana with your presence.

Sincerely,

James Earl Massey

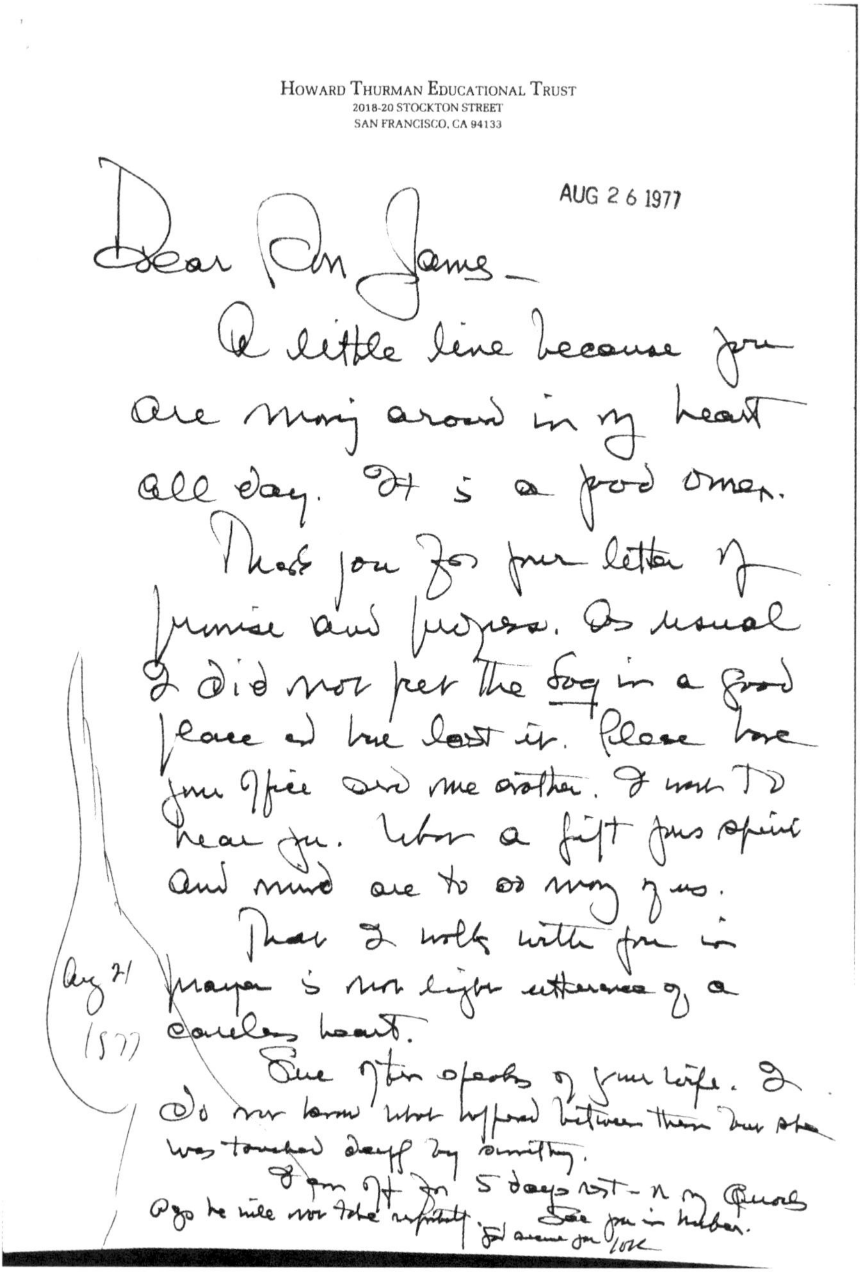

HOWARD THURMAN EDUCATIONAL TRUST
2018-20 STOCKTON STREET
SAN FRANCISCO, CA 94133

AUG 26 1977

Dear Dr. James—

A little line because you are moving around in my heart all day. It is a good omen.

Thank you for your letter of promise and progress. As usual I did not put the dog in a good place and have lost it. Please have your office send me another. I want to hear you. What a gift your spirit and mind are to so many of us.

That I walk with you in prayer is not light utterance of a careless heart.

Sue often speaks of your wife. I do not know what happened between them but she was touched deeply by something.

I am off for 5 days rest — in my [illegible] [illegible] he will not take [illegible]. See you in October. God [illegible] you. Love

Aug 21 1977

A hand-written letter from Howard Thurman to James Earl Masey, August 21, 1977.

Letter from Howard Thurman to James Earl Massey, August 21, 1977

Dear Son James,

A little line because you are moving around my heart all day. It is a good omen.

Thank you for your letter of promise and prayers. As usual I did not put the log[1] in a good place and have lost it. Please have your office send me another. I want to hear you. What a gift your spirit and mind are to so many of us.

That I walk with you in prayer is not light utterance of a careless heart.

Sue often speaks of your wife. I do not know what happened between them but she was touched deeply by something.

I am off for 5 days rest—or [as] my Quack[2] so go[es] he will not take responsibility. See you in November. God secure you. Love.

---

1. The word "log" refers to the log of radio sermons by Massey. In the letter prior, Massey notes that he has included a copy of the radio log.

2. "Quack" is a humorous reference to Thurman's doctor.

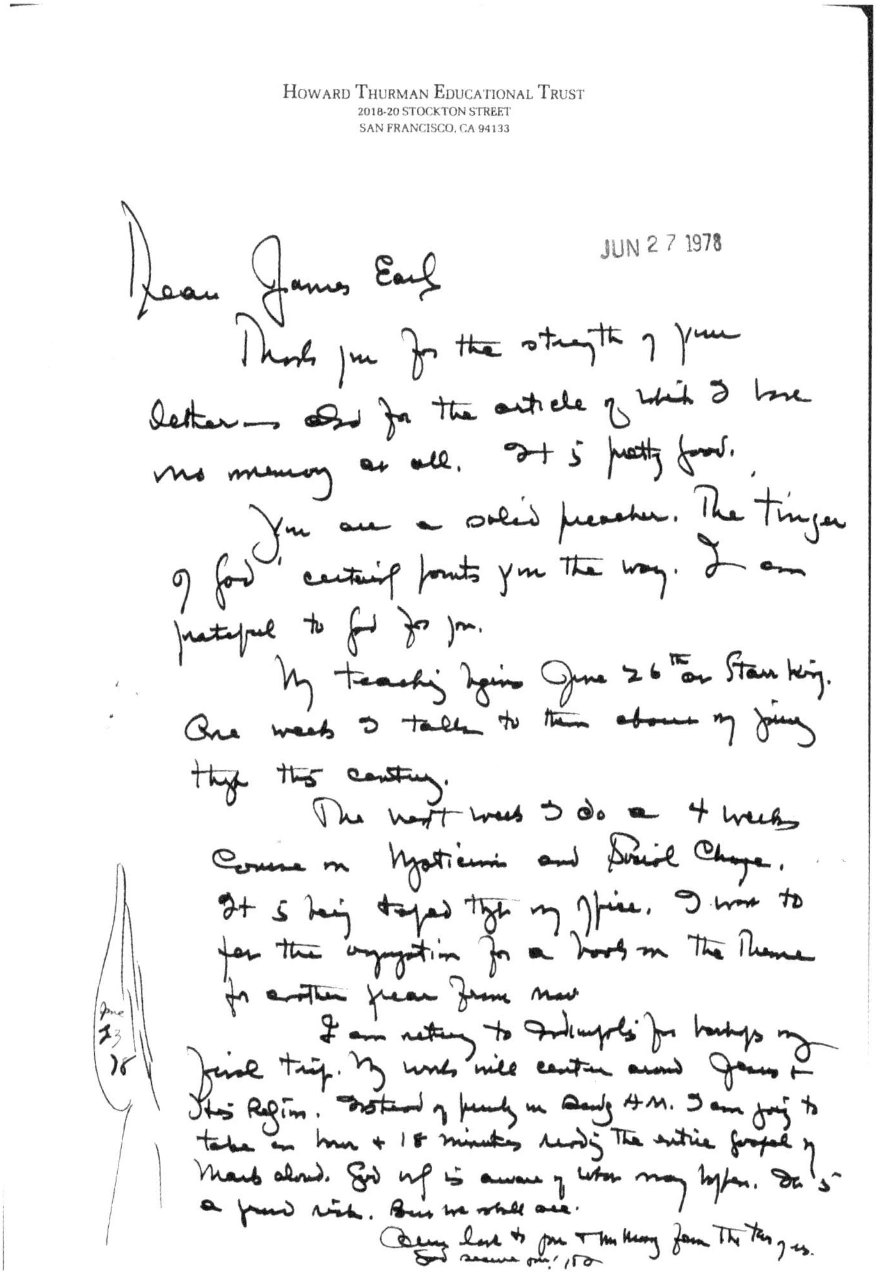
HOWARD THURMAN EDUCATIONAL TRUST
2018-20 STOCKTON STREET
SAN FRANCISCO, CA 94133

JUN 27 1978

Dear James Earl

Thank you for the strength of your letters and for the article of which I have no memory at all. It is pretty good.

You are a solid preacher. The finger of God certainly points you the way. I am grateful to God for you.

My teaching begins June 26th at Stanford. One week I talk to them about my journey thru this century.

The next week I do a 4 weeks course on Mysticism and Social Change. It is being taped thru my office. I want to put the organization for a book on the theme for another year from now

I am returning to Indianapolis for perhaps my final trip. My words will center around Jesus & His Religion. Instead of preaching on Sunday A.M. I am going to take an hour + 18 minutes reading the entire gospel of Mark aloud. God only is aware of what may happen. It is a grand risk. But we shall see.

Every love to you & the Massey from the two of us.
God sustain you! HT

June 23 78

A letter from Howard Thurman to James Earl Massey, June 23, 1978.

Letter from Howard Thurman to James Earl Massey, June 23, 1978

Dear James Earl,

Thank you for the strength of your letter—and for the article of which I have no memory at all. It is pretty good.

You are a solid preacher. The 'Finger of God' certainly points you the way. I am grateful to God for you.

My teaching begins June 26th at Starr King. One week I talk to them about my journey through this century.

The next week I do a 4 weeks course on Mysticism and Social Change. It is being taped through my office. I want to get the organization for a book on the theme for another year from now.

I am returning to Indianapolis for [the] lectureship[,] my final trip. My words will center around Jesus & His Religion. Instead of preaching on Sunday AM, I am going to take an hour and 18 minutes reading the entire Gospel of Mark aloud. God only is aware of what may happen. It is a good risk. But we shall see.[3]

Our love to you & Mrs. Massey from the two of us. God secure you! HT

---

3. The series of speaking engagements all agree with what is stated in the *Thurman Papers*, Vol. 5 Chronology.

SECTION TWO

Howard Thurman: This Luminous Life—James Earl Massey

Preface

Howard Thurman is a man whose composure and openness across many years have inspired the confidence and trust of others quite diverse from each other as well as from himself. It is not easy to deal with the secret of Thurman's attractiveness or compelling magnetism, but as one who has been influenced by his life, I have felt under necessity to at least try. Thus this book. The roots, pattern, and integrity of Thurman's religious thoughts are worthy of critical study, while his preaching and pulpit power deserve an extended assessment. Thus the theme and format of this study.

At a time when bitterness, hate, and competitive claims continue to splinter the groups in our land, Howard Thurman's work to affect human unity marks him as an exemplary person. Methodical, thoughtful, and committed, Howard Thurman has dared to share his religious convictions, his theology, and his full self. He did not know just where his dreams would carry him nor how God was leading him, but he trusted and worked with enthusiasm and faith. Aspects of his story are presented here and his thought is discussed.

Howard Thurman contributed directly to the preparation of this book, and the access I had to his files, tapes, journals, and manuscripts, together with many hours of conversation with him, has made my task much easier. In presenting his personal history, I have tried to see the details from an essential perspective, and I have tried to offer a responsible interpretation of the facts. In several instances interviews with Thurman yielded important additions to his thought on subjects, events, and people treated earlier in his published writings.

Portions of several chapters appeared in print earlier: sections of Chapter Two were published in the April 1972 issue of *The Journal of Negro History*, under title "Bibliographical Essay: Howard Thurman and Rufus M. Jones, Two Mystics"; portions of Chapter Seven were published in *Christian Scholar's Review* (Vol. I, No. 3, Spring, 1971) under title "Christian Theology and the Social Experience of Being

Black," and in *SPECTRUM: International Journal of Religious Education*, July-August Issue, 1971, under title "The Relational Imperative: Black Theology and Redemptive Relations."

The following persons were especially helpful in bringing this book through the many stages of its growth, and I thank them with all my heart: my wife Gwendolyn for her patience and encouragement; the typists-friends who by many drafts rendered my notes into intelligible typescript—Mabel Wilson, Mary Smith, and Eileen Clay. The final draft was prepared by Linda Foust.[1]

Finally, I express appreciation to the Danforth Foundation for the grant which made possible the leisure period for research and writing as an Underwood Fellow 1972-73.

JAMES EARL MASSEY
Anderson School of Theology
November 1977

---

1. **ED:** James Massey dedicated his book to his brothers: George, Raymond, Melvin, and Howard.

Chapter One

The Making of a Preacher

On Monday, May 23, 1955, Howard Washington Thurman was back in Daytona Beach, Florida, the place of his upbringing. He was one among more than 3,500 mourners there to attend the funeral service for Mary McLeod Bethune, the noted Black educator ranked during her lifetime among the fifty greatest women in the United States. Howard Thurman had returned to give the eulogy for this long-time friend and guide from his youth. His words that day, and the setting in which he spoke them, made him recall again the years when he was a child.[1]

Mary McLeod Bethune had known Howard as a thoughtful but high-spirited boy growing up in Daytona Beach fifty years earlier. She had been one of his guiding lights. The mourners gathered that day on the Bethune-Cookman College campus were many, and some of them reflected, as representatives, the esteem in which Mrs. Bethune was held by the national government and leading educational institutions across the United States, but few persons felt closer to her than Howard Thurman. Bethune had broadened his horizon; she was one of the first persons who helped him to understand that his black skin had nothing to do with the capacity of his brain or the worth of his life. This was very important as he lived through his boyhood years fearing the power of white people over his life. Howard Thurman began life as a very

1. **ED:** "Eulogy for Mary McLeod Bethune, 23 May 1955," in Fluker, ed., *Papers of Thurman, Vol. 4*, 123-131.

sensitive child who suffered much from the pressures imposed upon him by poverty and the ever-present fact of racial segregation. Mary McLeod Bethune had helped him to face his Blackness, his poverty, and his circumstances with responsible bearing. His eulogy at her funeral reflected his deep appreciation for her life and friendship.

The Daytona Beach Howard Thurman knew as a boy was a tourist town, a colony in the Winter season for white Northern businessmen and their families. He lived in a section called Waycross, an area racially separate from the rest of Daytona Beach; Ridgewood Avenue served as the dividing line. There were vast differences between the white world on the one side of Ridgewood Avenue and the Black world on the other. So many and so marked were those differences that if a Black person travelled in the white section after dark, they had to have a letter of authorization to do so.

Howard knew the "Negro" section of town and knew it well. Oak Street was there. Palm Street was there. Beach Street was there. There was Second Avenue, the main street of Waycross, but it was a rutted dirt road with unmanageable weeds growing all along it. Most of the houses in the Black section were frame buildings erected with minimal skill and placed without apparent pattern on the lots and yards. The area was very barely developed, but there were two redeeming features about it: the area allowed an open view of the ocean and it was rimmed by many palm and oak trees. The naming of Oak Street and Palm Street was quite apt. As a boy Howard Thurman began to regard the trees as a special part of the landscape. Watching the trees handle the stress of storms helped him to develop endurance. He even "befriended" one of the oak trees near the Thurman house and sometimes talked out his problems and feelings to that tree. Very early in his life Howard sensed within the world he knew a particular "aliveness," and he responded to that aliveness with imagination and interest.

Born on November 18, 1899, Howard Washington Thurman was the first and only son born to Saul and Alice Thurman. His father Saul worked for the Florida East Coast Railway and was part of a large labor force kept busy laying track and maintaining trackbeds. Saul's job kept him away from home for long periods of time so Howard and his sisters did not get to see their father very often. His father died when Howard was seven years old and that death made the family circumstances more crucial. His mother Alice was forced to find work, and her mother moved in with the family, presiding over its life with positive and ever-present control. As Howard grew older, he also worked, doing odd chores around town. In the Summer he caught fish and sold them; in the Fall he raked fallen leaves, collected discarded newspapers and magazines and took them to the city dump.

The death of his father left Howard the only male in the household. Outnumbered by females, he had to learn to live with women as the dominant figures around him. With his mother Alice (Ambrose) Thurman working for white families across town, during the days Howard developed a close relation with his strong, positive, and self-contained grandmother Nancy Ambrose.

Both mother and grandmother were ardent churchwomen, and both held high notions and hopes about the future of the Thurman children. Born as a slave, his grandmother lived until the end of the Civil War on a plantation near Madison, Florida. She was a woman of inward strength and outspoken convictions. She had pride, a sense of worth as a child of God, and was known to speak a decisive word that the entire Black community respected. She could sit on the porch of the house and control action along the entire block. Forbidden as a slave to learn to read, his grandmother lacked that skill. Howard had to read for her two or three times a week, and, by stipulation, always from the Bible. Although she could not read, he noticed that she nearly always told him what she wanted read: devotional Psalms, parts of Isaiah, and the Gospel accounts about Jesus. She had grown up with a deep sense of reverence for those particular parts she had heard her Black slave minister read and preach. After the grandson's reading sessions, she would meditate for extended periods of time.

Howard's grandmother was sensitive enough to recognize his abilities quite early. Having been denied so much herself, she was eager that the best would come to him. Believing that there is a magic in knowledge, she readied Howard daily for classes at the country school, made him recite his learning when he returned home each day, and kept reminding him about the seriousness of learning. She lamented the short school terms for Black children rightly seeing these as hindrances to a full education,[2] so she insisted that Howard must get all he could while in school. "My grandmother spoke compellingly about this

2. Henry Allen Bullock lists 123 school days per term for white children and 106 for Black children. See his *A History of Negro Education in the South: From 1619 to the Present* (Cambridge: Harvard University Press, 1967), 176-179.

matter, recalling her past and limitations. She insisted, with my mother, that I must go on." When he finished grade school in Daytona Beach, Howard's mother and grandmother had already discussed arrangements for him to attend high school. They chose the nearest private high school for African Americans; Florida Baptist Academy was a mission school one hundred and ten miles away in Jacksonville.

Howard's mother Alice was also strong. One quiet night after she had returned home and prepared herself for bed, young Howard chanced to discover one of the secrets behind her strength:

> When I was a little boy I chanced to enter my mother's room without knocking—my urgency was so great. My rush was arrested on the threshold by what I saw. The moonlight illumined one side of the room and there on her knees my mother was at prayer. What I saw in her face moved into the depths of me in a way that all the words and admonishings and teaching about prayer were never able to do. Deep spoke to deep, bypassing even the mind and the symbolism of the spoken word.[3]

Howard's mother and grandmother were two of a kind in many ways. Both lived by a sense of what was vital. Both worked to instill in their children the rules for wise living. Both laid stress on the need for honesty, thrift, carefulness of words, obedience, and respect for others. Both urged the children to live with regard for God. Both grandmother and mother encouraged nonviolence.

His grandmother once admonished Howard sternly against fighting, "No one ever wins a fight." He had been fighting on the street and came home showing sad evidence of the tussle. He described the fight: "I was something to behold. One eye was swollen, my jacket was ripped with all the buttons torn from their places, and there was a large tear in the right knee of my trousers. It was a hard and bitter fight. I had stood all I could, until at last I threw discretion to the winds and the fight was on." Thurman further recounted, "The fact that he was larger and older and had brothers did not matter. For four blocks we had fought and there was none to separate us. At last I began to gain in power; with one tremendous effort I got him

---

3. Howard Thurman, "Introduction," *Why I Believe There is a God: Sixteen Essays by Negro Clergyman* (Chicago: Johnson Publishing Co., Inc, 1965), vii.

to the ground and, as the saying goes, 'made him eat dirt.' Then I had come home to face my grandmother."

> Grandmother: "No one ever wins a fight."
>
> Howard: "But I beat him."
>
> Grandmother: "Yes, but look at you. You beat him, but you will learn someday that nobody ever wins a fight."[4]

It would be years before he learned to trust his fate to the weapons of love and nonviolence.[5]

His mother's morality code was so strict that she even forbade him to shoot marbles "for keeps"—a form of gambling. Thurman tells about the inward pain he experienced after disobeying her edict about this:

> It happens that I had sisters who found some mysterious use for all the marbles that I could accumulate. One day when I went to my cigar box I found that it was empty. I slipped out of the back yard and went down to the corner in quest of a certain boy. He was notorious in our community for his poor skill with marbles. But he always had many marbles because his parents were well-to-do. When I found him, I borrowed a few marbles from him and engaged him in a game "for keeps." As soon as I returned home, my mother, hearing my footsteps on the porch, called to me. My heart leapt to my throat. Great was my relief when she said, "I want you to run an errand." But all through that day and the next day there was a gulf between her and me. She was the same lovely person as always but now she was seen by me to be not my mother, but my judge.[6]

---

4. Howard Thurman, *Deep is the Hunger* (New York: Harper and Brothers, 1951), 10-11.

5. Thurman, *Deep is the Hunger*, 11. "Of all weapons, love is the most deadly and devastating, and few there be who dare thrust their fate in its hands."

6. Howard Thurman, "Keep Awake!" sermon, *The Christian Century Pulpit*, June 1937, 125; **ED.** Howard Thurman, "Keep Awake," in Walter Earl Fluker, ed., *The Papers of Howard Washington Thurman: Volume 2, Christian, Who Calls Me Christian April 1936-August 1943* (Columbia: University of South Carolina Press, 2012), 35.

Howard Thurman was four years old when Mary McLeod Bethune came to the Daytona Beach community in 1904. She came to establish a training school for African American girls, and this she did in founding The Daytona Normal and Industrial Institute for Girls. But in time Mrs. Bethune extended her concern and began to help young boys, especially those living in the "Midway" section of town where her school was located. Distressed daily by the sight of idle boys in the streets during certain seasons, she launched a Better Boys Club with a program oriented to the order of YMCA objectives.[7] Planned to supplement home life, school life, and church concerns, the Better Boys Club helped the neighborhood boys in reading, study, and social relations. The Club also helped them to have self-respect, a sense of responsibility, and race pride. Although never an official member of it, young Howard Thurman admired the club, shared some of its benefits, and even became known as "one of Mrs. Bethune's boys."[8] This might have been due, in fact, to his association with Albert, her son, who was about Thurman's age. Both Albert and Howard left town for high school studies: Howard to Jacksonville's Florida Baptist Academy, Albert Bethune to Augusta, Georgia, to Haines Institute, then afterward to the high school academy connected with Morehouse College.[9]

Another institution in the community that left its mark on Howard Thurman during his boyhood years was the family church. Daytona Beach had two Black churches then, one Baptist and the other Methodist. (A Roman Catholic congregation was started later.) The Thurmans were Baptists and were members under the Reverend Arthur L. James, an active leader in the community who exercised influence in several significant ways. He helped Mrs. Bethune get started in Daytona Beach and was one of the first trustees of her school.[10] Reverend James preached with feeling. In that setting, Howard began to sense the great drama that preaching and worship make possible.

---

7. Rackham Holt, *Mary McLeod Bethune: A Biography* (Garden City, NY: Doubleday and Co., Inc., 1964), 113-114.

8. Holt, *Mary McLeod Bethune*, 114.

9. See Edward Jones, *A Candle in the Dark: A History of Morehouse College* (Valley Forge: Judson Press, 1967), 98; Catherine Owens Peare, *Mary McLeod Bethune* (New York: Vanguard Press, Inc. 1951), 132.

10. See Holt, *Mary McLeod Bethune*, 59, 72-73.

Howard liked the preacher; he liked the freedom of the service. He responded openly to the influence of church life upon him and embraced faith when twelve years old during a children's revival service at the church. As was the church custom, all those who confessed faith had to appear before the deacon board of the church to be examined. When Howard went before the board, he confessed his faith, but with a statement that did not satisfy the board members. He was told that he should "go back" until he could confess a full Christian experience. Surprised, he reported this immediately to his mother and grandmother: "My grandmother brought me back to the meeting immediately and challenged the deacons with this statement: 'How do you know what God is doing in this boy's life? If he cannot join the church so as to learn from other Christians how to be a Christian, where else can he go?' They accepted me."[11] As a pre-teenager, then, Howard Thurman surrendered his life to God and began to follow Jesus. Thurman later explained:

> It is difficult to make clear precisely what happened to me during those formative years. Very early I distinguished between the demand to surrender my life to God and thus become a follower of Jesus, on the one hand, and the more prescribed demands of our local church, on the other hand.[12]

Howard's mother and grandmother discerned that God was at work in his life. They set themselves to sacrifice so that he could get an education for his role in life. The local principal also liked Howard and helped him complete eighth grade certificate studies, making him the first African American in Daytona Beach to achieve this result.[13] Howard left home in 1915 to stay with relatives in Jacksonville, attended school there, and earned his way through whatever jobs were available after school hours and on weekends.

---

11. Howard Thurman, *Footprints of a Dream: The Story of the Church for the Fellowship of All Peoples* (New York: Harper and Brothers, 1959), 17.

12. Thurman, *Footprints of a Dream*, 16.

13. **ED:** Daytona only funded Black students through the 7th grade. Since Black students could not complete the 8th grade, there was no public high school for Blacks. See Eisenstadt, *Against the Hounds of Hell*, 44.

Howard carried with him to Jacksonville a full but dilapidated trunk—shipped by courtesy of an unknown benefactor.[14] The clothes in the trunk were old and well-worn, nor did any of them match. He did not have one full suit or outfit. Howard lacked the usual items of affluence, but he got on well with his teachers. He also got on well with some students who saw his prowess in class and felt the impact of his eagerness and quick mind. Some other students tried to make him the target of their jokes, challenged, perhaps, by his evident abilities.

Thurman recalls a critical time in Florida Baptist Academy while studying plane geometry. All through the early part of the term he found it difficult to master the materials. Studying long and hard, he also sought help from anyone, teacher or student, whose grasp of the subject could make them helpful. At long last he began to see his way into plane geometry. As he tells it: "There came a day when the entire class was 'stumped' by a theorem that I could work. I raised my hand, shook my fingers, doing everything except calling the teacher's name. At last he called on me but not before he had reached my name in alphabetical order. I recited with a flourish. It was obvious to everyone but me that I was beside myself with arrogance." The classroom was silent. Howard assumed the teacher would express praise for his brilliance.

Finally the teacher spoke, "Will Howard Thurman stop by my desk when the bell rings." After the bell rangsignaling the end of the class session, Thurman approached the teacher's desk expecting that "the teacher was going to tell me that I had the makings of a great creative mathematician." The teacher spoke, "Howard, you must always do your own thinking but remember Wisdom was not born with you. That is all." Thurman reflects, "In these nineteen words there was held before me a mirror. What I saw I have never quite forgotten."[15] Howard was learning that knowledge in one area of inquiry does not give authority in every area of concern. He was learning respect for abilities and differences of gifts; he was learning reverence for truth and saw the need to escape arrogance and illusions of superiority.

---

14. A. J. Sullivan, "About Encounters: A Sketch of Howard Thurman," *Bostonia*, Fall Issue 1963, 7. **ED:** Thurman often recounted this story. For a fuller version see Thurman, *With Head and Heart*, 24-25.

15. Howard Thurman, *The Inward Journey* (New York: Harper and Brothers, 1961), 65, 66.

Doors of opportunity continued to open for Howard to find work. Tuition at the Academy was $1.50 a month and he always had enough work to earn and pay that amount. His health and strength held up, and both were tested daily since he had to walk two miles from home to school and back, four miles in all each day, with only one meal at home to sustain him. As problems arose, he prayed to God about them, just as he had done back in Daytona Beach. Again and again he recalled what his grandmother told him the day he left for Jacksonville. Having gathered his trunk, kissed his mother and grandmother goodbye, and was walking off to the station, his grandmother suddenly called him back. "Boy, there are some things I meant to tell you before you got away. Look up always. Look forward always. Don't look down. Remember everything you get you have to work for. And remember that God is as close to Jacksonville as He is to Daytona!"

Howard Thurman lived at Florida Baptist Academy and worked there scrubbing floors to earn part of his upkeep. This was arranged by the Academy principal who, impressed by Howard, wanted to help him reduce the problems in his path to preparation. During Howard's junior year the principal introduced him to a white benefactor interested in educating an African American boy. The benefactor had come to the principal seeking a student who showed promise of making good in life. "I have educated a Chinese boy," he said. "I have educated a Japanese boy. I have educated a Caucasian and all of them are making good. I want now to educate a Negro boy. Choose one for me from among your students." The principal replied instantly, "I have the boy. His name is Howard Thurman."[16] The man promised to help Howard forward as far as he was willing to go. He thereafter donated money to cover many of Howard's expenses through his senior year at the Academy.

On one of his visits to Florida Baptist Academy, Channing H. Tobias was told about Howard Thurman by the principal, who pointed him out as a lad of particular promise. Tobias was a distinguished religious leader and YMCA executive, whose word and respect strengthened the dream in Howard's teenage heart. In 1936, years later, Channing Tobias would reminisce about how they first met: "I met him first as a boy in his teens attending the Florida Baptist Academy, then located at Jacksonville. He was a serious student

---

16. Mary Jenness, *Twelve Negro Americans* (New York: Friendship Press, 1936), 150.

but showed keen interest in questions not directly related to his class work. He was the chief promoter of voluntary religious activities in the Academy and a debater of more than ordinary ability."[17]

The Student Years at Morehouse

Howard Thurman set his mind on Morehouse College in Atlanta, Georgia, long before he graduated from Florida Baptist Academy. There were many reasons behind that decision. Morehouse College was one of the most highly regarded institutions of higher learning for African Americans in the South at that time. It was a Baptist school, and he was a Baptist. It was the alma mater of some of his heroes and models. Morehouse also held a strong relationship with Florida Baptist Academy as one of the private secondary schools for Blacks in Georgia and Florida; many of the Morehouse students came from those secondary schools. Then, too, both the College and those secondary schools were all supported in part by the same American Baptist Home Mission Society. By arrangement with the Society, Morehouse offered annually two small scholarships for students from its related secondary schools who ranked highest in their graduating class and applied to the College for matriculation.[18] Howard Thurman received one of those scholarships when he enrolled at Morehouse College in September 1919. The scholarship was not large (only $25) but any amount was an incentive for this eager student.

Howard's eagerness was matched by an aptness for study and growth in learning. Both eagerness and aptness were needed because he had to work to support himself throughout his entire college career. Some additional financial help continued to come from the white benefactor who aided him while at Florida Baptist Academy. The man financed Howard's education during the Morehouse years, but the entire amount was never more than a hundred dollars a year, so it was always necessary for him to work for the rest of his needs.

Howard worked on campus for a while as office messenger for President Hope and Dean Archer. As he waited in his chair in the

17. Channing H. Tobias, "Some Outstanding Negro Christians," *The Missionary Review of the World*, June 1936, 295. Thurman was one of six African Americans that Tobias discussed and introduced to his readers.

18. See Jones, *A Candle in the Dark*, 34.

outer office, Howard was free to read and think. He had to utilize every free period because he was working thirty-six hours a week. Despite the daily pressure, he worked hard and earned excellent grades. He ranked first in his sophomore class and was elected president of it; he held first place during his junior and senior years as well. During his junior year Howard also won two honored prizes. One was the Willard Chamberlain Scripture Reading Prize, an all-departments competition, which yielded a $30 stipend for the winner. The second honor won was the Edgar Allen Poe Short Story Writing Prize.

There was something other than ambitious pride behind Howard's desire to enter the competitions. As his junior year began Howard saw that he needed some studies in philosophy, but the college offered nothing in that area except logic and ethics. He decided to try winning any of the cash prizes available on campus and thereby earn enough for Summer study at some university where courses in philosophy would be available to him. He decided that if he won the prizes, he would go to Columbia University in New York City. He won and went to Columbia. Living with a friend in Harlem, skimping on $.55 a day, Howard gave himself to philosophy, reading the works of Plato, Immanuel Kant, Spinoza, and Hegel, among others. There in New York City he had his first experience of studying beside white students. Filled with enthusiasm to learn, he assessed his gift of mind and thanked God for his brain. He was wide open to the insight flooding his mind that "a brain is a brain, and the package doesn't matter."[19]

Howard Thurman not only kept a job and gained excellent grades during his four years at Morehouse, he was also a valued member of the debate team during his senior year and a person to be feared in intercollegiate contests. He had been active earlier in the college Shakespearean productions. Under the direction of Louise Strong, his English professor, he acted a lead part in Hamlet in 1921 and in Othello in 1922. As for other activities, he was editor-in-chief of the Senior Class Yearbook during his senior year, president of the Morehouse YMCA, and president of the Atlanta Student Council—an interracial group with members from all of the colleges in Atlanta. He was also class valedictorian. All these opportunities for service were fulfilled even though he was still working thirty-six hours a week. Howard excelled because he had learned to discipline himself. Nor did he neglect friendships.

---

19. Jean Burden, "Howard Thurman," *The Atlantic Monthly*, October 1953, 40.

Howard was admittedly no ascetic. At night, after any activities that he had missed, Howard's friends would gather in his room to report: "They knew that I was interested and that I would be there studying."

Repeated invitations came from the social fraternities for him to join. Greek-letter fraternities were new on the campus when Howard entered Morehouse. He was asked to join during his first year there but he decided that he would not do so. There were several reasons behind that decision. Working as he did, there was no time for luxuries; he needed to give academic concerns priority over social possibilities. Poor as he was, there was no money for luxuries. Sensitive as he was, Howard did not believe that fraternities were democratic. Working for whom he did, he saw no reason for going against policies of the administration regarding fraternities. The Hope administration considered it illogical for Black students to set up social cliques among themselves when as an underprivileged group they needed the strength that only a sense of equality and solidarity can give. Lacking recognition from the administration, the Greek-letter fraternities operated off-campus. In later years, President Hope altered his policy of opposition and accepted the fraternities as worthy campus activities.[20] (Even then, although he was invited to join long after he had graduated, Howard politely refused the invitations.)[21]

Howard Thurman graduated with honors from Morehouse College in 1923. Along with Edward Swain Hope, eldest son of President Hope, and James M. Nabrit, Jr., Graham T. Perry, John W. Maxwell, Sr., among others, Howard Washington Thurman was a Morehouse man. He would see much of these men later, and he would know E. S. Hope and James N. Nabrit in settings of academic importance. He had heard President Hope's words to Morehouse students and had committed to memory the proud slogan of the campus "a Morehouse man cannot fail."[22] The President's chapel talks had made their point, and times of counsel with President Hope had given further guidance and timely encouragement.

As his senior year at Morehouse began, Howard applied to Newton Theological Seminary in Massachusetts requesting admission for

---

20. See Jones, *A Candle in the Dark*, 197-193.

21. Jones, *A Candle in the Dark*, 199.

22. Frederic R. Torrance, *The Story of John Hope* (New York: The Macmillan Co. 1948), 188.

ministerial training. He acted on information received while attending Florida Baptist Academy, both from visiting speakers there from the North who referred to that seminary in one way or another, and from many advertisements about Newton in magazines he found in the Academy library. His application for entrance was rejected on racial grounds. The letter of rejection suggested that he seek entrance to Virginia Union University, which as a Black school would better train him for the kind of leadership expected and needed by African Americans. He was being told that as a Black person he belonged with other Blacks. Disturbed by the rejection and its evident racism, Howard had gained painful insight into the world beyond the South. Applying soon afterward to Rochester Theological Seminary in Rochester, New York, he was gladdened by the reply that if his high grades continued during the senior year on the level of the three previous years, he would probably be admitted. He was told further, however, that acceptance could not be assured until the officials were certain that he was the best Negro to apply since the institution would only be admitting one. In late Spring 1923 Thurman received his letter of acceptance to Rochester Theological Seminary.

Upon graduation from college Howard Thurman knew where he would take ministerial studies. He also knew that he would be one of two Blacks attending that Northern seminary. The world of Blackness which he had taken for granted and only questioned now and then would soon come under examination as a matter of central consideration. Meanwhile, graduating with honors netted Howard a scholarship when he enrolled in seminary that Fall.

Seminary Student

The three years at Rochester was a period of questioning and questing along many lines: personal, social, and theological. Howard's experience as one of two Blacks in a white setting made his range of study far wider than he first imagined it would be. All considered, he was treated with courtesy and respect. Accepted by the other students, he did not find his color and race to be a forbidding problem as he did his studies. But being outside the Black world he had known all his life, he was forced to question the whole pattern of segregated church life. His white fellow students were training for ministry in white settings. He reflected, "This fact was omnipresent—the points of view in most of my class discussions, the attitudes of the fellows in the bull sessions, the etiquette of the place made this very clear, and this without hostility."[23]

Although the white students acted with freedom toward him in the study setting, he found that the church situation beyond the seminary was quite often otherwise.

There were occasional incidents of accommodation even in school, however. Thurman was invited once to move into a three-man suite by two white seminarians. When the administrative officer handling room assignments learned about this move, he said nothing to Thurman directly, but he reprimanded the two white roommates for the liberty they took inviting him to move in with them as the third man. This move represented a radical departure from what had been the dormitory rooming pattern. "Historically," Thurman explains, "the Negro students had always occupied two single rooms in the same wing on the theory that they needed to be close to each other for company and reassurance."[24]

As he assessed personal happenings in his life, watched social and racial process in northern church life, and delved into New Testament history and theology, Thurman took sharp issue with the accommodation of the church to faulty societal patterns. It became plain to him that the church was more of a secular institution than a responsible and open fellowship. He seriously searched to discover, "Where did Jesus of Nazareth and his gospel stand in all of this? Did the church part company with the Master in this particular emphasis on racial exclusiveness or not?"[25] He developed the thesis that segregation is not inherent in the Christian faith as Jesus intended it, that the message of Jesus had been given at first to the poor, the disinherited, and the dispossessed; that Jesus himself had been a poor Jew, thereby at one with the masses of people in the world; that Jesus had been a member of a minority race, and thus denied the rights and privileges taken for granted by citizens of the Roman Empire. He discovered that Paul, the first theologian of the church, was also a Jew but that his Roman citizenship gave him a freedom and privilege that Jesus could not know or experience as a noncitizen. This fact led Thurman to believe that such privilege

23. Thurman, *Footprints of a Dream*, 19.
24. Thurman, *Footprints of a Dream*, 20.
25. Thurman, *Footprints of a Dream*, 20-21.

influenced Paul's psychology and social philosophy causing him to even honor Rome's political system to the point of accepting slavery as a good.[26] Thurman took seriously the social context within which Jesus lived and taught, concluding that: "Christianity, in its social genesis, seems to me to have been a technique of survival for a disinherited minority."[27]

In 1935, following an address at the Annual Convocation on Preaching held at Boston University School of Theology, Thurman published his thought on this matter. Titled "Good News for the Underprivileged," that address was Thurman's response to the question about how Jesus' message was initially understood. Published in the journal *Religion in Life*,[28] it was the initial statement Thurman would expand across the years and finally issue as the book *Jesus and the Disinherited*.[29]

Howard Thurman decided during his senior year that he wanted to be an interpreter of religion. He wanted to help people discover spiritual insights by which to understand and shape their lives. This desire took root during his second year at Rochester, when

---

26. **ED:** Thurman "does not distinguish between the Paul of Acts and the Paul of the letters. Modern biblical critical biblical scholarship does make the distinction, however, and so there is a current debate as to whether Paul really was a Roman citizen, since he does not mention this fact in his letters." Lisa M. Bowens, *African American Readings of Paul: Reception, Resistance & Transformation* (Grand Rapids: William B. Eerdmans Publishing Co., 2020), 233, note 143. See also Peter Eisenstadt and Benjamin White, "The Apostle of Struggle: Reappraising Howard Thurman on Paul," *Church History* (2024), 93, 778–799; Allan Aubrey Boesak and Curtiss Paul DeYoung, *Radical Reconciliation: Beyond Political Pietism and Christian Quietism* (Maryknoll: Orbis Books, 2012) 14.

27. Howard Thurman, "Good News For the Underprivileged," *Religion in Life: A Christian Quarterly*, Summer 1935, 404. **ED.** Howard Thurman, "Good News for the Underprivileged, Summer 1935," in Walter Earl Fluker, ed., *The Papers of Howard Washington Thurman: Volume 1, My People Need Me, June 1918-March 1936* (Columbia: University of South Carolina Press, 2012), 265.

28. Thurman, "Good News For the Underprivileged," 403-409; **ED.** Howard Thurman, "Good News for the Underprivileged, Summer 1935," 263-270.

29. Howard Thurman, *Jesus and the Disinherited* (Nashville: Abingdon-Cokesbury Press, 1949).

Thurman met Grace Loucks, national director for YWCA conferences. Impressed after hearing him speak, she advised Thurman strongly that he should be heard in wider, larger settings. Thurman trusted her judgment and interpreted the invitations he received through her contacts as a way of reaching a larger field of service. Thus it happened that Howard Thurman became a popular leader in student conferences. Open to the new demands, he sought to appeal to all: Black and white, high school and college students, and young and old. He never liked being limited to only being a resource leader on race questions, but he was always delighted when summoned to serve in a religious role. When he graduated from Rochester Theological Seminary in 1926, the only Black in his class—and its top student—Howard Thurman was already a recognized and influential religious leader in student and college circles. He found himself accepted and admired on a wide scale and in quite varied settings.

The deepening desire to be an interpreter of religion rather than a "church" spokesperson put the young preacher in a position of jeopardy in some church circles. Dealing with universals was not always interpreted as he had hoped. This was especially the case in 1925 when, during summer work as student assistant to the pastor at First Baptist Church in Roanoke, Virginia, he was examined by a committee of ministers summoned by Pastor A. L. James in order to ordain him. The ministers were from the local Baptist Association. The interrogation did not so much involve Thurman's preaching abilities; having preached for several years he had developed some pulpit skills. Nor did the questions deal mainly with pastoral work. Pastor James had given Thurman a strong recommendation. Having tested him on the local scene, James considered Thurman trustworthy and ready. Bypassing pulpit skill and pastoral demands, they interrogated Thurman about his religious beliefs. The recent Scopes Trial had sensitized these church leaders to matters of doctrine. As Thurman gave his statement of beliefs and convictions, some of the ministers nodded approvingly at strategic points, some offered a verbal Amen. But one minister appeared to be dissatisfied with the statement and rose to his feet after Thurman sat down. He noted that the statement had mentioned nothing about the Virgin Birth, the divinity of Jesus, or the Resurrection! Nor, he stated further, had Thurman mentioned anything about the then hot subject of evolution! The dissenter spoke quite passionately for a while but the other ministers discerned that he was more emotionally involved than necessary, reasoned that he was reliving the Scopes Trial, and they tried to move on. After a few answers from Thurman about some points of question in his statement of belief he was finally dismissed from the meeting. The ministers voted that he should be ordained. When the ordination service was held, sometime later, Pastor Samuel A. Owens, from Thurman's boyhood church in Daytona Beach, came and preached the ordination sermon. Having filled his home church pulpit across several summers, Thurman had considered being ordained in his hometown, so that those who knew him from the start could share with him in the meaning of the event. But since Reverend James had initiated the process for his ordination there in Roanoke, Thurman thought it practical and timely to be ordained in Roanoke. He did request however that the pastor of the Daytona Beach church give the sermon and join the other ministers to ceremonially lay hands upon his head and offer prayers of blessing. "The laying on of hands was for Howard a charismatic experience," writes Elizabeth Yates. "Something was coming to him from each one, as well as from God. It had begun with the benediction that he himself had uttered, it continued through the laying on of hands. In wonder and amazement, Howard felt himself thoroughly anointed by the living Spirit of the living God. From this time on, he knew that he was a minister."[30]

The Oberlin Pastorate

Thurman's ability to interpret religious experience had good effect upon his first years in the pastorate. Answering a call from Mount Zion Baptist Church in Oberlin, Ohio, he went there as pastor after graduation, beginning his ministry in the Fall of 1926. Oberlin offered Thurman an open, historic setting within which to work. Founded in 1833, Oberlin was a religiously oriented settlement, named and chartered as "The Oberlin Society." There in Oberlin a tradition had developed for openness toward African Americans; in fact, Oberlin was a major way station along the Underground Railroad helping slaves reach freedom. At one time nearly one-fifth of the town's population was Black.

30. Yates, *Howard Thurman*, 76-77. **ED:** See Thurman's description in *With Head and Heart*, 58.

Mount Zion Baptist Church was also historic. Formally organized in 1886, the church had deep roots in the community and appealed particularly to Blacks not oriented to more formal types of worship in the town's white churches, none of which were organized along color lines. Under Howard Thurman's preaching the church complexion began to change, even literally. Although Baptist in background, the church became less denomination conscious under his ministry. Attendance increased and was integrated in pattern. Students from the college first began attending the services, then a few professors followed, coming regularly.

According to a section on Thurman in the published history of Mount Zion Baptist Church, "He was an impressive speaker, attracting many people from the entire community. Many times there was hardly standing room on Sunday morning because of the many townspeople and students who came to hear Rev. Thurman's excellent and mystifying messages."[31] Thurman has confessed:

> It was like refining fire to interpret religion each Sunday morning to a congregation which was composed of a few persons who could not read, many of very limited formal education, but also high school, college, and seminary students, and a few college professors. In addition to these educational categories, the racial categories were present also, Negro and white, with a few individuals each semester who came from beyond the seas.[32]

Thurman was at work living and teaching the spirit of inclusiveness. His church was Baptist, but he was helping the members to invest their background for richer dividends. The church was Black, but he was expanding its image and openness. Although an integrated service was the case, with admitted openness to receive any and all, Thurman thought it rather strange that "during that entire period, not a single white person ever joined the church."[33]

---

31. Fred L. Steen, "A Brief History of the Mount Zion Baptist Church of Oberlin, Ohio, 1886-1955," in *The Mount Zion Baptist Church: Golden Cornerstone Year*, privately printed, 1955, 27.

32. Thurman, *Footprints of a Dream*, 22.

33. Thurman, *Footprints of a Dream*, 21.

Thurman found that Oberlin offered opportunity as well for further theological study. Almost on the doorstep, as it were, of a famous center of theological education, the Oberlin College Graduate School of Theology, he enrolled in several courses there and came in direct touch with another major figure who was to do much for his inner life: Edward Increase Bosworth, dean of the Graduate School of Theology, and a scholar saint. Thurman recalls, "He was a man of medium height, with a relaxed face and quiet eyes, dapper in appearance in a saintly manner."

> I met him one day in the town haberdashery while he was in the act of selecting a necktie. The clerk informed me that it was a very painstaking task always when some article of wearing apparel was being chosen. I stopped by the counter for a word of greeting. "I am trying to select a necktie," said he. I believe that a man is under moral obligation to give to people who look at him, as completely satisfying an experience as possible. The clothes a man wears are also a part of the sacrament of living.[34]

Thurman considered Dean Bosworth a man of "crystal saintliness," so friendly and considerate that he sometimes walked two blocks out of the way just to say good morning to the janitor on the campus!

Thurman especially valued Bosworth as one who recognized the mystical element as part of a person's working equipment for a full life, and for his reasonable defense of that element as something other than a mere emotional state of mind. Dean Bosworth was known to talk personally as well as intellectually about being alive to God, feeling after God, numinous desire, and establishing God at the center of the self. Thurman discovered Bosworth as an experienced Christian mystic[35] and he read three of his major writings with deep interest: the book *What it Means to be a Christian* (1922), the pamphlet *What Prayer Can Accomplish* (1911), and an article published in *Religious Education* on "The Historic Jesus in our Present

---

34. Thurman, *Deep is the Hunger*, 157.

35. See Ernest Pyle, *The Biography of a Mind: Bosworth of Oberlin* (Chicago: At the Lakeside Press, R.R. Donnelley and Sons Co., 1948), 34-35, 219-301.

Religious Experience."[36] The studies had some effect upon Thurman's developing thought.

In one of his early books, *Deep is the Hunger*, Thurman reminisced about the death of Dean Bosworth in 1927:

> A few days after Dr. Bosworth's death, I went up on the campus to visit the library in Council Hall, the theological building in which Dr. Bosworth had had his office. I stopped at the entrance to chat with the janitor. I remarked, "We shall certainly miss Dr. Bosworth in the village." The janitor answered, "I don't think that anyone else will miss him in quite the way I shall miss him. During the many years that I have been here as a custodian, he was my friend. Many times in the winter, when I was shoveling snow, I have seen him walk across the campus, going two blocks out of his way just to tell me good morning. Every time he spoke to me, I felt that I was more of a man than I was before his greeting." The great Dr. Bosworth, honored on both sides of the Atlantic among countless students and others for his New Testament scholarship and the crystal saintliness of his beautiful life, walking two blocks out of the way to say good morning to the janitor![37]

Howard Thurman pastored the Oberlin Church for only two years. With widening contacts across the United States, and a growing concern for student life on high school, college and university campuses, he answered a call from President John Hope to return to Morehouse to serve as instructor in philosophy. He would also teach a biblical literature course at nearby Spelman College, a women's school, and be religious advisor for students at both schools.

Another factor that influenced Thurman's decision to return to the South was the poor health of his wife Katie. The family doctor advised a warmer climate in her interest. Kate Kelly had met and captured Thurman's eye when he was an undergraduate at Morehouse and she at Spelman. The sister of his close friend, Charles Kelly, Kate and Howard kept in touch through the years and married in 1926 when he graduated from Rochester Seminary. Thurman

---

36. See *Religious Education Magazine* (Vol. XX, No. 1), February 1925, 24-27.
37. Thurman, *Deep is the Hunger*, 158-159.

went to Oberlin with his wife. While there, a daughter, Olive, was born to them. After the move from Oberlin to Atlanta, Katie died in 1930. In the year prior to her death Thurman took a six-month study leave from his new post and went East to renew himself in the literature and discipline of mysticism. A scholarship grant from the National Council of Religion in Higher Education helped to make that leave for renewal and study possible. Thurman spent six months at Haverford College as a special student of philosophy under the noted Rufus M. Jones.

Chapter Two

At Haverford with Rufus M. Jones

Howard Thurman was honored by the Religious Education Committee of the Friends General Conference when he was invited in 1961 to give the Rufus Jones Lecture for that year. The address was later revised and enlarged for publication as a pamphlet in the Pendle Hill series. Thurman began by paying tribute to Rufus M. Jones, acknowledging the role Jones had played in helping him to understand the lines of life along which he was moving in the will of God.

> I would like to acknowledge in this Rufus Jones Memorial Lecture my indebtedness to him for so large a share in helping me to stake out the area of thought and the interpretation of experience which has been my formal concern for the past thirty years. In 1929, I was a special student with Rufus Jones at Haverford College. He gave to me confidence in the insight that the religion of the inner life could deal with the empirical experience of man without retreating from the demands of such experience. To state what I mean categorically, the religion of the inner life at its best is life affirming rather than life denying.[1]

Jones helped Thurman to better understand the elements of his spiritual quest and to interpret them more precisely for creative use.

1. Howard Thurman, *Mysticism and the Experience of Love*, Pendle Hill Pamphlet No. 115 (Wallingford, PA: Pendle Hill, 1961), 3.

The time at Haverford with Jones was the beginning of a long and deep relationship between two pilgrim mystics, an important period that would indelibly mark the rest of Thurman's life.

The six months at Haverford was the culmination of a request Thurman made to Rufus M. Jones after reading Jones's book *Finding the Trail of Life*.[2] The book was published in 1924. Thurman discovered the slender volume while attending a church conference on religious education in a town close to Oberlin, Ohio, where he was then pastoring. The book had been part of a pile of books placed for sale on a table during the conference. It cost only a dime, but as Thurman read the pages, he discovered that he had found a treasure. The reading also made him aware that he had found a new guide for his inner life, establishing an instant kinship with the author about whom Thurman yearned to know something more. Until then he had never heard or read that name, yet Thurman's reading of the book made him feel that he knew the spirit of Jones. Thurman read the book while he sat on the steps of the church building during a break in the conference schedule.

There in the book was the story of a man whose path was similar, whose experience had run near parallel to his own, whose thought was also centered upon a vital religion and godly experience. Thurman was further impressed that both he and the newly discovered author had a high but practical concept of God. The book made it clear that Jones was a Quaker but that was all it said regarding him. When he finished reading the book, and had reread certain special sections, Thurman set his heart upon finding the author one day to meet and talk with him. "He had what I wanted," Thurman said, "a combination of insight and social feeling."[3] In time, Howard Thurman finally realized his hope, meeting someone who knew Rufus M. Jones, and through that person met Jones himself. After corresponding with him at length, Thurman went to study under Jones during 1929, from January to June, as a special student in philosophy. He was given a room on the Haverford College campus.

The study at Haverford was a time of further learning about how to live from the inward depths. Thurman not only listened well to

2. Rufus M. Jones, *Finding the Trail of Life* (New York: The Macmillan Company, 1926).

3. Howard Thurman quoted in Jenness, *Twelve Negro Americans*, 154.

the great teacher, but he also spent unnumbered hours exploring his rich library. Jones had built up one of the most complete library collections in the United States on books dealing with mysticism.[4]

Jones was sixty-six years old at the time, seasoned and well-stocked in learning. He was also tired and ready for retirement, but he still felt "tremendously bound up with these men"—meaning the students with whom he was still vitally related as mentor and guide. In a letter to his friend John R. Mott, written during the same period of time, Jones commented on his situation, "I have found through my work here an amazing open door into lives and thoughts of students everywhere, and my interpretation of life and of God is ripening up in just the way I want it to." He also confided to Mott that "An intellectual task of spiritual interpretation does seem laid on me and I hesitate to go away and leave it."[5]

Howard Thurman, an African American, stood high among the students to whom Jones referred. With the rest of Jones's students, Thurman treasured his insights, responded to his enthusiasm, enjoyed his honest humor, and remained challenged by his scholarship and spirituality. There was a combination in Rufus Jones that Thurman had not found elsewhere in just that same blend. Heir to vast treasures from the classroom hours, Thurman reveled as well in Jones's library holdings on mysticism. He took especial interest in the books on the subject that Jones himself had written.[6]

Rufus M. Jones at that time was the leading historian of mysticism in the United States and he held status as a teacher in religious philosophy second only to William James. But Jones was more than teacher and historian. He was a reformer in the Society of Friends, a leader in Quaker world service, and an interpreter par excellence of vital religion. Thurman admired Jones's combination of spiritual insight and social concern, and took note that in 1928 Jones had led

---

4. Elizabeth Gray Vining, *Friend of Life: The Biography of Rufus M. Jones* (Philadelphia: J.B. Lippincott Co., 1968), 117.

5. Vining, *Friend of Life*, 228.

6. *Practical Christianity* (1899); *Studies in Mystical Religion* (1909); *Spiritual Reformers in the 16th and 17th Centuries* (1914); *The Inner Life* (1916); *The World Within Us* (1918); *Spiritual Energies in Daily Life* (1922); *The Church's Debt to Heretics* (1924); *Fundamental Ends of Life* (1924); *Finding the Trail of Life* (1924); *New Studies on Mystical Religion* (1927); and *The New Quest* (1928).

the American Friends Service Committee, as its longtime chairperson, into the work of bettering interracial relationships, among other things. Jones lived with a deep sense of responsibility to interpret the way of Christ to the world about him.[7] Howard Thurman was in the company of a man who was fully open to God and people. Writing to voice his concern to study under Jones, and to supply details about his previous training, Thurman had concluded the letter by reporting, "My color is Black."[8] Jones answered the letter without reference to that fact; he rather gave some details about housing and study.[9] Thurman's year at Haverford was with a committed, impartial, and uniquely resourceful Christian.

Life at Haverford allowed as well for the experience of worship in the plain Meetinghouse there. The focus of the customary silence helped Thurman to discover in a new way the creativity of silence. The friendliness of the worshippers after the meeting helped him to sense more deeply his involvement in a living fellowship.

There is much in Howard Thurman's later life and thought which suggests that Rufus M. Jones helped considerably to guide his thinking and deepen his life. Thurman's mysticism will be examined in a later chapter, but it is important to repeat here Thurman's acknowledged major legacy from Jones: "He gave to me a confidence in the insight that the religion of the inner life could deal with the empirical experience of man without retreating from the demands of such experience."[10] Rufus M. Jones helped Howard Thurman to stake out the primary area of enquiry for his thought, and under his guidance Thurman formalized the concern with which the rest of his ministry has been involved.

Thurman's sermons and writings show some of the influence of Jones's thought and teaching upon him. It is not possible to know just what aspects of belief were a part of Thurman's own thinking

---

7. Vining, *Friend of Life*, 224-225; see also Harry Emerson Fosdick's editorial introduction to *Rufus Jones Speaks to Our Time: An Anthology* (New York: The Macmillan Company, 1951), vii-xii.

8. Yates, *Howard Thurman*, 82.

9. <u>**ED:**</u> Thurman, *With Head and Heart*, 77. "During my entire time with Rufus, issues of racial conflict never arose . . . this aspect of my time with him remains an enigma."

10. Thurman, *Mysticism and the Experience of Love*, 3.

before the time at Haverford with Jones and what aspects of thought were entirely new formations during that season and immediately afterward. The growth or development of a theology is not always easy to trace. It is possible to indicate areas of thought and belief which show how Thurman and Jones correspond most surely in their writings and addresses.

There is an evident correspondence in their doctrine of God.[11] Jones and Thurman stand together on their doctrine of humanity. Their views accept some scheme of evolution, with the person as a child of God, not depraved (as in the classical Augustinian view), but a figure of dignity, an emergent part of a vital universe. Both Jones and Thurman hold strong reverence for human personality. Both agree essentially that formal creeds are usually divisive.[12] Both lay special emphasis upon the importance of ultimates, universals, and timeless truths for essential religious experience. Both Jones and Thurman joyously welcomed all aspects of truth as gifts from God, despite the corner of life or context of belief in which that truth first came to one's attention.[13] It is with purpose that Thurman recites so often those lines from Olive Schreiner about "The New Mother," placing emphasis upon the closing statement, "But shut your eyes to nothing that seems to them to be the truth."[14] Jones and Thurman can be seen in agreement at another point when they show a common dependence upon the inner light for guidance and authority, with but slight variation.

There are some points at which it appears that Thurman has been affected and influenced to some extent by Jonesian phraseology. The expressions suggest that Thurman not only listened with care to what Jones taught or guided him to read, but also to how

---

11. For a summary of Jones's theology of God, see Henry Nelson Wieman and Bernard Eugene Meland, *American Philosophies of Religion* (Chicago: Willett, Clark and Co., 1936), 121-129.

12. For Jones's view, see Vining, *Friend of Life*, 118; for Thurman's view, see *Footprints of the Dream*, 37-38, 54, and Howard Thurman, *The Creative Encounter: An Interpretation of Religion and the Social Witness* (New York: Harper and Brothers, 1954), 140-142.

13. Vining, *Friend of Life*, 227.

14. Olive Schreiner, *From Man to Man* (New York: Harper and Brothers, 1927), 158.

Jones phrased his insights. For example, there is a close relationship between Thurman's expression about "living one's way into life" and a statement Jones used in describing Buddha as having "lived his way down below the surface-life."[15] As another instance, Jones was fond of the figure about the inner and outer life, writing in one of his works, "So, too; there is an outer way and inner way and both are one." He added, "There is no inner life that is not also an outer life."[16] The same figure appears quite often in Thurman's works: a dedication line to his friend Eleanor Lloyd Smith in his book *Meditations of the Heart* lauds her as one "In whom the inner and the outer are one,"[17] while that image is given a more extended use in his book *The Creative Encounter*. The chapter headings are "The Inwardness of Religion," "The Outwardness of Religion," "The Inner Need for Love," and "The Outer Necessity for Love." Consider also the similarity of expression in the following titles: Rufus M. Jones titled one of his later books, *The Luminous Trail*, and Thurman titled one of his books, *The Luminous Darkness*.[18]

Other instances of likeness can be cited. Jones once wrote, "we muckrake for straws though a crown is just above our heads."[19] Thurman has often spoken about God having placed "a crown over our heads that we are forever growing tall enough to wear."[20] Such similarities in phrasing need not be the result of explicit borrowing. There is sufficient difference in the usage to show the marks of Thurman's imaginative insight even while it seems evident that he remained under the undeniable spell of Rufus M. Jones's poignant and picturesque imagery and speech patterns.

---

15. Rufus M. Jones, *Some Exponents of Mystical Religion* (New York: Abingdon Press, 1930), 22-23.

16. Rufus M. Jones, *The Inner Life* (New York: The Macmillan Co., 1916), viii-ix.

17. Howard Thurman, *Meditations of the Heart* (New York: Harper & Row, 1953), 5.

18. Rufus M. Jones, *The Luminous Trail* (New York: Macmillan Co., 1947); Howard Thurman, *The Luminous Darkness: A Personal Interpretation of the Anatomy of Segregation and the Ground of Hope* (New York: Harper and Row, 1965).

19. Jones, *Some Exponents of Mystical Religion*, 68.

20. Howard Thurman, *The Negro Spiritual Speaks of Life and Death* (New York: Harper & Brothers, 1947), 54-55.

Howard Thurman has continued to show variety, skill, and adaptability to his handling of themes and concepts. Consciously or unconsciously he has at times laid hold upon impressive data from his guided study under Rufus M. Jones; but in either case, Thurman would be eager to admit, with pleasure, that no idea is rootless and that there is no influence without its issue. If he has at times purposely utilized strains and lines from Rufus M. Jones, Thurman has done so with apt purpose, sensitive feeling, and sympathetic response to the great mind and spirit of a person to whom he is justly indebted.

The spiritual and intellectual togetherness of Jones and Thurman did not end when Thurman's special study leave at Haverford concluded. Correspondence continued between them across the years. On occasion they met to share ideas, interests, and projects.

One such project was of particular importance: it was an annual Prayer Fellowship in which both shared, together with ten other nationally known religious leaders. The Prayer Fellowship was convened by Glenn Clark in 1943, and Rufus M. Jones and E. Stanley Jones served as sponsors. A "Statement of Call" was issued to select persons whose lives "had been marked by a luminous trail as they moved about in the world."[21] The Statement read, in part:

> There are a number of sincere Christian movements of the Spirit abroad in America today, which have been born of the prayers of men and women that all Christians should be more spiritually ready to meet the challenging needs of today and the future. Some of these movements are within single denominations, some are interdenominational. All look to Christ as Lord and Savior, to prayer as a means of finding His will for us today, and accept the need to deepen our Christian experience, and then to apply it to our homes, in our daily work, and in the great political, economic and social problems that confront us.[22]

The Statement of Call suggested prayer as a means for creative change.

---

21. Rufus M. Jones, "Introduction," in Glenn Clark, compiler, *Together* (Nashville: Abingdon-Cokesbury Press, 1946), 7.

22. Jones, "Introduction," in Glenn Clark, compiler, *Together*, 9.

The first Prayer Fellowship meeting was held in Washington. The conveners hoped that a new thrust would spread out from the center of the national life. Having been invited, and serving at Howard University at the time, Thurman attended the first meeting. "That first meeting was intensely vital," Rufus M. Jones later commented, "and all who were there knew that it was the fresh initiation into a new stage of spiritual life of momentous importance."[23] The Prayer Fellowship continued across several years, meeting between Christmas and the opening week of each succeeding year. The group expanded as other people were invited to share. Soon, the range of interests within the group widened: correspondence was initiated with the President of the United States, representatives were sent to meet with ambassadors and other officials of other governments, and action was taken to send food to the hungry children of Europe. Along with these results, individual commitment and sense of adequacy deepened, thus helping to strengthen each member's ministry and effectiveness.

Thurman's contact with the Prayer Fellowship ceased when he left Howard University in 1944 and went to San Francisco as co-pastor of The Church for the Fellowship of All Peoples.[24] In 1946, however, Rufus M. Jones, Howard Thurman, and ten others from the group teamed in a writing project and put their concerns into print for the rest of the church. Titled *Together*, the book was published the same year, with Glenn Clark as compiler. The chapter Thurman submitted voiced a long-standing concern and gave his insights into a major church problem. The chapter was titled "God and the Race Question."[25]

---

23. Jones, "Introduction," in Glenn Clark, compiler, *Together*, 10.

24. **ED:** Thurman, Howard. Letter to James Earl Massey. 16 December 1970. *JEM Papers*. Thurman responded to a query from Massey regarding his research for the book that adds further detail for his reasons to end his attendance with the group. "I attended two of the Christmas meetings but did not ever feel myself to be organically a part of them. You see, James, there is something in me that rebels against the theory that I can call God up on the telephone and get Him to do what I want. I did not attend any group meetings after going to the West Coast."

25. Howard Thurman, "God and the Race Question," Glenn Clark, compiler, *Together*, 118-120.

Chapter Three

Campus Ministry 1930-1944

After the study with Rufus Jones, Thurman felt the need to learn still more about the inward journey and the mystic way. During the Summer of 1931, after his wife Kate's death, he went to Scotland for further meditation and travel in England as well. Desperately lonely after his wife's death in 1930, Thurman was seeking to transform his loneliness into solitude. What he wrote years later reflects that early experience of aloneness: "The observation may be correct that if one has never been solitary one has never been religious. It is the solitariness of life that makes it move with such ruggedness. All life is one and yet life moves in such intimate circles of individuality. The power of life perhaps is its aloneness."[1] He continued his reflection: "Each soul must learn to stand up in its own right and live. How blissful to lean upon another, to seek a sense of everlasting arms expressed in the vitality of a friend. We walk a part of the way together, but on the upper reaches of life, each path takes its way to the heights—alone." He came to the conclusion, "Ultimately, I am alone, so vastly alone that in my aloneness is all the life of the universe. Stripped to the literal substance of myself there is nothing left but naked soul, the irreducible ground of individual being, which becomes at once the quickening throb of God. At such moments of profound awareness I seem to be all that there is in the

1. Howard Thurman, *Meditations for Apostles of Sensitiveness*, 33; Thurman, *Deep is the Hunger*, 169.

world and all that there is in the world seems to be myself."[2] The lines are weighty and personal in tone and background.

While in England, Thurman had the chance experience of crossing paths with John Hope, the former president at Morehouse College during his student days. The two met in London. They saw each other across several days, attended some theatricals together, and, as expected, discussed racial affairs in the United States and the role of historically Black colleges and universities (HBCUs) in such a setting.[3] They talked in detail about Morehouse, Spelman, and Atlanta University[4] and about what Thurman's religious leadership could help effect on those campuses. As they parted, Hope was going on to visit Paris; Thurman was on his way back home to Atlanta.

Thurman's conversation with John Hope about his Morehouse and Spelman assignment is better understood when it is recalled that these two schools, together with Atlanta University, had affiliated in April 1929 to form The Atlanta University System. The new arrangement was to initiate a more economical and effective program of education. The three campuses were adjacent and operated by the same principles of interest. Morehouse and Spelman were to continue the undergraduate training of men and women, respectively, while Atlanta University was to function strictly as a graduate and professional school.

Dean of the Chapel: Howard University

Thurman did not remain long in the Atlanta area. He worked there until September 1932 when he accepted an invitation from Mordecai W. Johnson to join the faculty of Howard University School of Religion. Before leaving Atlanta, however, he married again. On June 12, 1932, he married Sue Bailey, a student secretary on the national staff of the YWCA, a long-time acquaintance since their undergraduate years. He was to teach Christian Theology, holding initial rank as assistant professor. Three years later he was named the first Dean

2. Thurman, *Meditations for Apostles of Sensitiveness*, 33: Thurman, *Deep is the Hunger*, 169-170.

3. Frederic R. Torrance, *The Story of John Hope* (New York: The Macmillan Co., 1948), 328-329.

4. **ED:** Renamed Clark Atlanta University in 1988.

of the Andrew Rankin Memorial Chapel. The new position seemed a logical move because of Thurman's aptness in chairing the University Committee on Religious Life, a responsibility he had carried along with his teaching load.

Howard University offered a cosmopolitan setting for higher learning and was oriented particularly to the education of African Americans. When Thurman went there in 1932 as a professor and leader of religious life, the University had a considerable number of Black faculty members and a predominantly Black student body. Since 1926 the University had been under the presidential leadership of Mordecai W. Johnson, the first Black to serve there in that capacity since the school was founded in 1867.[5]

Thurman viewed the Howard University assignment as a high compliment to his ministry. Mordecai W. Johnson was someone Thurman respected, looking upon him as a person of exceptional mind, distinctive accomplishments, strong character, wisdom, and as a skillful preacher and orator. Thurman had fallen under Johnson's spell shortly before graduating from high school, when, during a student conference at King's Mountain, North Carolina, he heard Mordecai W. Johnson speak. On that occasion, Johnson's background subject and style impressed the young Thurman. Speaking on the last night of the conference on the subject of the ministry as a vocation, Johnson's speech so moved Howard that he wrote Johnson a letter immediately afterward to ask advice on how best to implement his desire to be a preacher.[6] The letter bearing Johnson's answer came soon, and it was the first typed letter Howard Thurman had ever received.[7] He read it again and again, prizing it and contemplating the message it contained.[8]

---

5. To learn more about Mordecai W Johnson at Howard University, see Rayford W. Logan, *Howard University: The First Hundred Years*, 1867-1967 (New York: New York University Press, 1969), 242-244, 247ff.

6. **ED:** Howard Thurman, "To Mordecai Wyatt Johnson, 18 June 1918," in Fluker, ed., *The Papers of Thurman: Volume 1*, 1-4.

7. **ED:** Howard Thurman, "From Mordecai Wyatt Johnson, 8 July 1918," in Fluker, ed., *The Papers of Thurman: Volume 1*, 4-5.

8. **ED:** Eisenstadt, *Against the Hounds of Hell*, 291. Massey's first letter (1956) to Howard Thurman compared to Thurman's first letter to Mordecai Johnson.

Johnson, only ten years older, advised Howard to finish high school, go on to a four-year college, and then do seminary studies at a graduate school of theology. Young Thurman could hardly imagine a future at that point in his life—because getting as far as high school had been extremely difficult. But Thurman so valued the letter that he vowed to carry it on his person at all times during the years it would take to finish college, however many they be.[9] The letter remained a living link with a man for whom Howard held a deep sense of appreciation and respect.

It became evident across the years that the respect was not one sided. Just as Thurman had watched Mordecai W. Johnson, taking cues from his person and resourcefulness, Johnson had also watched Thurman's progress. Long before going to Howard University as president, while serving as pastor of the First Baptist Church in Charleston, West Virginia, Johnson had gone often to speak at Morehouse College, his alma mater. Thurman heard him during such trips and kept Johnson reminded that the instructions received from him some years earlier were being followed. Being elected in 1926 as the first Black president of Howard University increased Thurman's esteem for Johnson.

Meanwhile, Mordecai W. Johnson had taken note of Thurman's progress in the ministry. He had followed Thurman's occasional published articles,[10] and had noticed his wide ministry in distinguished speaking engagements in churches, college and university chapels, and conferences for youth. By 1932 when he appointed Howard Thurman to the faculty of Howard University's School of Religion, Mordecai W. Johnson had developed a high opinion of him as "an extraordinary personality."[11]

Thurman was on the Howard University campus at a time when great things of national and racial importance were in process. On the one hand, it was a time of economic problems across the land. Although Johnson appointed him for a specific assignment, he also hoped that Thurman's presence would attract more students for the seminary and also more support from new sources of finance.

---

9. Yates, *Howard Thurman*, 46-48.

10. See, for example, Howard Thurman's article on "Peace Tactics and a Racial Minority," in *The World Tomorrow*, December 1928, 505-507.

11. Logan, *Howard University*, 257.

The School of Religion needed that support because it could not receive government funding made available to the University's other schools and departments. A congressional act passed in 1928 forbade the use of government funds in religious categories at the University.[12] Increased support was needed from elsewhere to make the religion program match those of the other professional schools of the University. Although Howard Thurman was indeed a bright and attractive addition to the seminary faculty, even his presence did not help to bring the School of Religion any sizable increase from private philanthropy.[13] The Depression had left its indelible mark upon the national economy. Salaries throughout the University had been cut, necessarily. The School of Religion was especially ailing: four faculty members were doing the work for which eight were needed, and the total program needed further development to bring it to Class A level for graduate accreditation.

On the other hand, it was a time of educational and social ferment. The influence of the Harlem Renaissance was being felt most appreciatively at Howard University. As a leading educational center among Blacks, Howard University took special note of what was happening of a cultural and intellectual nature on the Black scene. In fact, some of the most outstanding persons involved in that cultural movement among African Americans were teachers on the Howard University campus, among them, E. Franklin Frazier the sociologist, Alain Locke the social philosopher-aesthete and anthologist, and Sterling A. Brown.[14] A race dynamic was at work among Blacks in the nation and the University was definitely involved in it.

Thurman's work was particularly significant at such a time. He knew the racial experience from the inside. He could relate most sensitively to the souls of Black folk. A person of open mind and sensitive spirit, he had the breadth of thought and concern to serve the entire campus, guiding in religious concern at a time of high

---

12. Logan, *Howard University*, 258, 272.

13. Logan, *Howard University*, 257.

14. See Logan, *Howard University*, 140, 320, 440-441, 492, 506, 539-540; John Hope Franklin, *From Slavery to Freedom*, Third Revised Edition (New York: Alfred A. Knopf, 1967), 506, 511, 558; and Harold Cruse, *The Crisis of the Negro Intellectual* (New York: William Morrow and Co., 1967), 22-23, 153-157, 171, 186.

hope on the one hand and strain on the other. Quiet, soft spoken, contemplative, but active, Howard Thurman worked on the scene to integrate an emerging social philosophy with a meaningful ethic. He wanted to match "cultural compulsives" with religious concerns.

The Howard University campus had a long history of interest in race, group esteem, and the strong demand for institutional self-control. The mood of the Black community in the United States found very literate and progressive expression there. The African American students at Howard, together with those of other leading Black liberal arts institutions, particularly Fisk University and Hampton Institute, had taken an informed and militant stance with respect to all these. The demand for staff to manage their own institutions began on those campuses as early as 1952 and led to frequent confrontations with controlling whites on the trustee boards and, in some cases, the faculties as well. Student unrest became so acute at Howard University that it led to the resignation of J. Stanly Durkee as President there in 1926, and the appointment of Mordecai W. Johnson, an African American, as president.[15]

Howard Thurman knew this climate and outlook. His years on Black campuses had helped him to value properly such a concern. The very nature of his own pilgrimage and experiences made him a ready ally. But while he was determined to work with student and race hopes in mind, he was firm in the will to deal with those hopes and concerns in his own way. He rejected cultural isolationism in favor of togetherness. He set himself to help the campus explore race concerns against a background of religious values and to build on an adequate spiritual basis. He knew that educational opportunities are more significant when balanced with insights from the religious dimension. In the classroom, chapel, and through counsel, Thurman worked to stimulate openness in matters of religion and race.

Involved particularly in African American education, Thurman gained insight into its patterns of excellence and its problematic areas. Interestingly, his first year at Howard University coincided with the publication of a new educational venture on the campus, the *Journal of Negro Education*, the first issue of which appeared in

---

15. See Logan, *Howard University*, 220-222, 231-244; and Robert H. Brisbane, *The Black Vanguard: Origins of the Negro Social Revolution 1900-1960* (Valley Forge: Judson Press, 1970), 101-107.

April 1932. Scheduled to appear quarterly, that Journal was to deal with the problems peculiar to African American life and education, together with thoughtful research and recommendations toward needed solutions. Later in Thurman's work at Howard, he was called upon often for his judgments and views as a Black religious educator and campus minister. One primary instance can be cited: a formal project dealing with religion in Black educational institutions, a study prepared by Richard I. McKinney as a doctoral dissertation and later published under the title *Religion in Higher Education Among Negroes*.[16] In the preface to his book McKinney paid special tribute to Howard Thurman's counsel and assistance during his research, commenting, "To Dr. Howard Thurman, Dean of the Chapel of Howard University, the writer owes a debt of gratitude for the stimulus of interest in and because of his wide contacts and knowledge."[17] He knew most of the institutions McKinney had studied. He knew something about financial expenditures in religious programs and studies, the policies of those institutions regarding religious programs, and the role of religious workers in those settings.

Thurman had more than a passing acquaintance with the religious situation in Historically Black Colleges and Universities (HBCUs) during the 1930s. It was he who assessed the scene as one of "religious illiteracy," explaining student rejection of religion on campus as due not to an irreligious attitude but rather to "complete lack of knowledge of the contents of the Bible itself, the great gap between what the person identifies as religion and what religion really is, and the absence of primary contact with people who themselves are having vital religious experience."[18] Thurman's words on this subject suggest and outline the scope of his concerns as religious leader while at Howard University. He wanted students and faculty to realize religion as a dynamic intelligible, and revolutionary experience. He attempted to do this in many ways, some of them traditional, some of them unique.[19]

---

16. Richard I. McKinney, *Religion in Higher Education Among Negroes* (New Haven: Yale University Press, 1945).

17. McKinney, *Religion in Higher Education Among Negroes*, vii-viii.

18. McKinney, *Religion in Higher Education Among Negroes*, 58.

19. Thurman, *Footprints of a Dream*, 24-28.

Shortly after McKinney's study was published, Thurman reviewed it for *Religion in Life*.[20] In one of the paragraphs from that review we have Thurman's early critique of U.S. education, the bearing of faculty social patterns upon the range of possibility for the educated African American, the frustrations that affect their outlook, and how the insights of religion can aid frustrated persons to deal with this problem. Thurman's paragraph is long, but it is worthy of being given in full. He begins his critique with an assessment of the value of public education:

> One of the functions of American education is to guarantee and to perpetuate the established patterns of American life. The presupposition is that the persons who are being educated are to function in the social order on the side of those who make the policies that determine the destiny of the country. The very fact that it is one of the common judgments of public-school education that it is well within the range of possibility of the most ordinary male student in the class to become President of the United States, is a case in point. This means that the degree to which American education is effective in the lives of the students marks the measure of the level of privilege and control for those who are exposed to it.

Next, Thurman speaks to the realities facing African Americans who complete the same education as their white counterparts:

> When a Negro boy comes through that same system, whether it be in Cambridge, Massachusetts, or Daytona, Florida, he is to some extent imbued with the same social estimate of his possibilities. When he is through with his education, however, he is faced with the problem that in broad outlook, there is no ceiling to his effective aspirations—he has the techniques and the philosophy that belong to the typical American—but he functions

---

20. *Religion in Life*, Autumn 1946, 619-620. **ED:** Howard Thurman, "Book Review: *Religion in Higher Education Among Negroes*, by Richard I. McKinney, September 1946," in Walter Earl Fluker, ed., *The Papers of Howard Washington Thurman: Volume 3, The Bold Adventure, September 1943-May 1949* (Columbia: University of South Carolina Press, 2015), 201-203.

> in society as a member of a minority. This fact is apt to issue in the profoundest kind of frustration affecting his total outlook.

Then he presents the impact of segregated education on the participant and the importance of a role for religion:

> In addition, if he has been educated in a segregated school, it means that the very conditions under which his education takes place are a constant denial of the basic assumptions by which his education is motivated. Therefore, the only possible justification for a segregated school in our country is the demand that in that kind of restricted environment, educators and students should test out techniques and methods which, when released in society, will be so revolutionary in their effect that they will destroy the very segregated institutions that made it possible to develop these techniques and methods. The Christian religion with its revolutionary ethic would be most reassuring and stimulating to the Negro student in such a dedication. It should mean that a revolutionary ethic of Christianity would be provided with a revolutionary technique. Unless religion in higher education among Negroes performs this function, it will not be able to challenge and inspire the loyalty and devotion of the most thoughtful administrators, faculty, and students on the various campuses.[21]

Given the climate of the campus, the city of Washington, DC, and the wider section beyond both campus and city, there were some who did not agree with Thurman's thesis and approach. Some students took issue with him. One student who had heard him speak about the importance of fellowship beyond race and color barriers sought him out after the chapel service and questioned Thurman about his honesty and claims. The student asked, "Just how far would you go with this fellowship?" Thurman paused before giving his answer, much aware of the student's forbidding mindset due to previous insults and psychological injuries as a Black man. He then matched his pause with a smile, and replied, "I would go

---

21. *Religion in Life*, 619-620. **ED:** Thurman, "Book Review: *Religion in Higher Education Among Negroes*," in Fluker, ed., *The Papers of Thurman: Volume 3*, 202-203.

all the way." He added, gently, "And I would not carry any escape clause in my back pocket."[22]

Occasionally some leaders took issue with Thurman's approach. A visiting Black preacher during his chapel sermon advised the students toward separatism as Blacks, basing his insistence upon Joshua 17:15, "If thou be a great people, then get thee up to the wood country, and cut down for thyself there in the land of the Perizzites and of the giants, if mount Ephraim be too narrow for thee" (KJV). The minister paraphrased the verse by saying, "If the borders of Ephraim be too narrow for thee, go ye out into the wilderness and hew down a place for yourself." That preacher was presenting what he thought to be an ideal response to the racial dilemma in the United States, offering students a challenge so to develop a pattern which would hold all power and authority within their own group life as Blacks. Instead of razing walls of separation he was erecting them, proposing a monument to separatism. Thurman has commented since on the problem contained in that preacher's advisement. "This is a form of charisma that always has a certain appeal to those who suffer from a consensus of rejection which segregation symbolizes. The fact that such separatism is not a practical procedure, that it cuts one off from the basic right to be a part of the common life, that it is falling away from the sense of participation in a collective destiny—all these are often forgotten."[23] Thurman set himself to not forget, intent to relate—and teach others how to do it as well.

For several years Thurman lamented the "tiny little office," out of which his work was done, but more adequate facilities became available when in October 1939 the School of Religion moved to the Carnegie Library.[24] The first office was small but great and memorable events happened there across the years: contacts, conversations of depth, commitments to God, corrections for life, and counsel of varied descriptions.

Thurman recalls a productive insight shared with him in his office by Dr. Cabot, the famous Harvard pathologist, who had come

---

22. Robert E. Luccock, *The Lost Gospel* (New York: Harper and Brothers, 1948), 11.

23. Thurman, *The Luminous Darkness*, 29-30.

24. Logan, *Howard University*, 355, 378.

to preach during the organ dedication services in the Howard University Chapel. As Thurman tells it:

> We were sitting in my tiny little office talking, and every five minutes a student would knock at the door. I'd go to the door and do a little counseling, and sit back down, and the buzzer would sound and I'd pick up the telephone. Dr. Cabot stood this for as long as he could, and then he said finally, "Would you do me a favor? Just for ten minutes, lock the door, and tell the young lady who buzzes you not to buzz. I want to tell you something." And he told me this. "Many years ago at a conference on social work, I lectured on the 'Limitation of Intake.' My thesis was that the number five bears the same relationship to infinity that five million bears. Now, human needs are infinite; if a man were to work 24 hours a day for a thousand years without ceasing, to counter these needs, at the end of the thousand years, human needs would still be infinite. . . . A wise man discovers he cannot make a quantitative impression on infinity—the only thing to do is try and make a qualitative impression on it. Now you can unlock the door, and tell the young lady you're in business again."[25]

Thurman treasures that experience as one of the most important encounters of his life.

Visting India and Gandhi

A trip to India opened earlier than Thurman had expected—and in a way he had not anticipated. In 1935, through an invitation from the American Student Christian Movement, Thurman was asked to head a delegation of visitors from the United States on a trip to India, Burma, and Ceylon, and to speak at their educational centers. The four persons involved in the trip were two African American

25. A. J. Sullivan, "About Encounters: A Sketch of Howard Thurman," in *Bostonia*, Fall 1963, 9-10; see also recorded television presentation over WHDH-TV, Channel 5, Boston, Massachusetts, for Friday, December 15, 1962 (unedited transcript made available from the Office of the Dean of Marsh Chapel).

married couples: Howard and Sue Thurman, and Edgar and Phenola Carroll. Formally designated as a Friendship Delegation, the four sailed out of New York in September 1935, and returned six months later in March 1936. While on their trip the group visited fifty-three educational centers in Ceylon, Burma, and India.

Thurman had heard and read about Mohandas Gandhi. Prominent individuals from the West had discussed the Indian leader, some admiring him as a stalwart and wily politician, some others as a saint. Still others demurred, critical of both his motives and his strategies. Thurman had listened, read, and thought about the critiques of the famed Asian leader. Mindful of the scars on his own spirit, he knew them too well to miss seeing a basic identification between the struggles of Indians under British rule and the continued subjugation of Blacks in the United States. Gandhi was fighting a system; so were Blacks. Gandhi had found a framework within which to stand and work with all moral urgency and undergirding. African Americans needed to find a framework for their active quest for freedom. Thurman reasoned that Gandhi might well influence African Americans to find a proper method and plan of action for needed freedom, so he began to think that Gandhi was a man he needed to meet.

Thurman had heard about Gandhi's interest in the social problems African Americans faced and remembered that leader's message which appeared in the July 1929 issue of *Crisis Magazine*:

> Let not the 12 million Negroes be ashamed of the fact that they are the grandchildren of slaves. There is no dishonour in being slaves. There is dishonour in being slaveowners. But let us realize that the future is with those who would be truthful, pure and loving. For, as the old wise men have said, truth ever is, untruth never was. Love alone binds and truth and love accrue only to the truly humble.[26]

Thurman also knew that Gandhi's nonviolent methodology was then under discussion by Black leaders as a practical way of resisting injustice and segregated patterns. Thurman was one Black leader

---

26. Mohandas Gandhi quoted in *Crisis Magazine*, July 1929 (Vol. 36, No. 7), 225.

who believed that Gandhi could give some direction in the plight of African Americans.

It came to Thurman's attention that Miriam Slade, a member of Gandhi's inner circle, was on a lecture tour of the United States seeking to interpret his work to the West.[27] Misrepresented in the West by limited reports and slanted views intended to present the British cause in the best light, Gandhi had sent Mirabehn (a name bestowed upon Slade by the Indians) on an extended tour of England and the United States to counter misinterpretations of him and his work. The trip was calculated to serve more than one purpose: rally those already supporting Gandhi's cause, allay fears among those who were apprehensive about his intentions, and inform those who needed more understanding about his methods.

Miriam Slade was an English woman of privilege, the daughter of a British admiral. She had become a follower of Gandhi, renouncing her way of life to live by his side as student, servant, and sharer in community. All of this occasioned a shock to the British conscience. Howard Thurman knew about her. Given his delegation's planned trip to India, he arranged to meet her and engaged her as a campus guest and speaker at Howard University. It was Slade's first trip to the United States. Her itinerary was arranged by John Haynes Holmes at her request.[28] Headquartered at the Henry Street House Settlement, she received an inside view of New York.[29] Her entire tour included over twenty major gatherings and five radio broadcasts. According to her own report, "The meetings were much bigger than in England, and everywhere extraordinary interest was shown in Bapu as a person. Every sort of question was asked about him, while the political aspect, so much to the fore in England, was of secondary importance to the American audience. Gandhi the man, the Teacher, the Apostle of Truth, was what they sought, and with such thirst and earnestness!"[30] She added, "It was this deep interest, and the overflowing openheartedness and affection, that kept me going to the end of the fortnight."[31]

27. *The New York Times*, October 4, 1934, 13.

28. Madeleine Slade, *The Spirit's Pilgrimage* (New York: Coward-McCann, Inc., 1960), 186.

29. *The New York Times*, October 11, 1934, 26.

30. Slade, *The Spirit's Pilgrimage*, 187-188.

31. Slade, *The Spirit's Pilgrimage*, 188.

When John Haynes Holmes arranged for her to go to Washington, DC to meet with Eleanor Roosevelt at the White House, Slade also acted upon Howard Thurman's invitation and thus spoke on the Howard University campus. Before leaving Washington, she talked encouragingly to Thurman about his visit India. She added, "And when you come you must meet Gandhiji." He assured her that such an encounter would be one of his main concerns.

Thurman has referred to this trip in several of his books, mentioning some of the rich insights which accrued to him as he traveled, and confessing how the trip made him search his own soul and reassess his plans for his ministry.[32] The trip led to changes in Thurman's thinking and theological priorities, while it deepened some of his major convictions, especially his desire to bring people into experiences of unity. His friend Channing Tobias later reported some of the trip results, writing: "Enthusiastic comments on the extraordinary services rendered on this mission have come not only from the Indian leaders but from E. Stanley Jones and other well-known missionaries."[33]

There were two particular conversations that Thurman would always remember from his trip. The first was a five-hour long conversation with the principal of the Law College, University of Colombo, Ceylon, after he had given a talk there on civil disabilities under the states' rights system in the Southern United States. The second conversation was a three-hour long encounter with Mahatma Gandhi during which they talked about Jesus, Christian missions, and life for Blacks in the United States.

When Thurman ended his remarks at the Law College, University of Colombo he was invited by the principal to have coffee. The principal confronted Thurman:

> What are you doing over here? I know what the newspapers say about a pilgrimage of friendship and the rest, but that is not my question. What are *you* doing over here? This is what I mean.

---

32. See *Jesus and the Disinherited*, 13-15; *Footprints of a Dream*, 22-24; see also Yates, *Howard Thurman*, 94-111. **ED:** See also Thurman, *With Head and Heart*, 103-136.

33. Channing Tobias, "Some Outstanding Negro Christians: Howard Thurman," *The Missionary Review of the World*, June 1936, 296.

> More than three hundred years ago your forefathers were taken from the western coast of Africa as slaves. The people who dealt in the slave traffic were Christians. One of your famous Christian hymn writers, Sir John Newton, made his money from the sale of slaves to the New World. He is the man who wrote "How Sweet the Name of Jesus Sounds" and "Amazing Grace"—there may be others, but these are the only ones I know. The name of one of the famous British slave vessels was "Jesus."
>
> The men who bought the slaves were Christians. Christian ministers, quoting the Christian apostle Paul, gave the sanction of religion to the system of slavery. Some seventy years or more ago you were freed by a man who was not a professing Christian, but was rather the spearhead of certain political, social, and economic forces, the significance of which he himself did not understand. During all the period since then you have lived in a Christian nation in which you are segregated, lynched, and burned. Even in the church, I understand, there is segregation. One of my students who went to your country sent me a clipping telling about a Christian church in which the regular Sunday worship was interrupted so that many could join a mob against one of your fellows. When he had been caught and done to death, they came back to resume their worship of their Christian God.

Then the principal focused in on Howard Thurman and closed his argument: "I am a Hindu. I do not understand. Here you are in my country, standing deep within the Christian faith and tradition. I do not wish to seem rude to you. But, sir, I think you are a traitor to all the darker peoples of the earth. I am wondering what you, an intelligent man, can say in defense of your position."

Thurman noted that their conversation continued for more than five hours. He reflected: "The clue to my own discussion with this probing, honest, sympathetic Hindu is found in my interpretation of the meaning of the religion of Jesus. It is a privilege, after so long a time, to set down what seems to me to be an essentially creative and prognostic interpretation of Jesus as religious subject rather than religious object. It is necessary to examine the religion of Jesus against the background of his own age and people, and to inquire into the content of his teaching with reference to the disinherited and the underprivileged."[34] This conversation became a catalyst for Thurman writing *Jesus and the Disinherited*.

The second life transforming conversation took place with Gandhi at Bardoli where Gandhi was stopping over on his way to Wardha. Thurman's delegation met him there by prearrangement. Interestingly, Gandhi broke with his usual custom of remaining inside to receive his guests and rather walked out to greet the Black delegation. He then invited the Thurmans and Carrolls into his tent where they joined him sitting on the floor. Gandhi's secretary was present and made notes as the group talked.

The full discussion during the visit with Gandhi involved several crucial areas of concern. The portion of the discussion about color prejudice and race conflicts in the United States was later published in Gandhi's paper *Harijan*. I present this in the form of a conversation.

> **Gandhi**: "Is the prejudice against colour growing or dying out?"
>
> **Thurman**: "It is difficult to say because in one place things look much improved, whilst in another the outlook is still dark. But the economic question is acute everywhere, and in many of the industrial centres in the Middle West the prejudice against the Negro shows itself in its ugliest form. Among the workers there is a great amount of tension, which is quite natural, when the white man thinks that the Negro's very existence is a threat to his own."
>
> **Gandhi:** "Is the union between the Negroes and the whites recognized by law?"
>
> **Edgar Carroll:** "Twenty-five states have laws definitely against these unions, and I have had to sign a bond of 500 dollars to promise that I would not register any such union."
>
> **Thurman**: "But there has been a lot of intermixture of races as, for 300 years or more, the Negro woman had no control over her body."

34. Thurman, *Jesus and the Disinherited*, 14-15.

Thurman: "Did the South African Negro take any part in your movement?"

Gandhi: "No, I purposely did not invite them. It would have endangered their cause. They would not have understood the technique of our struggle, nor could they have seen the purpose or the utility of nonviolence."

Thurman: "Is nonviolence, from your point of view, a form of direct action?"

Gandhi: "It is not one form, it is the only form. I do not, of course, confine the words 'direct action' to their technical meaning. But without direct active expression of it, nonviolence to my mind is meaningless. It is the greatest activist force in the world. One cannot be passively nonviolent. In fact, 'nonviolence' is a term I had to coin in order to bring out the root meaning of *ahimsa*. In spite of the negative particle 'non', it is no negative force. Superficially we are surrounded in life by strife and bloodshed, like living upon life. But some great seer, who ages ago penetrated the centre of truth, said: it is not through strife and violence, but through nonviolence that man can fulfill his destiny and his duty to his fellow creatures. It is a force which is more positive than electricity and more powerful than even ether. At the centre of nonviolence is a force which is self-acting. *Ahimsa* means 'love' in a Pauline sense and yet something more than the 'love' defined by St. Paul, although I know St. Paul's beautiful definition is good enough for all practical purposes. *Ahimsa* includes the whole creation and not only human. Besides, love in the English language has other connotations too, and so I was compelled to use the negative word. But it does not, as I have told you, express a negative force, but a force superior to all the forces put together. One person who can express *ahimsa* in life exercises a force superior to all the forces of brutality."

Thurman: "And is it possible for any individual to achieve this?"

Gandhi: "Certainly. If there was any exclusiveness about it, I should reject it at once."

Thurman: "Any idea of possession is foreign to it?"

Gandhi: "Yes. It possesses nothing; therefore, it possesses everything."

Thurman: "Is it possible for a single human being to resist the persistent invasion of the quality successfully?"

Gandhi: "It is possible. Perhaps your question is more universal than you mean. Is it not possible, you mean to ask, for one single Indian, for instance, to resist the exploitation of 300 million Indians? Or, do you mean the onslaught of the whole world against a single individual personally?"

Thurman: "Yes, that is one half of the question. I wanted to know, if one man can hold the whole violence at bay?"

Gandhi: "If he can't, you must take it that he is not a true representative of *ahimsa*. Supposing I cannot produce a single instance in life of a man who truly converted his adversary, I would then say that is because no one had been found to express *ahimsa* in its fulness."

Thurman: "Then it overrides all other forces?"

Gandhi: "Yes, it is the only true force in life."

Thurman: "Forgive now the weakness of this question, but may I ask how are we to train the individuals or communities in this difficult art?"

Gandhi: "There is no royal road, except through living the creed in your life which must be a living sermon. Of course, the expression in one's own life presupposes great study, tremendous perseverance, and a thorough cleansing of one's self of all the impurities. If for mastering of the physical sciences you have to devote a whole lifetime, how many lifetimes may be needed for mastering the greatest spiritual force that mankind has known? But why worry even if it means several lifetimes? For, if this is the only permanent thing in life, if this is the only thing that counts, then whatever effort you bestow on mastering it, is well spent. Seek ye first the Kingdom of Heaven and everything else shall be added unto you. And the Kingdom of Heaven is *ahimsa*."

Sue Bailey Thurman: "How am I to act, supposing my own brother was lynched before my very eyes?"

Gandhi: "There is such a thing as self-immolation. Supposing I was a Negro, and my sister was ravished by a white or lynched by a whole community, what would be my duty?—I ask myself. And the answer comes to me: I must not wish ill to these, but neither must I co-operate with them. It may be that ordinarily I depend on the lynching community for my livelihood. I refuse to co-operate with them, refuse to co-operate with even my brother Negroes who tolerate the wrong. That is the self-immolation, I mean. I have often in my life resorted to the plan. Of course, a mechanical act of starvation will mean nothing. One's faith must remain undimmed whilst life ebbs out, minute by minute. But I am a very poor specimen of the practice of nonviolence, and my answer may not convince you. But I am striving very hard, and even if I do not succeed fully in this life, my faith will not diminish."

Sue Bailey Thurman: "We want you to come to America. We want you not for White America, but for Negroes; we have many a problem that cries for solution, and we need you badly."

Gandhi: "How I wish I could, but I would have nothing to give you unless I had given an ocular demonstration here of all that I have been saying. I must make good the message here, before I bring it to you. I do not say that I am defeated, but I have still to perfect myself. You may be sure that the moment I feel that call within me, I shall not hesitate."

Thurman: "Much of the peculiar background of our own life in America is our own interpretation of the Christian religion. When one goes through the pages of the hundreds of Negro spirituals, striking things are brought to my mind which remind me of all that you have told us today."

Gandhi: "Well, if it comes true, it may be through the Negroes that the unadulterated message of nonviolence will be delivered to the world."[35]

---

35. Originally published in *Harijan*, March 14, 1936. This text is from D.G. Tendulkar, *Mahatma: A Life of Mohandas Karamchand Gandhi, Vol. IV, 1934-1938* (Delhi and Bombay: Government of India Publications Division, 1952), 48-51. See also Mohandas K. Gandhi, *Non-Violence in Peace and War, Vol. I* (Ahmedabad: Navajivan Publishing House, 1948), 113-116.

The 1935 trip to India sensitized Howard Thurman as never before to the multifaceted realities of missions, social process, and human culture. Gandhi told Thurman that the greatest enemy in India against Jesus Christ was Christianity. He was not belittling well-intentioned Christian missionaries or the development of meaningful missionary enterprise in his country; rather was he questioning the view of those who sought to transform Indians into Christians at the expense of their own significance as Indians. He was also calling attention to explicit failures by Christians to follow in full the principles and practices of Jesus Christ himself, as being untrue to the Sermon on the Mount and to the spirit of Jesus.

Speaking further, Gandhi did not feel that Christian missionaries took sufficient notice of the font of ideas and values already at work within the culture of his country; he was intent to argue for greater interrelation and reciprocity between Indian life and Western religious concerns. He openly criticized Christianity in its Western form as an agent of Western materialism and the expansion of Western culture. As he viewed it, pure Christianity would not be foreign to his people; it could be integrated with Indian life and culture. Thurman listened well to Gandhi's criticism, agreeing that developmental relationships were imperative if social process in India was to fulfill itself along authentic lines of spiritual significance.

The discussion with Thurman about race problems in the United States allowed Gandhi to draw upon insights from his experience with racism in South Africa. He knew firsthand that color prejudice and economic concerns had influenced Christians in race contacts, and that unfair dealings of whites with people of color made it necessary for the victims to voice their grievances, criticize the system, and form protest movements. His advice about nonviolence highlighted that method as politically discreet, clearly ethical, creative, and especially suited to the prevailing condition in the United States. For him, nonviolence represented both an expedient and an attitude akin to the spirit of Jesus. Thurman had already committed himself to this approach earlier while doing his work on the home scene in the United States. In fact, he had published an article on "Peace Tactics and A Racial Minority" in the December 1928 issue of *The World Tomorrow*. Now, in 1935, firsthand discussion with Gandhi helped to deepen his convictions and confirm his judgment about the practical and spiritual values of nonviolence.

It has been too long overlooked that Howard Thurman was one of the first Blacks to urge that African Americans use the Gandhian method of nonviolent direct action for addressing the Black situation. It was to Thurman that Gandhi suggested that it "may be through the Negroes that the unadulterated message of nonviolence will be delivered to the world." This prophetic statement came into increased prominence years later when Martin Luther King, Jr., succeeded in using Gandhian methods to change the segregated setting of the Southern United States.[36]

The trip through India prodded Thurman to do some thinking and planning about his own ministry as a Christian leader. He was stirred especially by the question put to him everywhere about why he remained in the Christian church when he was being segregated as a Black person from religious fellowship with whites. "In almost every city we visited, in varied ways the same question was raised—why is the church powerless before the color bar? All answers had to be defensive because there was not a single instance known to me in which a local church had a completely integrated membership! The color bar was honored in the practice of the Christian religion. From a 10,000-mile perspective, this monumental betrayal of the Christian ethic loomed large and forbidding."[37]

The question so haunted Thurman that he knew he had to find an answer, find it soon, and then make it visible in the United States. The answer came during a high moment of insight at a scenic spot their group visited during the trip. As Thurman himself has explained it:

> Near the end of our journey we spent a day in Khyber Pass on the border of the northwest frontier. It was an experience of vision. We stood looking at a distance into Afghanistan, while to our right, and close at hand, passed a long camel train bringing goods and ideas to the bazaars of North India. Here was the gateway through which Roman and Mogul conquerors had come in other days bringing with them goods, new concepts, and the violence

---

36. Lerone Bennett, Jr., *What Manner of Man: A Biography of Martin Luther King, Jr.*, rev. ed. (Chicago: Johnson Publishing Co., 1968), 3-5. Bennett cites Gandhi's statement, but has neglected to name the one to whom Gandhi spoke.

37. Thurman, *Footprints of a Dream*, 24.

> of armed might. All that we had seen and felt in India seemed to be brought miraculously into focus. We saw clearly what we must do somehow when we returned to America. We knew that we must test whether a religious fellowship could be developed in America that was capable of cutting across all racial barriers, with a carryover into the common life, a fellowship that would alter the behavior patterns of those involved. It became imperative now to find out if experiences of spiritual unity among people could be more compelling than the experiences which divide them.[38]

The travel-weary delegation returned with a deepened sense of priorities. Thurman moved back to the Howard University scene with a renewed commitment to the dream of community among all people.

The return from India coincided with his third year as professor of theology and chairperson of the University Committee on Religious Life. Named "Dean of the Chapel" after his return, Thurman's new appointment matched a newness he applied to his responsibilities. Inspired by his new dream, he began working on a new format for the worship service, a format that would provide not only for the sermon and hymns, but also meditation, quiet, and the enrichment of prayer. In time he drew upon the resources of fine arts, devotional readings, verse-speaking choirs, and even aesthetic or liturgical dance forms—a daring, hazardous, but finally rewarding venture in the interest of experienced unity of quest. As hoped, chapel attendance increased, with a mixed crowd of skeptical and awed observers as well as anticipating worshippers. But again and again it happened: the ingredients of the service were so selected and managed that a meaningful claim was made upon each human spirit. "It was as if a wall was removed and we became one people, feeling one thing."[39]

These initial successes encouraged him to believe that he was finding ways to unite people of great diversity in religious backgrounds, providing them with religious experiences more compelling than those ideological and denominational concerns which had previously walled them off from each other. The environment was

38. Thurman, *Footprints of a Dream*, 24.

39. Thurman, *Footprints of a Dream*, 26.

under his control, increasingly, and to that extent his experimentation in worship patterns was to some extent artificial, but he still felt assured that he was seeing his dream for community fulfill itself in a common setting of worship. Thurman was making his way with the insight that religious experience should unite and integrate, undermine the sense of separateness, and predispose the worshipper toward multiplied experiences of unity. It is within this dimension of intent that Thurman's nine and one-half years of ministry as Dean of Rankin Chapel must be interpreted and understood.

Chapter Four

The San Francisco and Boston Years

In the Fall of 1943 Howard Thurman received a letter from A. J. Muste, Executive Director of the Fellowship of Reconciliation, asking his help to secure a young Black seminary graduate, to serve a small and somewhat diversified neighborhood church in one of San Francisco's blighted areas. Muste thought that Thurman could help him find such a person. A. J. Muste was writing for Alfred G. Fisk, a Presbyterian minister who had been working part-time with the group for a few months. Fisk's work as professor at San Francisco State College did not allow sufficient time to nurture the young group, so he had written to A. J. Muste asking his advice and help to find someone for full-time ministry there.

With reference to Muste's letter to him, Thurman reports that "at first there was no 'pick up' either in my mind or imagination. I saw no connection between this 'stirring' in San Francisco and the quest upon which I had been engaged for so long a time."[1] But after the person Thurman first suggested declined the assignment, Fisk contacted Thurman directly and asked for further suggestions. For the first time he began to think about the personal challenge of the matter. "It was now for the first time that there was kindled in my mind the possibility that this may be the opportunity toward which my life had been moving. The conception was limited but I thought I saw in it

1. Thurman, *Footprints of a Dream*, 31.

the germ of the great possibility."[2] After careful thought, prolonged discussion with his wife Sue, and a prospecting trip to San Francisco taken by Sue, Thurman developed an interest in joining the small group there as full-time leader. He applied for a leave of absence from Howard University and left for San Francisco, California in July 1944.

The Church for the Fellowship of All Peoples

San Francisco was a strategic center during the war years. The climate of the national life was felt there in many dimensions of sensitivity and conflict. Work opportunities brought thousands of newcomers to the area, most of them Blacks and whites from some of the southern states. This in turn forced a direct encounter there between whites, Blacks, and foreign-born laborers. War production kept employment demands high, but this caused problems in available housing, job conditions, union membership, zoning agreements, and social contacts. The results were social friction, housing discrimination, residential restrictions, overcrowding, inadequate recreational facilities—in short, a situation of constant threat developed against neighborhood rapport and social harmony.

Actually, it was to help heal hurts caused by such social friction that Alfred G. Fisk established the neighborhood church. Locating in the Fillmore Area, the group began to meet together in 1943. There was no formal membership at that time. The rather loose structure of the group made the future of the project somewhat uncertain. The San Francisco presbytery supported Fisk in his work with the group. Through the Presbyterian Board of National Missions, Fisk gained rent free use of some property the Board owned at 1500 Post Street. The living room had been converted into a chapel and an upstairs apartment was available for a resident minister. The Board even underwrote the project financially. Upon learning that Thurman had committed himself to join the group on a full-time basis, the Presbyterian Board of National Missions provided $3,600 for salaries during the first year, $2,400 for Thurman and $1,200 for Fisk's part-time services.

Thurman's move to San Francisco from his university post meant a radical alteration of the family's way of life. The church opportunity was in line with his deep-seated dream about unity, but certain

2. Thurman, *Footprints of a Dream*, 31.

privations kept all the family members aware of the risks they had assumed. He had left a secure and tenured position at Howard University, daring to move himself, his wife Sue, and their two daughters, Olive and Ann, across the continent into a new venture in a precarious setting and uncertain conditions. The reactions of friends differed as they learned about his move. "When the announcement was made public, I received letters from friends in the San Francisco Bay Area expressing a real interest in the new undertaking. Many friends in the East rallied to the dream and its possibilities. There were others who were skeptical of this decision and thought I was sick in mind."[3]

Howard Thurman's desire and eventual decision to accept Fisk's invitation "goes much deeper and antedates Dr. Fisk's letter by many years." Thurman reflects:

> Ever since I began to give serious thought to the meaning of religion I have been deeply puzzled by its apparent inability to make a radical impact upon the tensions and the tragedies of human relations, particularly those obtaining between racial groups in America. Was this paralysis due to the nature of religious experience in particular? Or was it due to the breakdown in techniques and methods of implementation? Why cannot religion make a difference in the way groups deal with each other? More specifically, why was the church itself among the chief of sinners in the matter of racial separateness and prejudice?

As early as 1936, while in India, the Thurmans had decided that they would need to "leave the relative particularism of an academic atmosphere and move into a situation in an environment not under control where an honest attempt could be made to test the validity of the religious faith of men of good will, who drew their major inspiration from the genius of their own faith. It was obvious that a nucleus of interested and committed persons would have to be found and developed." Howard Thurman notes, "My faith to make a bold venture without such a nucleus was too weak and indefinite. To do this would require becoming a part of a community somewhere and on the basis of belonging to seek to develop such a group." Upon hearing about the community in San Francisco, Thurman says, "I felt that

3. Thurman, *Footprints of a Dream*, 33.

this was the opportunity if I dared to accept it. Mrs. Thurman and I agreed that this was precisely the kind of opening for which we had hoped and prayed. The result was I secured a leave of absence from my work and sallied forth without any assurance beyond a dream in my heart and mind and a small group with which to work."[4]

One of the first things Thurman did was to guide the group into a stable organizational structure which would allow formal membership in keeping with some agreed terms. The individuals comprising the group had backgrounds of specific variety: Baptists, Methodists, Presbyterians, Congregationalists, and Episcopalians. Some people there had never belonged to any denomination, but most of them had some kind of church background. They had to deal with the question of what kind of church they would be. "It was my idea," Thurman reports, "to project a church that would go beyond the boundaries of a denominational church, a church that would have a more creative and inclusive basis of membership. As difficult as it might seem to fulfill, that was my idea." Fisk and Thurman wrote out a basic statement of membership, which was acted upon favorably after two months of thought and discussion within the group. Revised sometime later, that statement was known as "The Commitment."[5]

Under Thurman's guidance, the group moved from self-inventory to formal organization, and finally to an independent status and operation. The desire for independence grew out of the group decision to be more inclusive than a denominational church. In the light of that decision, the financial arrangement between the group and the Presbyterian Board of National Missions became problematic and embarrassing. At first it seemed reckless to break with the Board and lose needed financial support, yet the members knew that denominational funds could not be supplied forever without a final denominational commitment on their part.

The logic of Presbyterian Board support spoke loudly about the Board's desire for the neighborhood group to become a Presbyterian mission church. The local committee of the Presbytery had shown special interest in the young group: besides the salary support to

4. From a 1951 issue of *Growing Edge* magazine, as cited in a feature story on The Church for the Fellowship of All Peoples, "Trumpet Ready in the West," *The Christian Century*, September 12, 1951, 1041.

5. Thurman, *Footprints of a Dream*, 37-40, 52.

Thurman and Fisk, plus the rent free use of the chapel and living quarters on Post Street, the Presbytery committee even helped the group find larger facilities when the chapel could not accommodate the larger crowds that attended after the church's inaugural service as an incorporated fellowship.[6] In spite of these persuasions, however, the members of Fellowship Church—as it was now called—decided to cast their votes for an independent status. The vote was taken in August 1945, and it included a provision that affiliation with some religious body would remain an option to be considered in the future if the members so desired.

Independence gained, Fellowship Church had to raise its own budget, provide its own chapel, support the ministers, and shape its own future. The members rallied, friends from near and far gave gifts, and organizations made contributions. Thurman himself took speaking engagements across the nation to aid the church and supplement his own salary.

Thurman's absence from the Howard University scene had its negative effects, especially where the School of Religion was involved. The School of Religion had not yet recuperated from the resignation of Dean Benjamin E. Mays who left in June 1940 to become president of Morehouse College. The nation was enduring the war years, and the campus was affected by the many wartime emergencies. Because of the draft, fewer men were enrolled at the School of Religion. When Thurman decided not to return to the campus but rather to stay in San Francisco, this was an additional problem for the growth of the School of Religion. Rayford W. Logan, in his history of Howard University offered comment about Thurman's resignation.

> The reasons for his resignation as Dean of the Chapel and Professor in the School of Religion cannot be precisely stated because the Executive Committee on June 7, 1946, accepted his resignation without recorded comment. Probably one reason for his action was a blunt remark by President Johnson that Howard University was not to be "used as a basis of operations." Persons in the employ of the University owed their primary obligation to Howard. After the meeting in which this remark was made (the

6. There were several other factors at work, however, that made the change of location necessary. See Thurman, *Footprints of a Dream*, 43-46.

> author was present) Dr. Thurman said that President Johnson was talking about him.[7]

Howard University had first granted Thurman a year's leave of absence, effective July 1, 1944. Not pleased with the timing of the leave, and questioning the wisdom of it, President Mordecai W. Johnson had nevertheless let Thurman have the leave of absence, really expecting him to return to the campus scene tutored by troubles, and wiser for his Chapel and teaching role. Thurman's choice to stay on in San Francisco after the initial leave was a blow to the older friend's plans and hopes for the university. Johnson did not get over Thurman's resignation easily.

Thurman did not enter upon his San Francisco task cold. He was armed with more than a dream and a hope. His concerns were informed in part by his discovery of other "fellowship" efforts in several places across the nation. In 1936, one year after his Pilgrimage of Friendship to India, Thurman learned about an interracial religious fellowship in Philadelphia sponsored by the American Friends Service Committee. The interracial venture was actually labeled "Fellowship Church." He discovered that the Philadelphia group held monthly meetings during the winter months, and that the meetings were held at Black and white churches on an alternating basis. The leadership responsibility was also shared on an alternating white-Black basis. Although the pattern followed some of the lines of a distinct "church" life, Thurman could see that "the idea was not to establish a regular church in the community but rather to give a genuine testimony in the field of group relation."[8] Not long afterward, these ventures in interracial religious fellowship spread to other cities, particularly in the Eastern United States.

Thurman watched the new movement and its apparent effects. As he did so, he discerned a crucial difference between his own concern for an interracial church and the ventures illustrated by the movement in the East: he wanted to shape an interracial congregation whose life and witness would be a permanent and full-time reality under regular

---

7. Logan, *Howard University*, 379.

8. Howard Thurman, "The Fellowship Church of All Peoples," *Common Ground*, Spring 1945, 29. **ED:** Thurman, "The Fellowship Church of All Peoples, Spring 1945," in Fluker, ed., *The Papers of Thurman: Volume 3*, 125.

and full-time leadership. This was a broader and deeper thrust than the earlier efforts he had been watching. Thurman wanted to develop an incorporated and community-based church fellowship that could take its place within the framework of North American Protestantism and solidly rooted there, directly challenge separatism and segregated religious life by its radically open fellowship.

Under the guidance of Fisk and Thurman as co-pastors the congregation grew in numbers and a sense of normalcy. The color bar was surmounted: not just overlooked or ignored but faced, regarded, and surmounted. Both leaders and people began to see over and over again that experiences of unity can undermine and topple barriers. Through Fellowship Church, Blacks were worshipping with whites, and both with Asians, and a common life together had developed between them under one God. Little by little this living demonstration began to cast its image upon the diverse life of San Francisco and finally the rest of the religious world in the United States. Called upon to both speak and write about the new development, Thurman prepared interpretative articles for publication. After only four years from its inception, *Time* magazine covered the story of the church, lauding its dynamic differences as a church multicolored in composition, interfaith, interdenominational, and intercultural. At the time of that feature story in 1948, Fellowship Church was using a rented meeting hall, but the dynamism at work in the group and its worship caused one of the members to remark to the magazine reporter that coming into that hall was "like coming into a cathedral."[9]

From the beginning, Thurman's design was to have spiritual leadership of the church vested in two co-pastors of different ethnic backgrounds. This was a deliberate plan written into the church constitution. "In order to appreciate the meaning of the provision," Thurman has explained, "it must be remembered that the usual policy of a congregation seeking its leadership was here reversed: it was the minister or ministers who called the congregation."[10] The plan took advantage of the presence and work of Fisk. Given the original

---

9. "Fellowship Church," *Time*, July 26, 1948, 40-42. **ED:** Thurman, "*Time*: "Fellowship Church, 26 July 1948," in Fluker, ed., *The Papers of Thurman: Volume 3*, 275-278.

10. Thurman, *Footprints of a Dream*, 97.

relationship between this group and Fisk, there was no question about the fact that his ministry must be continued. The organizational plan for co-pastors undergirded this concern. But it did more: it guaranteed the presence of another white leader should Dr. Fisk find it necessary to leave the scene.

Although Howard Thurman and Alfred Fisk served the group as fully accredited co-pastors, this arrangement had some built-in problems and both recognized those problems for what they were. For instance, Fisk's work as professor at San Francisco State College meant that he was restricted to a part-time work relationship with the church. On this basis alone the co-pastorate was not being completely tested so as to prove itself, Thurman has explained:

> This early arrangement, nevertheless, served two important purposes. The co-pastorate symbolized the kind of integration we wanted to obtain in all the church relationships of all the members. It was also a test of whether or not a community of fellowship within the congregation could be achieved that would offset the tendency to separateness which was the common experience of the members' lives in the workday communities. It was crucial to discover whether or not there could be developed a bond of such authentic community that—contrary prevailing social patterns notwithstanding—the Caucasians would not gravitate to Dr. Fisk's leadership and the non-Caucasians to mine. The fact that this kind of gravitation did not take place gave the church, at its very inception, a spirit that sustained it through the many crises that were to come.[11]

Once it was seen that the membership pattern in the church would remain interracial the co-pastors began to believe that the leadership pattern could shift or be changed without any significant difference in the composition of the church. This was tested when Dr. Fisk found it necessary to resign from his leadership responsibilities as co-pastor. After his resignation, the church adapted to a senior pastor plan with Thurman carrying final authority and others working with him as associates and assistants.

Thurman's indefinite leave of absence in 1953 to go to Boston University could have shaken the congregation far more violently than it

11. Thurman, *Footprints of a Dream*, 98.

did had it not been for two other aspects of organizational structuring for which he was originally responsible. One was the system of small group meetings of the membership on a sectional basis. These meetings allowed for free discussion and involvement of every member in church planning. The other was the internship program which gave in-depth ministerial training to young seminary graduates.

The small group meetings were especially helpful to the official board in planning for the church. The sectional group meetings operated as follows:

> Those persons who lived in Berkeley and Oakland met in a group in that area and those down the peninsula met in a group in that area so on until the entire membership had the opportunity of involvement. With the help of persons trained in group discussion techniques, groups throughout the membership thus discussed matters that needed to be brought up at the scheduled town meeting of the congregation as a whole. At the big meeting, the entire group was informed of whatever had taken place in each of the smaller discussion groups. All matters affecting the church, including its leadership, came under careful scrutiny. It was a sober and enlightening experience for the minister to sit through a town meeting and hear what the congregation had to say about his sermons and his other services as pastor. The net result of all this was a quality of experience healthy for the congregation and for the future of the church. Out of it came a way of dealing with any crisis that would allow the time needed for full discussion.[12]

The internship program developed very early in the organization of the church. The plan was to allow young ministers an opportunity to work within a multiracial and multicultural setting controlled by a common religious commitment. The intent was to help the ministers learn from the experience of inclusiveness so that their future ministries would be geared always to that spirit and interest. Expenses to cover the internship program came first from friends who liked the idea and its implications for the wider church. In time, Fellowship Church itself budgeted for the expense. There were occasions

---

12. Thurman, *Footprints of a Dream*, 99.

when interns remained as assistant ministers by invitation of the church and the official board. This was the case with Robert Meyner, a young Congregational minister, who was the first ministerial student to intern at Fellowship Church.[13]

It was also the case with Francis Geddes, a white minister who served two summers as an intern before he graduated from Yale Divinity School. After his graduation the church invited him to join the staff as an assistant minister. Still later, following an interim ministry there by Dryden Phelps, Francis Geddes succeeded Howard Thurman as pastor.[14] Several others interned at the church, some being supported through a plan arranged between Fellowship Church and the intern's respective denomination.[15]

> In addition to these interns, students from a neighboring theological seminary, The Pacific School of Religion, worked as student assistants in various capacities. All of this meant that during the first ten years more than a dozen persons who have subsequently become professional workers in regular churches were acquainted with the problems and the significance of Fellowship Church. It is difficult to overestimate the far-reaching effect these people will have on the future of American Christianity.[16]

Thurman believes that the Fellowship Church experience in unity really came of age during the early months of 1948. He had risked a lengthy absence from the group while serving as guest professor at the University of Iowa. Upon his return—with his stipend already volunteered for church needs—he noticed that the members were not calling it "Fellowship Church" or "the Church" but were referring to it in a rather matter-of-fact way as "our Church." This made him know that they had reached a place of essential growth, on the one hand, and a stealthy pride, on the other. He knew that he would have to work now to keep the church from "freezing" its genius and gains.

---

13. Thurman, *Footprints of a Dream*, 100.
14. Thurman, *Footprints of a Dream*, 102, 132-133.
15. Thurman, *Footprints of a Dream*, 100-102.
16. Thurman, *Footprints of a Dream*, 103.

Seven years from its humble beginnings The Church for the Fellowship of All Peoples had 345 resident members and 1,105 "members at large." The "members at large" were persons living outside of San Francisco in other parts of the nation who wanted to be formally identified with the church as national affiliates. Among such national affiliates or associates were Eleanor Roosevelt, President of the United Council of Church Women Harper Sibley, Mary McLeod Bethune, South African novelist and antiapartheid activist Alan Paton, and Channing M. Tobias, to name only a few. Over half of the resident members were white, about 40 per cent were Black, and there were several Asian members. Interestingly, however, the larger proportion of those who attended the worship services at that time were Asians. By 1949 they were supporting a program guided by a paid staff of three full-time and two part-time persons. By 1951, its seventh year, The Church for the Fellowship of All Peoples had become one of the most talked about churches in the religious life of San Francisco. The church was rightly cited that year in a feature article in *The Christian Century*.[17]

That witness to fellowship was not always honored by some people touched by its impact. Some onlookers criticized the group: Blacks, because they thought the church should be a social whip; radicals, because they wanted to see the group wage an open fight against social pressures and problems; traditionalists in religion, eager to pin a label on the group and thus classify it; emotionalists, who thought that Thurman's preaching and services were too highbrow. Interestingly, there was seldom any outright criticism of the interracial stance of the church! Yet that stance did constitute a test to all who sought to benefit from the life of Fellowship Church. In this connection Douglas V. Steere reports an incident within the Fellowship Church life that Thurman once shared with him.

> A woman from the congregation asked him to call on her, and when he came, proceeded to outline to him seven reasons why she could never join the Fellowship Church. The seventh reason was that she simply could not stand Negroes! Howard Thurman

---

17. "Trumpet Ready in the West," *The Christian Century*, September 12, 1951, 1040-1045.

> laughed and told her he hoped that none of these reasons would keep her from at least continuing to attend the church, and added that none of us could ever be quite sure what God might do with our objections. Now and then in the course of the next months, this woman appeared in the line of those who spoke to him after the service, and there were cryptic reports that, "Number one is gone," or, "Five has disappeared," but always with the addition, "Seven is still there." Finally one Sunday she came to him and said, "Oh, Thurman, even seven is gone, and I want to join the church."[18]

Thurman was wise enough across his years of ministry in San Francisco never to claim more for the venture than he should, despite the apparent successes he and the congregation kept witnessing in their life together. Fellowship Church became known across the nation for its active and inclusive fellowship. Given the climate of racial separateness in the United States at the time when the church was formally incorporated, and given the conflicts witnessed by pastor and people in living out the dream of fellowship, the story of that church is of compelling significance. So is the spirit of Howard Thurman whose unique gifts helped that group in its quest to fulfill the dream.

Campus Ministry at Boston University

Howard Thurman's appointment as Dean of Daniel L. Marsh Chapel at Boston University was an event heralded across the nation. The appointment was a kind of "first" in that university's history because Thurman was the first African American to fill a full-time faculty post there. He was given the rank of full professor and, being Dean of the Chapel, he headed a six-member board of preachers. His designation "Professor of Spiritual Disciplines and Resources" excited interest across the academic world. In announcing the news event in *The Christian Century*, one of the editors commented, "We are not so much impressed by this appointment of a Negro to this faculty post as we are by the title of his post. A 'professor of spiritual disciplines

---

18. Douglas V. Steere, *Dimensions of Prayer* (New York: Harper and Row, 1962), 96-97.

and resources' sounds like something most theological seminaries have needed for a long time. No one is more likely than Dr. Thurman to be able to make this intriguing but vague professorial assignment a valid academic discipline."[19]

The Boston University campus, with its sixteen schools and colleges, was a highly complex educational center. The students, drawn from across the world, and numbering more than 25,000, had religious needs, and the university had long had a tradition of concern about those needs along with its educational emphasis. President Harold C. Case, himself a Methodist minister, had known Howard Thurman across several years and believed that Thurman would work well in such an interracial, intercultural, interdenominational, and interfaith setting. Thurman's success in shaping and leading The Church for the Fellowship of All Peoples made him a natural choice for the Boston venture. In being appointed Dean of Marsh Chapel, Thurman succeeded Franklin H. Littell, first Dean of the Chapel after it was completed in 1950.[20]

When Thurman went to Boston, a new era was beginning to take shape on the national social scene. He began his work at Marsh Chapel at about the time Martin Luther King, Jr.—a young, vigorous, and scholarly Black preacher destined to become the nation's leading advocate of nonviolent resistance was completing his course requirements for the PhD degree at the Boston University School of Theology. Although Thurman knew the King family in Atlanta, his path and that of Martin L. King, Jr., did not regularly cross. Both men were too involved in their assignments to have time for lengthy contacts that first year. Thurman's major ministry to King would come later, even as King's major service would only later take shape under the pressure of circumstance, necessity, and public call. Thurman and King did see each other occasionally that first year, but the task of research on his dissertation limited the younger man's time, as did the weekend preaching trips after January 1954 to Montgomery, Alabama, where later he was to pastor.[21]

---

19. *The Christian Century*, April 8, 1953, 406.

20. Richard Morgan Cameron, *Boston University School of Theology 1839-1968* (Boston: Boston University School of Theology, 1968), 137. The book was a special edition of *Nexus* (Vol, XI, Nos 2 and 3), May 1968.

21. Bennett, Jr., *What Manner of Man*, 48-51.

As for the new social era about to emerge in May 1954, the Supreme Court issued an epochal decision that segregation in the public schools was unconstitutional, forcing the entire nation to make a reappraisal of Black-white relations on many levels. A new spirit was at work in many places. Thurman was one of many agents of that Zeitgeist.

Howard Thurman was the right person for the Boston University assignment. Utilizing techniques and insights he had gained at Howard University, Thurman had the background of experience out of which to project a plan and program for Marsh Chapel. In both places of service Thurman proved himself a pioneer. As the first Dean of Rankin Chapel at Howard University, Thurman shaped his work by experimentation, trial and error. In the Boston assignment as second Dean of the Chapel he had to pioneer again as an African American serving in a predominantly white setting.

Thurman went to Boston to establish in a large urban university a center of worship and religious life with which all the varied members of the academic community could relate. The situation was one of emotional strain initially, best classified as life in a "fish bowl," as he termed it.[22] But the years had prepared him well for his assignment: the twelve years at Howard University, the nine and one-half years at the San Francisco church, and the still earlier years of seeking his place as a thinking Black person. Thurman majored in the crucial art of human relations, exercising his ability to relate religious resources to personal and social problems encountered on his way through the world. He knew how to deal with academia, moving with concern and competence among professionals and colleagues, and he knew how to deal with the student mind, identifying and treating students' religious needs with insight and integrity.

Thurman worked with a well-developed general philosophy for his assignment. He knew campus culture. He knew his area of counseling.[23] He had a healthy respect for cultural differences and

---

22. Thurman, *Footprints of a Dream*, 131.

23. **ED:** Eisenstadt, *Against the Hounds of Hell*, 145: "Throughout his career, Thurman was in demand as a mentor and advisor. . . . Thurman clearly had a special calling for it, less a matter of dispensing advice than assuming the role of a spiritual psychologist, helping others to find their inner voice, what

distinctives, having worked intimately with what he called the "challenging cross-section of people" who made up the membership of that interracial, interfaith, intercultural congregation in San Francisco.[24] He had learned how to move beyond the surface of human togetherness under guidance of religious distinctives.

Marsh Chapel was the religious center of the campus. As the Dean of Marsh Chapel, Thurman was the designated University official responsible for the total religious life of the university community. He coordinated the religious aspect of freshman orientation to the university setting. He chaired the university board of preachers and religious counselors, which was known officially as the United Ministry to Students. He also held responsibility for preaching at the Sunday Morning Service of worship in the Chapel, as well as for planning and conducting special services on various occasions as required in the life of the University. Beginning on a Sunday near the start of each new school year, and continuing thereafter throughout the academic year, an All-University Religious Service was available for the campus community—and interested town folk. During the years of Thurman's tenure there, many from both campus and city came under the influence of his ministry through Marsh Chapel.

The regular Sunday Bulletin held a significant statement that alerted every worshipper to the context in which their worship was to take place.

> The Sunday Morning Service addresses itself to the deepest needs and aspirations of the human spirit. In so doing it does not seek to undermine whatever may be the religious context which gives meaning and richness to your particular life; but rather to deepen the authentic lines along which your quest for spiritual reality has led you. It is our hope that you will come to regard the Chapel not only as a place of stimulation, challenge, and dedication, but also as a symbol of the intent of the University to recognize religion as fundamental to the human enterprise.

---

he later called the 'sound of the genuine,' and to assist them in formulating and answering their own questions."

24. Howard Thurman, *The Growing Edge* (New York: Harper & Row, 1956), x.

The format of the regular Sunday Morning Service allowed for creativity on the part of the leaders and worshippers, and for necessary interaction between organist, choir, and preacher. Thurman tried to keep the worship structure minimal, in order to keep worship experience central. Max Miller, organist, and Allen C. Lannom, Director of the Chapel Choir, worked responsibly with a well-trained and devoted choral unit, and sometimes instrumentalists and a small chamber orchestra. The Choir had such training and versatility that the choral repertoire ranged from Gregorian Chants to Brahms' German Requiem, Bach's B Minor Mass, and to contemporary composers.

The digest of the ministry of Marsh Chapel for the academic year 1956-1957 contained a statement from Allen C. Lannom about the spirit of the choir he directed.

> Devotion is perhaps the key word in the Marsh Chapel Choir experience. Devoted to each other, to the spirit of great music, and to the purposes of the Chapel program, choir members made whatever sacrifices and adjustments were necessary to breathe into the rehearsals and services an inner "something," undefinable, but pulsating with the urgency of creative activity. In this group, duty was never the measure of accepted responsibility, but opportunity, charged with the imperative of growth, led every participant into an enormous area of service.[25]

The spirit of the total service had a great deal to do with such a result. As Thurman has explained, "A genuine effort was made to recognize that the congregation of that urban university Chapel must be addressed at the level of the deepest needs and the most fundamental aspirations of the human spirit." He was intent to be profound yet simple and universal, working within the context of the Judeo-Christian tradition with such universality that all those of such diverse cultures and ethnic differences could realize their oneness and equality in the Presence of God. Thurman's own heartfelt concern was at one with the thrust of the inscription over the door entering the Sanctuary of Marsh Chapel: "Let this chapel at the center of the university campus signify forever the centrality both

---

25. Boston University, *Marsh Chapel: The Program*, 1956-1957, 9.

of intellectual and experimental religion in education and also of devotion to God's righteous rule in human lives." The words were those of Daniel L. Marsh after whom the Chapel was named.

In addition to directing the Chapel program and preaching during the Sunday Morning All-University Religious Service, Thurman also began in November 1957 to give a meditation each Friday morning at 11:15 a.m. over Station WHDH Television Channel 5 as part of the "We Believe" series. Sometimes guest speakers from the Graduate School of Theology were called upon to share with him in the television program. His presentations were transcribed weekly and mailed to a large list of people who requested them. Some of these people also attended the services at Marsh Chapel on Sundays or listened to the service when broadcast live over the University's own radio station WBUR-FM. Airing the service allowed those within a fifty-mile radius of Boston to receive from the ministry of Marsh Chapel. Later in his ministry as Dean, Thurman also broadcast a 15-minute meditation hour each Friday evening over WBUR. The flavor and accent of his voice was well known both on the campus and beyond it in the Greater Boston area. In 1962, President Case credited Thurman with having "given National prestige to the pulpit in Marsh Chapel."[26]

The worship pattern used at Marsh Chapel was designed to appeal to a wide range of participants. Thurman notes, "In the course of a year, a host of people from our own country and beyond the seas attend the Sunday morning religious services in Marsh Chapel. Each Sunday morning the congregation consists of persons from the Orient, Africa, the Near East, Europe, South America, Canada, and the United States."[27] This fact influenced the structure of the services, the spirit of the services, and all the methods, meditation materials, and activities. This fact also influenced the basic substance of Thurman's sermons.

Although the All-University Religious Service on Sunday morning in Marsh Chapel was the heart of the Chapel program, the services that contributed to it and those that issued from it were many indeed. Among those services necessary for the Chapel program was the singing of the volunteer Chapel Choir. There was also the

26. Marsh Chapel Bulletin, Sunday, September 16, 1962, 4.
27. Thurman, *The Inward Journey*, 7.

Liturgical Dance Choir whose aesthetic services were occasionally utilized as a Vesper experience toward spiritual togetherness in worship. Like the Chapel Choir, the Dance Choir was also comprised of volunteers who met weekly for rehearsal and strategic training. Recognizing that dance is a basic and universal language, Thurman initiated a liturgical dance choir into the Chapel program in 1953. He had tested this medium as an aid to worship while at Howard University. The purpose was to create through movement and space the substance of worship, and to reestablish dance as an integral part of the active worship of God—as it was once known in ancient Israel's past. The choreography was sometimes a group development and sometimes the direct planning of the dance group leader. Services were rendered by the Liturgical Dance Choir at select points during the annual calendar: an occasional Daily Chapel Service, a Thanksgiving Day Service, a Christmas Choral Vesper Hour, or a service wholly used by the Dance Choir and an interpretative reader, usually Dean Thurman himself.

The Chapel Ushers provided a meaningful ministry on Sunday mornings. The ushers were volunteers from the several schools and colleges of the University or members in the congregation who came from the Greater Boston Area. Social meetings of the usher group occurred occasionally as well as when the ushers periodically joined the Chapel Choir for dinner at the Thurman home.

A Children's Chapel operated concurrently with the Sunday Morning Service, a direct result of the initiative of parents who attended the Sunday services. At first, parents of the children formed the guiding committee, but later skilled leadership was provided through volunteer teachers and students from within the campus community. As interest deepened, and as the group of children increased, each school year closed with an annual picnic held for the children, the teachers, and the families involved in the program.

The Coffee Hour after each Sunday Morning Service was a weekly treat for the Marsh Chapel congregation. The sense of community formally realized during worship was experienced informally over coffee shared together in the Conference Lounge of the Chapel building. Thurman would position himself near the door to welcome those who entered. The coffee time was admittedly a community idea.

The Women's Committee of the Chapel delegated members of the Committee to serve as hostesses during the Sunday coffee time. Organized in 1954, the Chapel Women's Committee gave what Thurman called "the magic touch of personal sensitiveness" to the Chapel program: securing flowers for the altar, keeping guest books with records of Chapel visitors, serving at special times of celebration, decorating for special events, sharing with the Dean and Mrs. Thurman when groups were given hospitality at their home. The Chapel Women's Committee also developed a program of aid for refugees around the world, selling arts and crafts and Christmas cards to aid them in their enterprise.

Under Thurman's administration as Dean of the Chapel, an All-University Weekday Morning Service also developed. The request for this came in 1956 from a group of concerned students. Starting as an experiment, the Daily Chapel Service was conducted by students and volunteer faculty members from 8:45 to 9:00 a.m. As with the Sunday Morning Service, the Daily Chapel was conducted on an interfaith, nonsectarian level.

Every Wednesday evening during the academic year, from 7:30 to 9:00 p.m., a Weekly Discussion Group convened informally to consider religious subjects. The time was divided into two periods of interest: a quiet and informal worship session in Robinson Chapel, after which the group arrived to a circle of chairs in the Conference Lounge for questions and discussion. Dean Thurman and his graduate assistant from the School of Theology guided the period.

Chapel Retreats were held periodically for representatives from the various Chapel organizations and members of the congregation. The first such retreat was held in October 1961, with about twenty-five people attending, and was mainly focused upon a congregational and programmatic self-appraisal of the Chapel life and work. The sharing permitted many aspects of the Chapel program to be further interpreted by the Dean, while it also allowed the voicing of suggestions for strengthening the program and life of the Chapel. The second retreat involved more of the congregation than the first, and was held at the University's Conference Center.

The Dean's residence was a place of hospitality, fun, and fellowship. There was an "open door policy" for students, in particular, which continued a practice from his years at Howard University. Informal dinners were shared monthly with the Chapel staff, the

Choir, and the Chapel Ushers. Additional courtesies in the home took the form of luncheons, teas, "Nationality Dinners," and coffee hours with many other campus groups, clubs, international students, community groups, and the Dean's classes from the School of Theology. Thurman's Boston years not only revealed his spiritual expertise but also his social graces. The strategic ministry of Sue Bailey Thurman in this regard must also be highlighted. Besides assisting the Dean, she worked to foster better understanding and appreciation of peoples and cultures around the world among college students. Her use of rare dolls from around the world called attention to significant aspects of culture and, as well, the plight of certain peoples, particularly refugees. In 1961, *Ebony Magazine* 'honored Sue Bailey Thurman's work in this area with a feature story."[28]

The work of the Chapel during the 1960s had to take into consideration the social revolution in the United States. Always alert to deal radically with the social sickness of racial prejudice and discrimination through the insights of the Christian faith, Howard Thurman continued to address himself "to the deepest needs and aspirations of the human spirit"—including the quest for freedom and the need for community. Through a special gift to the Chapel, Thurman planned and promoted a series of special dinner meetings in order to bring campus and community together for strategic discussions. In January 1962, John Hope Franklin, then Chairman of the Department of History at Brooklyn College, spoke informatively about "A Century of Civil War Centennial Celebration and the Image of the Negro." In February a second dinner was held, and guest leaders of the conversation period were Attorney and Mrs. T. Emory Daniel, formerly Assistant Prosecuting Attorney of DeKalb County, Georgia, whose topic was "Atlanta, Georgia—A Small Oasis in a Big Desert." Among other things, the speech helped to interpret some of the recent experiences of Martin Luther King, Jr., in the DeKalb County court, and some attendant events that helped to start significant change in the course of the nation's history.[29] The third dinner meeting speaker, in April, was A. Philip Randolph, President of the International Union of Pullman Porters and Dining

---

28. "Dolls For Democracy: Toys Aid Thurman's Campaign for Understanding," *Ebony*, December 1961, 93-96, 98.

29. Bennett, Jr., *What Manner of Man*, 117-119.

Car Attendants, using a topic central for information and discussion, "The Civil Rights Revolution in the United States." The dinners were all held in the Faculty Club of the University and all the 250 people present from the campus and the wider community were guests of Howard and Sue Thurman.

During the same period as the dinners, Thurman preached on Sundays about the religious dimensions of the problems, needs, and aspirations lifted to view by the dinner speakers. Under the collective title "Quests of the Human Spirit," he concerned himself with the quest for freedom, values, truth, security, authority, integrity, identity, peace, and God.[30] Considered against the background of the times, these topics were strategically chosen and presented with essential timeliness. The settlement of the Brown vs. Board of Education case by the Supreme Court in 1954 had been an event on the side of wholeness and community. So had the 1955 Montgomery, Alabama, boycott under Martin Luther King, Jr. So was the Civil Rights Act of Congress in 1958, and the Freedom Rides in the South in 1961. In his activities as Dean, preacher, and professor, Thurman was eager to stand against that which divides, and to work and speak for justice, wholeness, and community.

As Professor of Spiritual Disciplines and Resources, Thurman mapped out a new three-hour course in the seminary curriculum. During his nine years as professor at Boston, he experimented with many ways of teaching on the subject. He lectured, distributed selected readings for the class, engaged the members in discussion, and guided them in meditation. He pinpointed certain devotional classics and highlighted them for their resourcefulness. He probed the nature of religious experience and guided his students in the creative use of silence, music, and worship occasions. He scheduled conferences in private for those students who wished to go further into the subject than class sessions allowed. Howard Thurman was at his best when interpreting religious experience and dealing with the raw materials of daily life as doors into the Presence of God. His book *The Creative Encounter* (1954) shows some of his structured thought on the meaning of religious experience. His book, *Disciplines of the Spirit* (1963) was a more direct outgrowth of his classroom work and experience. It was because of this background

30. Boston University, Marsh Chapel Program, 1961-1962, 10.

that Thurman dedicated the book "To the students in my course on Spiritual Disciplines and Resources, 1953-1962."[31]

Thurman's Marsh Chapel schedule was flexible enough to allow him to accept and handle a few special lectureships at other colleges, universities, and church associations. Among the lectureships these should be listed:

- 1953 Merrick Lecturer, Ohio Wesleyan University
- 1956 Ware Lecturer, American Unitarian Association
- 1957 Ratcliff Lecturer, Tufts University
- 1958 Beach Quiet Hour Lecturer, Bangor Theological Seminary
- 1959 Earl Lecturer, Pacific School of Religion
- 1960 Smith-Willson Lecturer, Southwestern College
- 1961 Willson Lecturer, Nebraska Wesleyan University; Mendenhall Lecturer, DePauw University; Rufus M. Jones Memorial Lecturer, Society of Friends.

But of all the lectureships that Thurman fulfilled, perhaps none of them quite matched his experience years earlier in 1947 when he was the Ingersoll Lecturer on The Immortality of Man, at Harvard University. The assignment was doubly meaningful: Thurman was the first African American to give the Ingersoll Lecture, and the preparation of the lecture for publication in the Harvard Divinity School Bulletin led to a new aspect of ministry for him—the writing of books. Thereafter many of his lectureship assignments reached a wider public in book form: 1948 Mary L. Smith Memorial Lectures at Samuel Huston College became *Jesus and the Disinherited*, 1954 Merrick Lectures at Ohio Wesleyan University became *The Creative Encounter*, and 1960 Smith-Willson Lectures at Southwestern College became *Disciplines of the Spirit*.

Thurman had another writing experience that was also a kind of "first" for him and for African Americans. He was the first Black preacher to take part in the publication of a major commentary on the Bible. *The Interpreter's Bible*, popularly classified as "Christendom's Most Comprehensive Commentary," was a landmark of biblical scholarship. The commentary project began with a somewhat

---

31. Howard Thurman, *Disciplines of the Spirit* (New York: Harper and Row, 1963), 5.

casually asked question during dinner as George Arthur Buttrick sat talking with Pat Beaird, the business manager of Abingdon-Cokesbury Press. The Methodist publisher asked Buttrick, "What, in your judgment, is the most urgent task in religious publishing today?" The scholarly pastor answered, "A new commentary on the Bible which would bridge the gap between the exegetes [interpreters] and the rank & file teachers and preachers."[32] Under the general editorial direction of Buttrick, the entire project took about fourteen years to complete, and at a cost of more than $1,000,000. Howard Thurman was one of thirty-six consulting editors for the project. He was also a contributing writer (one of 129), and the only African American involved in the commentary project.[33] Thurman prepared the exposition for the books of the two Minor Prophets Habakkuk and Zephaniah, which appeared in Volume VI of the commentary.[34] His gifts and insights were especially apt for that assignment.

Along with prestigious lectureships and writing assignments, Thurman received many academic honors during his years at Boston University. Before his Marsh Chapel ministry he had been honored twice with conferred honorary doctorates: Morehouse College, his alma mater, conferred an honorary Doctor of Divinity degree upon him in 1935, and Wesleyan College did the same in 1946.

The Wider Ministry

On September 1, 1962, Howard Thurman went on leave from active duty as Dean of Marsh Chapel, free to pursue other assignments that would carry him into other parts of the nation but especially to other parts of the world. The "global ministry" plan was his response to

---

32. "Biblical Landmark," *Time*, October 22, 1951, 75. See also Walter Russell Bowie, *Learning to Live* (Nashville: Abingdon Press, 1969), 209-211.

33. **ED:** Massey, *Aspects of my Pilgrimage*, 423-425. Massey served on the updated project for *The New Interpreter's Bible*. "How pleased Howard Thurman would have been to see me serve as a writer and working editor for the new commentary series planned to supplement and update the older series for which he had been a writer and a consulting editor (424)."

34. *The Interpreter's Bible, Volume VI*, edited by George A. Buttrick, et al. (Nashville: Abingdon Press, 1956), 979-1002, 1013-1034.

many calls from institutions in countries Howard and Sue Thuman had visited and served during his sabbatical leave in 1959-1960. When President Case approved the leave, he publicly interpreted Thurman's services abroad as an extension of the ministry of the Chapel. In fact, two weeks after Thuman began his leave, President Case wrote a statement about the Wider Ministry Plan which appeared in the Marsh Chapel Sunday Bulletin for September 16, 1962, referring to the Dean of the Chapel as being on loan from the University "to preach to the nation."

The leave covered a two-year period fulfilling many significant assignments in many strategic institutions and areas of the world. Friends in Boston, San Francisco, and elsewhere underwrote the expenses of the program for the two years. Before leaving Boston, Thurman videotaped enough programs to cover his period of absence from the weekly "We Believe" series on Channel 5. Guest preachers handled the Sunday worship responsibilities at Marsh Chapel. Thurman also vacated his residence on campus since "it was the general understanding with the administration of the university that at the end of the two-year period, inasmuch as I would be eligible for formal retirement from the university, I would not resume my responsibilities at the Chapel."[35] An announcement was later made that Robert H. Hamill was dean designate and would succeed Thurman in ministry at Marsh Chapel.

Thurman retired from deanship at Marsh Chapel in 1964 at the close of the second year of the Wider Ministry and was honored with the title of "University Minister-at-large." At a testimonial dinner given by the University in his honor in May 1965, Thurman was cited for his work by President Harold C. Case and the Honorable Joseph Palmer, Director General of the Foreign Service of the United States. In the presence of four hundred personal friends gathered for the occasion, Case commended Thurman for his ministry to the University, and Palmer commended him for his ministry to the nation and world.

Howard Thurman went to Boston University to establish a campus center of worship that would cut across all lines that divide—lines of culture, class, race, creed, and religion. There is abundant

35. Boston University Marsh Chapel Annual Report: The Wider Ministry, 1962-1963.

evidence that he fulfilled his assignment well. The University held his ministry in such esteem that upon retirement Thurman was named Dean Emeritus of Marsh Chapel. The Church for the Fellowship of All Peoples had already honored Howard Thurman as Minister Emeritus. During the 1967 commencement Boston University conferred upon him an honorary Doctor of Divinity degree. Having retired, he was, as he put it, "free now from the restraint and security of a portfolio," but he would never be free from the communal ties of regard from his unique campus and church ministry.

Chapter Five

Thurman as Preacher

In 1953 a board of judges under the auspices of *Life* magazine listed Howard Thurman as one among the twelve greatest preachers in the United States.[1] This assessment was based upon a carefully conducted poll taken among ministers, priests, and theological schools of the major faiths. The inclusion was reasonable and warranted, highlighting the skill of one whose preaching has been contagious, inspiring, unique, and legendary in his own time.[2]

Howard Thurman's preaching bears the unmistakable imprint of his personality: it is thoughtful, singular, explicit, brooding, and captivating. Recognized widely as one of the ablest living interpreters of classic religious experience, early in his ministry Thurman adopted a style of presentation and delivery that would match both his sermon subject matter and his personality. The "brooding quality" in his sermons has been misinterpreted at times by some hearers as a kind of studiedness. It is as if Thurman is feeling his way or trying

---

1. *Life*, April 6, 1953, 128.

2. <u>ED:</u> Through the years, Massey shared widely in lectures and publications about Howard Thurman as a preacher. Two examples that draw on this chapter are: James Earl Massey, "Thurman's Preaching: Substance and Style," in Henry James Young, ed., *God and Human Freedom: A Festschrift in Honor of Howard Thurman* (Richmond, IN: Friends United Press, 1983), 110-121; and James Earl Massey, "Howard Thurman," in William H. Willimon and Richard Lischer, eds., *Concise Encyclopedia of Preaching* (Louisville: Westminster John Knox Press, 1995), 484-487.

to recall what he has planned to say next—since there are no manuscript sheets or notes before him when he preaches. But Thurman's brooding is rather part of his personal exposure during the service as a fellow worshipper with the people. As he has explained it: "For me the sermon is an act of worship in which the preacher exposes his spirit and mind as they seek to reveal the working of the spirit of the living God upon them. It is a searching moment! The atmosphere is one charged with dynamics of worship and the surrender and commitment which worship inspires."[3]

Howard Thurman's sermons are best described as religious tracts that deal creatively with aspects of life in the light of God. They are planned and delivered with concern to help the hearers to understand life and gain confidence for handling themselves as persons responsible to God.

Thurman is a master interpreter and guide on the inner life. No one who has heard his sermon on "The Dilemma of Commitment" or his sermon on "The Single Mind" can question his sense of what is central, nor escape the need to make a commitment to God and ensure a quality life in the world. Thurman's sermons are provocative, calling hearers to examine their crucial link with God. Quite early in his ministry, Thurman decided to preach only what will help us truly to worship and to fulfill the kind of life true worship inspires.

The typical sermon pattern in Thurman's preaching involves a single idea or insight. Seldom does his sermon involve more than one point to which every aspect of the sermon directly and logically relates. A concern is stated, then it is underscored by religious principles, practical illustrations, and the logic of common experience. He has never forgotten the teaching of his homiletics professor at Rochester Theological Seminary who advised the class that a preacher is never under obligation to preach a great sermon, but that they are always under obligation to wrestle with a great idea.[4] Howard Thurman's sermons betray such wrestling, and some of his sermons have become justly great.

Thurman usually prefaces his sermons with a meditation-prayer, drawing together the aspirations of his own heart and those of the

3. Thurman, *The Growing Edge*, ix-x.

4. Thurman, *The Growing Edge*, x.

people. He sometimes offers in addition (or instead) a short but centered reading as a prolegomenon to the sermon. The reading may or may not be related directly to the sermon theme or meaning, but it is purposed "to aid the listeners in bringing their minds into focus upon some searching insight and to make available the centered spirits."[5]

Howard Thurman's preaching is characterized by clear speech. Thurman tries always to remove the strangeness, difficulty, and unfamiliarity of religious concepts and make them understood for practical use in experience. While it is true that his sermons are vehicles of philosophic, existential, and religious truths, he works always to make vital religion understood for direct experience. Those who hear him preach are left with no misunderstanding about the demand for commitment to God. Thurman's preaching carries the hearer well beyond the claims of custom, convention, and culture. He interprets, reminds, invites, educates, and feeds.

For Thurman, the spoken word is a vital tool. He has a highly developed speech pattern. He risks himself in his words. He makes the speaking event a personal, lyrical, and dramatic moment of confrontation. In preaching to help people grasp truth—and be grasped by truth—Thurman counts seriously on the spoken word, the personal witness, the expression. Style is important to his statement. Pauses are crucial to accent the depth of the thought. Obsessed with the power of the spoken word, Thurman did not begin to stir himself as a writer until late in his career; even then he molded his writings in a form determined by his meditational speaking approach. One needs only read aloud the deceptively simple prose found in Thurman's sermons and you will sense immediately the same liveliness and favor which characterize his books of meditations. The sermons of Howard Thurman are an event of living language and they encourage a lively hearing.

The quality of aliveness in his preaching is deepened and extended by several means. For one thing, Thurman does not rush through a sermon. He does not preach long, but he exercises a deliberateness which has caused some hearers to criticize him as long-winded. This deliberateness, a characteristic feature across many years, helps to affect a felt sense of pause, quietness, intimacy, lingering over

5. Thurman, *The Growing Edge*, ix.

meanings, and waiting in the presence of God, before the hearer moves to deal again with the world that waits outside the place and time of worship.

For another thing, Thurman makes those who hear him study his words with him as he speaks to them. He is not concerned merely with speaking and speaking well, but to listening anew with the other worshippers to catch aspects of insight that he had not seen while preparing the sermon. Thurman does not view forethought for preaching as the final thought in preaching, nor is initial meaning ever terminal meaning. His interest is never general but specific. His words rise from deep within him, from those deep places touched by life and tutored by God in the midst of life. His words rise slowly, as if heavily freighted with meaning and concern. They are spoken with passion and extend their meaning through form and detail, but slowly, ever so slowly, as if reluctant to be exposed to a world that might not give them welcome.

Another aspect of aliveness in Thurman's preaching is his emotionally expressive delivery. Thurman does not shout nor does he gesture violently. He does not use the contrived rhetoric of arousal. His facial gestures and the graphic movement of his hands correspond with the carefulness, style, and tone of his thought.

There is emotional expressiveness in his illustrations and the choice metaphors he employs. Thurman can "feel" with his hearers and anticipate their reactions and unasked questions. A part of the wisdom of this might well lie in the background tradition in which Thurman was raised as a boy. In the family church in Florida, Thurman grew up accustomed to a worship service in which there was a definite feeling tone between the preacher and the worshippers. Pastor James was free in his preaching and his speech was zestful and engaging. The preacher sometimes gave such vivid descriptions of biblical events that one could think they had been there on the scene when it all first happened. The whole church would get caught up in the contagion. To the listening church, and especially to young Howard, the drama was exhilarating—"it was so real, so real."[6] He had witnessed the impact of the power of words. He still remembers sermons that helped him experience a climax of impression. He learned early that a sermon can be an experience of truth.

6. Yates, *Howard Thurman*, 37.

It was this same quality of aliveness in his sermons that made Howard University's Rankin Chapel a popular place when Dean Thurman preached there. That aliveness helped The Church for the Fellowship of All Peoples to grow across the years of his ministry in San Francisco, and it kept Marsh Chapel at Boston University full during Thurman's service years there as Dean of the Chapel. An observer reported that Marsh Chapel had never been full until Howard Thurman came there to preach regularly as the University Preacher.[7]

Built in 1949, Marsh Chapel's Gothic structure offered an atmosphere of beauty and spacious accommodation. Those who came there to hear Thurman's first sermon as Dean of the Chapel knew that they would have to return again and again to hear him, finding his style unique and his content gripping. One reporter commented on Thurman's preaching at Boston University, lauding "the power of his speech, the original and forceful symbols he evokes, his strong sense of humor, and the breadth of his philosophy."[8] He added, "It would be hard to find a more accomplished speaker; in fact without in the least impugning his sincerity, he may be called a spell-binder."[9]

Howard Thurman preaches with integrity and appeal. His rhetoric, imagery, illustrations, deliberateness of timing; his sincerity and sermonic voice—with its infinite gradations of tone and measured cadence; all these combine when he preaches and they produce a vision for the hearers; and they affect a climax of impression.

Thurman likes to preach sermon series. He favors this method because his thought ranges widely and his themes are usually multifaceted. It is a good method in handling sustained preaching themes, either as church pastor or university preacher. Some of Thurman's sermon series first saw the light of day as single sermons. Examples abound, but one instance is sufficient at this point. In 1939, one of the sermons Thurman preached at Howard University was published in a special college edition of the *Christian Century Pulpit*. Titled "What Shall I Do with My Life?,"[10] the sermon treated Jesus' temptation

7. "Offering of the Heart," *Yankee*, December 1953, 19.
8. "Offering of the Heart," *Yankee*, December 1953, 20.
9. "Offering of the Heart," *Yankee*, December 1953, 21.
10. *The Christian Century Pulpit*, September 1939, 210-211.

experience drawing lines of relation between his temptations and the temptations of the college student. The sermon highlighted the way Jesus handled himself under stress, advising that what Jesus achieved remains possible for the student under stress. In 1962 he preached a series of five sermons on the levels of the temptations of Jesus during the last month of his nine-year ministry as University Preacher at Boston University.[11] Among the many series he has preached across the years, Thurman has especially liked to deliver series of sermons about Jesus.

Thurman is a master at illustrating his insights. He sometimes restates illustrations he has used before, but quite often the restatement opens some aspect of thought within the illustration that was not lifted to the hearer's attention before. This can be seen in the following illustration, drawn from his own personal observation:

> One day I saw city workmen doing an emergency job on the sewer pipes that were deep beneath the surface of the street in front of our home. As I watched the process, I was struck by the fact that about five feet of sewer pipe was completely enmeshed by a thick network of large and small roots. It was impossible even to see the section of the pipe. After much chopping and "uprooting," the pipe was uncovered—but not quite, for some of the roots had found their way inside the joints and had grown so profoundly within the pipe that it was impossible for water to flow. The whole section of the sewage was blocked. It developed that the roots had come from a tree more than 500 feet away. Deep under the ground they had caught the scent of water from the sweating pipes and found what they sought. The book of Job says of a tree stump, "Yet through the scent of water it shall sprout again and bring forth boughs like a plant." It is always dangerous to read into the behavior of nature some great design or plan and to apply that design or plan to human life. Nevertheless it is good to know that life in any form seems to have

11. Howard Thurman, *Temptations of Jesus: Five Sermons* (San Francisco: Lawton Kennedy, printer, 1962). Four paragraphs from the original single sermon became six pages (15-20), three paragraphs on the second temptation became seven pages (25-31), three paragraphs on the third temptation became seven pages (37-43).

> a little way of its own, moving with quiet assurance to some special end.[12]

Appearing in print first as a meditation, this same illustration appeared again in the study (growing out of sermons) dealing with "Commitment" as a personal spiritual discipline. The form is shortened and the point immediately put.

> Many years ago when I lived in Oberlin, Ohio, I noticed workmen digging a large hole in the street in front of my house. When I went out to watch what was going on, I saw that a large section of sewer pipe had been exposed; around it and encircling it was a thick network of roots that had found their way inside the pipe by penetrating the joints in many places. The tree was more than four hundred yards to the other side of the house, but this did not matter to the roots. They were on the hunt—for life.[13]

The illustration helped him to move from a general law of nature to discuss a law for spiritual growth and development.

There is another much repeated illustration that Thurman uses with great effectiveness. It is the story about one of his students who had been a deep sea diver.

> Some years ago, one of my university students who had been a deep-sea diver, wrote a very interesting sketch. In it he described one of his experiences on the Caribbean Sea. He was on the ocean bottom. It was very beautiful down there. The water was clear, and he was in the midst of a coral rock garden. Since he was in no particular hurry, he sat down to look around. He sat; he looked. Occasionally, a fish would swim up to take a close look at him and would pass the word along to his friends, who were also curious. After an indefinite time, he lost track of all time awareness. Then he discovered that he was sitting in the midst of a very beautiful flower garden. There were plants of many shapes, and things that looked like blossoms. It was wonderful. He could enjoy the beauty for a long while; but he realized that he

12. Thurman, *Deep is the Hunger*, 26-27.
13. Thurman, *Disciplines of the Spirit*, 13.

> couldn't stay there forever, so he stirred to go about his business. And, as soon as he moved, every plant disappeared. Apparently there were living things that were in mid-passage between the vegetable and animal world. They emerged only when he was completely still.[14]

The illustration was used to teach the importance of silence as a resource during prayer time, as a means for seeing life in focus. In still another use that illustration helps Thurman highlight the luminous quality of the darkness surrounding the diver, enabling him to see and thus relax his fears.[15]

Thurman draws his illustrations from several sources: his wide and deep reading, his travels, his insights into Scripture texts, nature, science, art, news stories, poetry, novels, drama, but mostly from his own personal experiences. He has an uncanny instinct for tracking down ways of making his meanings clear. With a unique perception Thurman can comb the most common facts and find rich specimens of unsuspected meaning. His retentive memory enables him to recall his materials at will, turn them over in his mind again and again and see fresh meanings so that he can use even the same illustration to point up more than one aspect of meaning.

Howard Thurman seldom uses quotes as he preaches. If a quotation is sometimes used, it is not used to give him authority. The reason appears in a statement Andrew W. Blackwood recalled Thurman having said. "Why do you quote so many authorities in your new book? If what you are saying is true, you do not need the authorities. If what you are saying is not true, all the authorities in the world cannot make it true."[16] The few quotations that do appear are relevant, pointed, and a means of moving further into his subject.

Thurman generally uses Scripture in his preaching but it must be said that the text does not always form the center of his consideration. He is not a textual preacher in the usual sense. He does not preach to exegete or expose a textual meaning mainly. Although he has been an apt student of biblical literature and is among front-rank

---

14. Thurman, *The Growing Edge*, 40-41.

15. Thurman, *The Luminous Darkness*, vii-viii.

16. Andrew W. Blackwood, *Doctrinal Preaching for Today: Case Studies of Bible Teachings* (Nashville: Abingdon Press, 1956), 148.

expositors of Scripture meanings,[17] Thurman is not a biblical preacher in the traditional sense. His sermons usually blend philosophical, existential, and religious truths. This follows his dedication to deal with the universals of religious experience.

This kind of thrust comes out clearly, for instance, in his sermon "Prayer and Pressure." Intent to be exegetically honest, he first explains what the Parables of the Importunate Widow and the Friend at Midnight do not mean, concluding after his quick but careful sketch: "I think this says something about God that is unworthy; terribly unworthy! The point of the stories is not as is often indicated that God must be subjected to pressure in order to act on our behalf."[18] Then he goes on in the sermon to suggest what is the real meaning of prayer.

Thurman takes occasional liberties in his use of Bible passages and texts, but when he does lift them out of the initial context of meaning he is careful to confess that he is doing so. The introduction to his sermon on "The Love of God" is an instance. The background for the sermon is the story of the Prodigal Son. Thurman first clears away false notions which hinder a clear understanding of that parable.

> The most important thing in the story is not so much the fact that the prodigal son was forgiven by his father, though that is important and crucial, and very exciting and wonderful, and very redemptive. But the thing that I see in it always is that the boy had to purify himself by his self judgement because of the way in which he had violated the relationship between him and his father. His father forgave him, but how could he forgive himself? He had to find ways by which he could redeem his life from the lacerations inflicted upon it by his own willfulness. Meanwhile, the creative attitude of his father's love held firm the context, the climate, the atmosphere, in which the boy could work out his salvation.[19]

Then, after that foundation statement, Thurman sets forth the meaning he sees in concept and experience of the love of God. Speaking personally, he affirms:

---

17. See Thurman's exposition of Habakkuk and Zephaniah in *The Interpreter's Bible*, Vol. VI, 979-1002, 1013-1034.

18. Thurman, *The Growing Edge*, 50.

19. Thurman, *The Growing Edge*, 67.

> In quietness, in prayer, I become aware of the meaning of the love of God. I may see it or find it as I discover the world of nature, as I observe the pattern of life-behavior around me. I may see descriptive pictures of what seems to me the manifestation of the love of God as I watch this expression in personality, or that expression in personality. I look over the whole stretch of human history and see movements toward creativity and redemption and, central to it all, the redemptive love of Jesus. But the moment when I discover the meaning of the love of God is not in the context of a million minor coincidences, but in the moment when I, as a human being, am able to experience the sense of being completely and totally understood in the Presence of God. This bottoms all the adventure of my life. This is the ultimate immunity against isolation. This is the only bulwark against the stark devastation of affliction. No argument, no series of "for instances" in my own life, no aspects of my behavior pattern, are as important as this. I must know for myself that I am not alone; that in the solitariness of my own existence, when I am stripped to whatever is in me that is literal and irreducible—that here, in that ultimate outreach of my spirit, I am understood.[20]

At a time when sermons no longer hold the center of public attention as earlier in history, and when sermons lack the appeal commonly linked with the great divines of the past, it is interesting to observe that Howard Thuman's preaching has continued to have appeal and his audiences have remained steady across the years. Even his oratorical styles deliberately paced, have not fallen into disrepute in a day of flaming rhetoric. Just what is it that continues to attract people to him and to his way of worship and preaching?[21]

---

20. Thurman, *The Growing Edge*, 68.

21. **ED:** Massey, "Thurman's Preaching," 119, stated regarding Thurman, that his "approach to homiletics posed a problem when he went to Boston University ... (and) was asked to serve as a team member in teaching homiletics there. . . . Thurman threw up his hands. 'In the first place, he objected, 'I don't think homiletics can be taught, and certainly not by the team approach.' . . . He did agree to work with five students . . . to help seminarians learn what he saw as all-important about preaching—the communication of meaning and the sharing of a mood. . . . Some of the seminarians did learn this

The answer must take into consideration the combination of qualities and gifts in Thurman's life. The answer will involve something more than his learning and the ability to frame interesting and provocative patterns of thought for the hearer. The answer will have to do, fundamentally, with the contagion Howard Thurman generates within those who dare to listen to him. Thurman preaches as one who knows, making worship an engagement. Howard Thurman is a religious personality and he preaches as such, reacting totally in the service of worship as a worshipper. This characteristic tone and attitude carry conviction. It inspires confidence in his leadership and trust in his words. The phenomenon of his own openness to God and the gathered group is immediately evident in the meditation prayer that precedes each sermon and provides us with a window on Thurman's spiritual life. Sometimes introspective, sometimes overtly social in reach, the meditation-prayers are always open, simply stated, poetically related to life, and honest. Ethical and religious dimensions are obvious in his prayers—and the hard places of life are frankly admitted. To state it briefly, one part of the reason for the appeal in preaching is when preachers carry a true spirit of worship. They exalt God without diminishing the image of any human being; and they help us rise before God, ready to take courage for another step in the divine will. Thurman's pulpit composure encourages this.

His themes also encourage this. For him the God of life is the God of religion, and religion and life creatively intersect. He goes about his preaching task with the insight of a mystic, the joy of a believer, the articulateness of a teacher, and the concern of a pastor. The pastoral element is unmistakably evident in his sermons. It is not incidental that one of his sermons on love was republished in a sermon anthology of pastoral preaching at its best.[22]

As Thurman sees it, the Christian pastor must be concerned in the main with two important areas of focus, namely the content of the Christian faith and the inner life. So in the first place we "must be

---

communication, but some others reacted as if Thurman's approach to the art was strange, unorthodox, and inappropriate."

22. Howard Thurman, "The Greatest of These," in Charles F. Kemp, *The Preaching Pastor* (St Louis: The Bethany Press, 1966), 123-127. Also in Thurman, *The Growing Edge*, 24-28.

taught the content of the Christian faith. Such questions as: Who was Jesus? What precisely did he teach? What are the historic Jewish-Christian insights with reference to God and the meaning of life and the interpretation of human experience? What is man and what is the nature of his responsibility? How must one interpret the true significance of the various political, economic and social arrangements under which men live?"[23] In the second place, regarding the inner life Thurman asks: "What is the significance of spiritual exercises? Precisely what is prayer and how does one pray? What techniques and methods are available for deepening one's sense of the presence of God and how may one work in the world courageously and intelligently on behalf of a decent world, without despair and complete fatigue? What are the resources for personal rehabilitation and renewal?"[24] Thurman answers such questions for his hearers when he preaches, seeking seriously to articulate religious insight, evidence pastoral concern, and illustrate the social dimension of the witness he gives.

A part of Thurman's appeal can be traced as well to his craftsmanship in phrasing sermon topics that excite interest. The topics and titles are usually brief, suggestive, and sufficiently "open" to permit the surprise element that he will invariably introduce as he speaks. Sometimes a title will accent some particular universal for the hearer. Sometimes a question forms his title: "What Shall I Do with My Life?," "Why Hast Thou Forsaken Me?," or "Who is My Neighbor?" The very putting of the question is a promise that he will supply an answer for those who listen. Sometimes the topics are but a phrase suggesting a religious concept, a doctrine, an aspect of the life and teaching of Jesus, a social issue, a personal need.

There is considerable diversity reflected in the following topics and titles from Thurman's sermons: "Affliction," "Freedom," "Forgiveness," "Equality," "The Religion of Jesus," "The Great Delusion," "Jesus Prays," "Keep Awake!," "The Great Moment," "The Great Feast," "Seeking and Finding," "Finding God," "The Radical Test," "Pain and Crisis," "The Gothic Principle," "Vignettes of Life," "The Light That Is Darkness," "Faith the Tutor," "Time Still Flows," "The Judgment," "The Lost," "The Quest for Maturity,"

---

23. Thurman, *Deep is the Hunger*, 32.
24. Thurman, *Deep is the Hunger*, 32.

"The Journey into Fulfillment," "In Favor With God," "In Favor With Man," and "A Glass Darkly."

Thurman's preaching program while Dean of Marsh Chapel at Boston University allowed him to work quite regularly with series. This was especially important to his purpose and the needs of the campus community. During the 1957-58 school year, Thuman preached several series of sermons: "Seeking and Finding—God" (three sermons), "Seeking and Finding—Forgiveness" (two sermons), "Seeking and Finding—the Self" (four sermons), "The Moment of Truth" (two sermons), "The Moment of Crisis" (six sermons), "The Modern Challenges to Religion" (three sermons), "Intentional Living" (two sermons), and "The Creative Encounter" (six sermons). During the 1959 school year he delivered his now famous series on "Jesus and the Disinherited" (twelve sermons). Another series was "Quests of the Human Spirit" (eleven sermons), dealing with the quest for God, freedom, truth, peace, values, authority, integrity, identity, among other themes. Thurman has also developed an illuminating series of sermons on "The Mystics."[25]

Across the years of his ministry, Thurman has released single sermons occasionally for use in preaching magazines like *The Christian Century Pulpit*[26] and *The Pulpit Digest*,[27] but it was not until late in his career that he published a volume of his sermons. *The Growing Edge*, his first volume of sermons, was published in 1956. The book contained twenty-four sermons arranged under six main topics: I. Concerning Enemies, four sermons; II. Concerning Prayer, three sermons; III. Concerning God, four sermons; VI. Concerning Peace, three sermons; V. Concerning Festivals, four "spot" sermons for Hanukkah, Christmas, New Year, Easter; VI. Concerning Christian Character, six sermons. The sermons are in typical Thurman style, which is to say that they are short, perceptive, aptly titled, suggestively treated, simply worded, and timeless in concept and content.

---

25. <u>**ED:**</u> Howard Thurman, *Walking with God: The Sermon Series of Howard Thurman, Volume 2: The Way of the Mystics*, ed. Peter Eisenstadt and Walter Earl Fluker (Maryknoll: Orbis Books, 2021).

26. *Christian Century Pulpit*, June 1937, 125-127; September 1939, 210-211.

27. *Pulpit Digest*, May 1957, 13-19; December 1962, 13-16, 66.

One of the special features of *The Growing Edge* is the inclusion of the setting or "worship pattern" in which each sermon was used. That pattern involves the meditation-prayer which preceded the sermon, the special reading Thurman gave as a prelude to delivery, and the closing prayer to the sermon. The sermons were transcribed from tapes made during delivery and carefully edited afterward. Apart from this procedure, the book would have never taken shape since Thurman always preaches without a written manuscript or notes. In preparing for the pulpit, Thurman thinks his subject through without the use of writing. This has been his custom since leaving seminary.

Some of the sermons in *The Growing Edge* have been used across many years, worked and reworked in many different settings, and now stand in print as approved specimens of Thurman's vision and craftsmanship. Both his vision and artistry were honored when upon publication in 1956 *The Growing Edge* became a Pulpit Book Club selection.

In 1962 a second volume of Thurman's sermons was published under title *The Temptations of Jesus*. The five sermons in the book represent the last preaching he did at Marsh Chapel, marking the end of his nine-year preaching ministry there. As always, the preaching reflects Thurman's desire to affect "the illumination of the imagination, the stirring of the heart, and the challenge to live life meaningfully."[28]

Quite apart from his prowess, success, and appeal as a pulpiteer, Howard Thurman has been criticized by some church leaders for the noticeable absence of the Christian kerygma from his sermons. By his own admission, Thurman has been concerned about the universals of religion rather than doctrines and dogmas peculiar to any one faith. Some Evangelicals have questioned whether or not nonkerygmatic preaching can be rightly classified as Christian. As for the criticism, it is true that Thurman does not highlight the theme and details of the kerygma. His sermons are purposely cast as vehicles of philosophic, existential, and religious truth; they deal with the universals rather than the doctrinal particulars of the Christian faith. He has explained that he wants every and any worshipper to feel at home in his preaching service, whatever that worshipper's

28. Thurman, *Temptations of Jesus*, 5.

religious background and orientation, his conviction being that worship and religion must serve to unite rather than divide, and that "total Christianity," as he phrases it, is inclusive rather than exclusive. Even at risk of being considered syncretistic, Thurman has insisted on being interfaith, as well as interracial and intercultural. This rationale stands behind his development of The Church for the Fellowship of All Peoples.

When he was pastor of Mount Zion Baptist Church in Oberlin, a Chinese gentleman who had been attending the services there across an entire semester came to the parsonage one day to speak with Thurman. The two had never met until the man came to tell the pastor goodbye, and to express his appreciation for the openness that had characterized the services of worship at the church. The man said, "I am a Buddhist. I did not expect to find a Christian service in which I could worship. This year your church has provided that kind of experience for me and I take back to my country a genuine gratitude for what you have given me."[29] The comment cheered Thurman who interpreted it as a kind of validation of his quest to relate with openness and regard for all people, honoring their background and context of life. Some of Thurman's critics have rather viewed such experiences and his non-kerygmatic sermons as indications of the extent to which he stands outside the context of Christian particularity and claims.

Thurman has explained his whole approach to worship and life as follows: "It is my belief that in the Presence of God there is neither male nor female, white nor Black, Gentile nor Jew, Protestant nor Catholic, Hindu, Buddhist, nor Moslem, but a human spirit stripped to the literal substance of itself before God."[30] This orientation has been criticized as syncretistic.[31] Thurman rather considers it as an exercise in "total Christianity."

Howard Thurman has long held the reputation of being a renowned orator and pulpiteer. He can so articulate his chosen theme that the very essence of religious experience stands exposed

---

29. Thurman, *Footprints of a Dream*, 22.

30. Thurman, *The Creative Encounter: An Interpretation of Religion and Social Witness* (New York: Harper & Brothers, 1954), 152.

31. See critique by Joseph R. Washington, Jr., *Black Religion: The Negro and Christianity in the United States* (Boston: Beacon Press, 1964), 105-112.

in his words and by his very manner of speaking to them. As a preacher, Howard Thurman is poetic, polished, mystic, and prophetic.[32] Many would agree with Marcus Hanna Boulware that "When under the spell of the man's oratory, a listener can hardly imagine an equal."[33] Although the kerygma does not form his horizon, Thurman's preaching opens doors of insight. "The sermons are food, not froth."[34] Dorothy Henderson has aptly summarized Thurman's pulpit artistry: "When Howard Thurman holds up an idea for you to look at, it becomes like a brilliant jewel. He turns it for you this way and that, and as he throws differing lights on its many facets, you see things there you've never seen before. Soon from the heart of it you come to see Truth, and not only Truth, but you yourself in relation to that Truth."[35]

---

32. **ED:** Martha Simmons and Frank A. Thomas, eds. *Preaching with Sacred Fire: An Anthology of African American Sermons, 1750 to the Present* (New York: W.W. Norton & Company, 2010), 492. "Arguably the ablest and most renowned African American practitioner of contemplative preaching was Howard Thurman, a man who was one of the high peaks in a range of Christian mystics who served in strategic pulpits." James Earl Massey served as a contributing editor on the volume and wrote the section on Howard Thurman.

33. Marcus H. Boulware, *The Oratory of Negro Leaders: 1900-1968* (Westport, Conn: Negro Universities Press, 1969), 186.

34. Ibid., 185.

35. Dorothy Henderson, *Biographical Sketches of Six Humanitarians Whose Lives Have Been For the Greater Glory* (New York: Exposition Press, 1958) 163.

Chapter Six

Thurman as Theologian

It can be said of Howard Thurman, as it was said about another learned contemporary, that he owes his reputation as "theologian" to his power as a preacher.[1] Thurman was a preacher before he gained fame as a writer. People heard his theology before they ever read it. People have listened to and thought with him as he has wrestled with great ideas and imperatives, but they have done so because of the expectation he excited within them and the depth of thought to which he has introduced them. Having worked intently to first grasp a notion and sift it for content and meaning before releasing it in speech, Thurman has revealed himself as a person of reflective mind and deeply rooted theological understanding. From early childhood, as we have seen, he was stirred to deal seriously with religion and objective reality, and he has learned to see not only what life does but also what life means and how it is to be used. His biographer Elizabeth Yates has rightly termed him "a practical dreamer."[2] Always alert to "the deepest needs and aspirations of the human spirit,"[3] Howard Thurman has responded with sincere interest to the human quest and hunger for God. It is correct to say

1. That learned contemporary is Reinhold Niebuhr. See Paul Scherer, "Reinhold Niebhur—Preacher," in *Reinhold Niebuhr: His Religious, Social, and Political Thought*, ed by Charles W. Kegley and Robert W. Bretall (New York: The Macmillan Co., 1956), 312.

2. Yates, *Howard Thurman*. ED. Book subtitle, *Portrait of a Practical Dreamer*.

3. Thurman, *The Inward Journey*, 7.

that this has been his one theme. The major accents of his theology reflect this.

Although he has been classified rightly by some as a theologian, it must be said that Thurman's primary interest has not been to explicate a theology but to live an effective life. He has thus become recognized as a religious personality of intellectually responsible thought and ethically demonstrative actions. In terms of category, Thurman can be classified in part as a philosophical theologian. Philosophically he is a monist. Theologically he is a theist. Experientially he is a mystic. Historically he is a Christian. Moving well beyond the structural and substantive aspects of theology as a field of study, Thurman stands rooted in a theology of experience and hope that celebrates God and life.

Some Basic Beliefs

The Aliveness of Life. Howard Thuman's thought has been preoccupied with the phenomenon of Life. "It is a matter of profoundest significance to me that life itself is alive."[4] This is a fact so obvious that one can miss the tremendous import of it! "Observers of nature are apt to be much more consciously aware of this than the average person."[5] Thurman's sermons and writings are filled with his thought on this theme, pointing to the processes of life from the standpoint of religion, on the one hand, and nature, on the other. Again and again he takes aspects of nature and explains them theologically, and yet again he takes theological concerns and uses aspects of nature to illustrate them.

The notion that life is alive is rooted in a kind of theological biology that sees in organic existence a dynamic process indwelt and sustained by God. In Thurman's view, it is as reasonable to speak of a theological biology as it is to speak of a philosophical biology[6] or a philosophical cosmology.[7] For him, the aliveness of life is syn-

4. Thurman, *Deep is the Hunger*, 168.

5. Thurman, *Deep is the Hunger*, 168.

6. As in the case of the book, Hans Jonas, *The Phenomenon of Life: Toward a Philosophical Biology* (New York: Harper and Row, 1966).

7. For example, see Milton K. Munitz, *The Mystery of Existence: An Essay in Philosophical Cosmology* (New York: Appleton-Century-Crofts, 1965).

onymous with vitality, and vitality is an aspect of "the givenness of God." This "givenness of God," as he calls it, sustains the living process and thus enables life to continue, prevail, and fulfill itself. Thurman comments that we are "rooted in the same basic aliveness (and) God's care of the individual has its basis in the very structure of life itself."[8]

God sustains a vital relation to all that lives. God is within life. Thurman's words about this could at times cause some undiscerning person to conclude mistakenly that he is making "life" nearly coterminous with God. Thurman does not intend such a meaning. He is not a pantheist. His vision is rather upon the unity between the inner and the outer, between source and issue, between even natural life and supernatural life since these never appear to be free and independent of each other—that is, insofar as they can be viewed presently by humanity.

God Is the Source of All Life. This is the foundation principle in Thurman's theology. Since it is from God that all life derives and is sustained, then there must be an underlying unity and an essential kinship between all that lives. This interpretation was given published expression in 1927 in one of his sermons "Finding God."[9] The lines of a universal theology are clearly marked off in his earliest formal preaching. Thurman proclaims: "First of all, if God is the source of all of life, if out from Him emanate all creation, then there must be an underlying unity for all of them, and wherever one digs in honestly, living up to the limit of the light that one has at the particular time, one does make contact with that unity." Thurman makes it personal. To find God, to find fulfillment "in a world like this, I must have demands within myself for the kind of energy that God releases, and that energy must be with reference to a need which calls it forth and which will not let me rest until I find it."[10]

8. Thurman, *Deep is the Hunger*, 168.

9. Howard Thurman, "Finding God." In Francis P. Miller, editor, *Religion on the Campus: The Report of the National Student Conference, Milwaukee, Dec. 28, 1926 to Jan. 1, 1927* (New York: Association Press, 1927) 48-52. **ED:** Howard Thurman, "Finding God, 1927," in Fluker, ed., *The Papers of Thurman, Volume 1*, 110-114.

10. Howard Thurman, "Finding God." In Francis P. Miller, editor, *Religion on the Campus*, 50, 52. **ED:** Thurman, "Finding God, 1927," in Fluker, ed., *The Papers of Thurman, Volume 1*, 111, 113.

Some years ago when the Institute on Religion in an Age of Science was planning a volume to discuss the impact science had made on religious beliefs, Howard Thurman was one of a group of seventeen theologians, educators, and laypersons chosen to explore the question and point out aspects of that impact.[11] Howard Thurman prepared a chapter from his angle of insight and gave freely from the data of his own experience, his formal training, his own convictions, and the persuasions arrived at through the eyes of others. Thurman wrote on "The Meaning of Purpose in Religious Experience." The book was published in 1964, forming a companion volume to one published four years earlier titled *Science Ponders Religion*.[12]

That particular essay by Thurman presents an extremely perceptive programmatic statement. He discusses purpose as a sense of direction determined by the fixed life principle of goal seeking. He first illustrates this characteristic on several levels of life and then shows this at work in the life of humanity, where purpose takes on its most complex character and meaning due to one's capacity to determine and influence their own conscious functions. The essay is much too long and involved to allow extensive sampling, but the two final paragraphs clearly show Thurman's views about how one apprehends God in the midst of life:

> Life at its deepest and profoundest seems to be kind and in that sense personal. And this is the claim of religion, that God cares for man and that man is not the creation of some blind impersonal force, but there is purpose, intent, at the heart of reality, which addresses and confirms that which is at the very center and core of personality. There is in the life of man the kind of potential that is actualized at its fullest in the full-orbed sweep of the religious experience. Just as his body is the actualized potential of organism, so his mind and spirit are the same thing

---

11. Howard Thurman, "The Meaning and Purpose in Religious Experience," in Edwin Booth, editor, *Religion Ponders Science* (New York: Appleton-Century, 1964), 266-278. Benjamin E. Mays was one of the other contributors. **ED:** Howard Thurman, "The Meaning and Purpose in Religious Experience, 1964," in Fluker, ed., *The Papers of Thurman, Volume 5*, 108-117.

12. Harlow Shapley, ed. *Science Ponders Religion* (New York: Appleton-Century-Crofts, 1960).

> in a different dimension and in another universe of discourse. It would seem to follow quite directly that what man as a part of the universe experiences as actualized potential cannot be foreign to that which is characteristic of the universe itself. Man experiences purpose in his own profoundest fulfillment and this provides him with the crucial clue to the understanding not only of his own life but of the world about him. Always he seeks the clue to meaning in all about him, always he seeks a rational active ingredient in all manifestation that will give him understanding of all phenomena. On the basis of this he reads the history of life on the planet and the history of the planet and of the cosmos itself; he understands and relates to the present and predicts the future.
>
> For the religious man the all-encompassing reality which contains and sustains his body is a part of an intent at the very heart of existence. The order within his body gives the content of order to his mind, and the order in his mind makes him seek for order in his world of men and things. He becomes predisposed to harmony, which is the conscious meaning of order—thus he is not only a sharer in values, but is a creator of values. The time and the place of his life on the earth is the time and place of his body, but the meaning, the significance, the purpose of his life is seen in its grandest dimension when he has the experience of being a part of a larger life, a larger consciousness, a larger reality which can only be compassed by the terms "divine, holy, God."[13]

The essay is apparently autobiographical at many points. The permitted freedom of treatment allowed for this result. Thurman was treating insights of his own from across many years of discovery and testing. His early intuitions, his real experiences, and the theory he formulated afterward with reference to the hunger of the heart and life for God are given clear statement in his essay. While scientific in method, his statement was still personal and solidly confessional.

This Is God's World. Thurman accepts the universe, and he accepts it with joy. The universe is here and we are in it. The wise

13. Thurman, "The Meaning and Purpose in Religious Experience," 277-278. **ED:** Thurman, "The Meaning and Purpose in Religious Experience, 1964," in Fluker, ed., *The Papers of Thurman, Volume 5*, 116.

person holds an attitude of acceptance toward the universe. Thurman makes it personal to us, "It does mean that I and every other man must accept the fact of our existence in the world, the basic structure of which we did not in any way create or determine. In this acceptance there should be no fear, but a quiet confidence in the reliability of life."[14]

We and our world belong to God. We are in a process of development. Thurman affirms that "Our life represents essential process . . . We seem always to be on our way."[15] Thurman accepts the givenness of the world and life, and he seeks to build a relationship with the given world and its offerings as part of "the givenness of God." He asserts, this is what Jesus did.

> To Jesus, God breathed through all that is. The sparrow overcome by sudden death in its evening flight; the lily blossoming on the rocky hillside; the grass of the field and the garden path; the clouds light and burdenless or weighted down with unshed waters; the madman in chains or wandering among the barren rocks in the wastelands; the little baby in his mother's arms; the strutting arrogance of the Roman Legion; the brazen queries of the craven tax collector; the children at play or the old men quibbling in the marketplace; the august Sanhedrin fighting for its life amidst the impedances of Empire; the futile whisper of those who had forgotten Jerusalem; the fear-voiced utterance of the prophets who remembered—to Jesus, God breathed through all that is. To Jesus, God was Creator of life and the living substance; the Living Stream upon which all things moved; the Mind containing time, space, and all their multitudinous offsprings. And beyond all these God was Friend and Father.[16]

Thurman's statement about God is not pantheistic, nor is his statement about purpose one of blind determinism. God is immanent in the world of life, but God is apprehended by humanity as Person. God deals personally and privately with the individual. The

14. Thurman, *Deep is the Hunger*, 55.

15. Thurman, *Deep is the Hunger*, 140.

16. Thurman, *The Inward Journey*, 30; Howard Thurman, *The Centering Moment* (New York: Harper & Row, 1969), 12.

residue of the meaning of God is both universal and particular. God sustains existence and guarantees every aspect of the living process, especially humanity who is created and shaped in God's image.

Life is given. The world is given. It is to be experienced by being accepted in truthfulness. "Man must experience life; he must feel it run through his whole being that life belongs to him and he to life. The experience of life not in life will teach a man not to fear life but to love life."[17]

Thurman's notion about the aliveness of life is not to be understood as a statement of mere robust naturalism or nature mysticism. The real world has impressed him with its vitality, properties, solidity, aliveness, order, variety, events, and evident dependability. Thurman is careful, however, to insist upon cause as well as observed phenomena, and cause is always credited to God. It is Thurman's belief that God is the living substance within the life process. But when asked how is it that God so relates to that process, Thurman's answer is given in terms of scientific fact. Among other ways, he affirms that God relates to the created world as energy. Energy constitutes the moving power at work within life. In Thurman's thought, the aliveness of life relates to energy, and energy is an express relation between God the Creator and this ordered, orderly world. The energy can also be understood, then, as an expression of the reality of God; it is an aspect of God's "givenness."

It is interesting that energy became for Thurman a clue about the reality of God at work in the world. Energy can be measured, and its manifestations can be both predicted and controlled. Then, too, the interactions between energy and matter can be traced. Energy appears in so many roles: as matter, as chemical reaction, as impulse, as spiritual power. Matter is bound energy. Spiritual power is free or boundless energy because, "Life is alive and every tiny rootlet and every tiny nerve all charged with the energy of the eternal."[18] God makes energy available in life, but certain conditions must be met before it is released. The conditional demands press upon all living things and all living people. Just as energy is available to growing things as they seek to unfold, provided the proper conditions are observed. "When a man is able to bring to bear upon a single purpose

17. Thurman, *The Inward Journey*.
18. Thurman, *Deep is the Hunger*, 142.

all the powers of his being, his whole life is energized and vitalized," Thurman asserts. "In fact, it is my view that the general insight becomes profoundly particularized in religious commitment and that the 'general law' reaches its apotheosis in man's religious experience, in the surrender of his life to God. This is the focal point to which all the other manifestations of the insight quietly call attention."[19]

Thurman spells out even wider reaches of this insight in the chapter on "Commitment" in his book *Disciplines of the Spirit*.[20] God's world "is a living world; life is alive, and as expressions of life we, too, are alive and sustained by the characteristic vitality of life itself. God is the source of the vitality, the life, of all living things. His energy is available to plants, to animals, and to our own bodies if the conditions are met. Life is a responsible activity. What is true for our bodies is also true for mind and spirit." Thurman identifies our role, "At these levels God is immediately available to us if the door is opened to Him. The door is opened by yielding to Him that nerve center where we feel consent or the withholding of it most centrally. Thus, if a man makes his deliberate self-conscious intention the offering to God of his central consent and obedience, then he becomes energized by the living Spirit of the living God."[21]

Taking a general law of life, Thurman has applied it to many levels of observed experience, ending with a significant statement about how the energy granted by God works on the level of our self-consciousness and purposed intent. Our relation to God, then, is essentially akin to our relation to life: it is a given relation, but a relation where conditions must be met—and cooperation established—so that what is given can be fully realized and experienced. "If life is to manifest itself in a particular form, it poses the conditions, the discipline, essential to that end."[22] This is God's world, and God has established the laws by which both humanity and the world will find fulfillment. Thurman expresses here a sacramentalism reminiscent of William Temple's notion of a "sacramental universe."[23]

---

19. Thurman, *Disciplines of the Spirit*, 19.
20. Thurman, *Disciplines of the Spirit*, 13-37.
21. Thurman, *Disciplines of the Spirit*, 21.
22. Thurman, *Disciplines of the Spirit*, 16.
23. William Temple, *Nature Man, and God* (London: Macmillan and Co., Ltd., 1935), 473-495.

Human Freedom Must Be Disciplined to Be Fulfilled. The phenomenon of human freedom takes on added dimension when considered in the light of divine purpose. Our ability to know alternatives and options as we live, and the pressure to choose responsibly between them, can make one feel threatened and exposed by life. But "where there is no sense of alternatives or sense of option, there is no freedom. It does not of necessity follow that there must be the active realization of option, which may be impossible because of circumstances over which the individual, at the moment, is unable to exercise any positive control; but the sense of option must be preserved even though the exercise of option may be prohibited."[24]

Human freedom is a given factor; our freedom is a responsibility. It also entails the demand for willingness to take responsibility for the use of freedom. Thurman admits, "It may be that this is the most difficult of all the responsibilities of Freedom. The tendency to separate oneself from the responsibility for one's actions is very persistent in human life. It is a hard lesson to learn."[25] It is at such a point that many fail in life. Some of them fail repeatedly, never able to take the radical step and act responsibly about the alternatives that life places before them. But always, life demands decisions on our part.

Some decisions are difficult because the issues involved in making them are complex. The facts available might be limited, thus understanding and consideration are affected. Fears might influence one facing the demand to make the decision. Or perhaps a habit of indecision stands in the background of the person who must decide. Thurman further explains that decisions vary in weight, as when a matter is viewed as either minor or very important and crucial. The same person can react to similar situations in very different ways. But decisions are critical affairs because they exact of us what is truly personal. Thurman notes, "A person likes to feel that he made up his own mind and not that he has been pushed or forced into a decision either by events or by other persons."[26] He continues, "Always the intimate relation between taking responsibility and making up one's

24. Howard Thurman, *Apostles of Sensitiveness: The Ware Lecture* (Boston: American Unitarian Association, 1956), 10-11.

25. Thurman, *Apostles of Sensitiveness*, 13.

26. Thurman, *Meditations of the Heart*, 113-114.

mind must be held steadily in view."[27] Decision is an insistence of life. It is a demand grounded in the very nature of creative freedom.

Thurman stresses that decisions are fulfilled in deeds and actions. The integrity of those deeds and actions depends upon several factors.

- First is one's chosen purpose: "The mind must be centered upon a goal, a purpose, a plan. Of all possible goals, purposes, plans, a single one is lifted above the others and held as one's chosen direction. Then the individual knows when he is lost, when he has missed the way. There emerges a principle of orderliness which becomes a guide for behavior and action."[28]
- Second is a sense of personal responsibility for the deeds: "The act of a person finally involves the person and he is required at last to back his deed. Therefore, to do the true thing places a searching liability on the integrity of the person who does the deed."[29]
- Third is action with a will that is set on achieving the chosen goal and purpose: "An important part of living is the process by which the individual will brings under its private jurisdiction the behavior of the individual. . . . It is important to make the full conquest of one's life pattern to the end that one's deeds will flow more and more from the center of one's intent. . . . In such a climate, the most natural desire of the heart is the quiet utterance to God: Let not my will be set to sin."[30]
- Fourth is the decision and courage to act: "Here at last is the place where a person may discover what manner of man he is—here he may sense the independence of the self—here he may stand in his own right as a person—here Life claims him as a part of its vast creative power. It may be that in the integrity of the act a man knows for himself that he is created in the image of God, the Father of all that lives. Shrink not from your heritage by holding back when your time comes to act—for to act is to claim your true sonship."[31]

---

27. Thurman, *Meditations of the Heart*, 114.
28. Thurman, *The Inward Journey*, 63.
29. Thurman, *Meditations of the Heart*, 166-167.
30. Thurman, *The Inward Journey*, 69, 70.
31. Thurman, *The Inward Journey*, 81.

- Fifth is the refusal to let one's life be lived at cross purposes with the will of God: "At long last the only redemption from the paralysis of the cross-purpose is to seek with all possible intent to link one's deepest desire with one's choice of goal and to make of one's life a dedication to such an end. Ultimately a man's responsibility is to God; the God a man worships is the God he must face. And when he stands before Him, what shall he say?"[32]

In singling out aspects of Thurman's thought about the character of personal deeds and actions, we clearly see his stress on the nature and importance of personal action in shaping history. Decisive actions are never unilateral. They always involve others as well as the actor themself.

> It is never enough merely to act responsibly oneself, or to be willing to pay the price for one's own deeds, but we are ever under the tireless obligation, where others are concerned, to place no burden upon others the consequences of which are not seen by them as clearly as we may see them ourselves. Despite the deep solitariness of life, in the intricate pattern of human relations no man lives to himself, nor indeed does he die to himself, or to himself alone.[33]

Here again we see Thurman's thesis regarding the unity of life. The discussion here is admittedly limited and sketchy but it does show Thurman's stress upon our involvement in our own destiny by means of decisions, both about our response to God and the divinely ordained laws that pertain to life at its best.

A human being is a creature of free will, a decision maker—and so much depends upon one's wisdom or ignorance in deciding some course of action. Where a course of duty and action is clearly seen and understood, we are under responsibility to so act. At such a time, for Thurman, "What is needed is not more information, more facts, but an aroused will. The facts need to be charged with concern, with emotion. Knowledge must be shot through with dynamics, urgency and zea1."[34]

32. Thurman, *The Inward Journey*, 75.
33. Thurman, *Deep is the Hunger*, 26.
34. Thurman, *Deep is the Hunger*, 36.

Thurman appeals again and again to the person of Jesus in discussing how an authentic life should be lived. For life as God wills it we need a sense of aliveness—aliveness to ourselves, to nature, to other people, to the Bible, even to other religions than our own, but especially an aliveness to Jesus.[35] Jesus lived, behaved, and achieved with distinction in God's sight. His life is both a challenge and a judgment. His performance was an expression of his openness to God; it was an affirmation of his faith in God. Jesus had no special gift by which he overcame. We all can say: "But I had no special gift of God by which I can overcome the world."[36] Thurman asserts that Jesus won the approval of God because he set himself to live life on God's terms. This constitutes the challenge and judgment of his life. "It is clear that God was the answer to all that Jesus sought and quested for in life. Anyone who is as sure of God as was Jesus, can hear for himself: 'Thou art my son, my beloved, this day have I begotten thee.'"[37]

In another place Thurman states: "What he did with life, others can do—if they are willing to use the tools that are at hand. When that emphasis is given to Jesus, he becomes the source of inspiration and humiliation. Inspiration—because those who come after him have so much in him and make so little of it. In a man's confusion and frustration, it may be easier to worship Jesus than to walk in his steps."[38] In yet another passage Thurman writes of Jesus as one who was "free to experience [himself] as a child of God and to experience all other men as children of God. Of such is a part of the miracle of Jesus. Men came to him with the searching question, What must I do? How may I? He made the life of God contagious!"[39]

In terms of human decision, Thurman highlights Jesus' use of "a working paper" for life.[40] The working paper helped Jesus to establish the lines along which his life is to be lived. It enabled him to "mingle his strength with the forces of history and emerge with

35. Thurman, *Footprints of a Dream*, 82.
36. Thurman, *Deep is the Hunger*, 172.
37. Thurman, *Deep is the Hunger*, 173.
38. Thurman, *Footprints of a Dream*, 82.
39. Thurman, *The Luminous Darkness*, 108.
40. Thurman, *Jesus and the Disinherited*, 110.

a name, a character, a personality."[41] The working paper is essential for every person because it keeps us alert against carelessness in attitudes, slovenly reactions and responses to life, and half attempts in the face of God's demands. "Each person is under obligation to do to the limit of his powers, the very best thinking, the most honest feeling of which he is capable, as he faces even the simplest alternatives of life."[42] Thurman suggests that Jesus is an exemplar:

> Such a figure was Jesus of Nazareth. To some he is the grand prototype of all the distilled longing of mankind for fulfillment, for wholeness, for perfection. To some he is the Eternal Presence hovering over all the myriad needs of humanity, yielding healing for the sick of body and soul, giving a lift to those whom weariness has overtaken in the long march, and calling out hidden purposes of destiny which are the common heritage. To some he is more than a Presence; he is the God fact, the Divine Moment in human sin and human misery. To still others he is a man who found the answers to life's riddle, and out of a profound gratitude he becomes . . . humanity's answer and his life the common claim. In him the miracle of the working paper is writ large, for what he did all men may do. Thus interpreted, he belongs to no age, no race, no creed. When men look into his face, they see etched the glory of their own possibilities, and their hearts whisper, "Thank you and thank God!"[43]

The issue of decision-making finds a near classic statement in that prayer meditation Thurman titled "Always Making Decisions."

> Always, I am making decisions. There are some decisions that are deliberately negative. They cut across everything in me that is positive and affirming. They may involve much or little as far as my immediate destiny is concerned. It is a crucial thing to come to a point of decision, to weigh causes of action, to sense the meaning of direction. It is in such a moment that man knows whether he is on the side of life or death, and the choice is his to

41. Thurman, *Jesus and the Disinherited*, 111.
42. Thurman, *Deep is the Hunger*, 22.
43. Thurman, *Jesus and the Disinherited*, 112.

> make. To affirm life is to accept growth, to accept challenge, to move with all of one's full-orbed intent in response to the deepest that stirs within. Then the miracle takes place. The deepest thing in man somehow makes contact with the deepest things in life, and he knows that the decision is right, that the decision is on the side of life and not death. Of course, a life-giving decision may be difficult. It may cause much heartache and disturbance, even upheaval, but the issue is never in doubt. It is a terrible thing to make a decision which one knows, somewhere in the profound recesses of one's being, is against life. Teach us to overcome our fear of life and in that freedom may we learn to understand life and in our understanding of life, to love life. Steady us, our Father, that we may cast our vote for life and not against life. "Let the words of my mouth and the meditation of my heart be acceptable in thy sight, O Lord, my rock and my redeemer."[44]

God Is Always Near. The notion of the sense of the Presence of God is also crucial to Thurman's theology. We are close to our best only when we live by a sense of the Presence of God. As Thurman declares: "This sense of Presence must be a reality at the personal level as well as on the social, naturalistic and cosmic levels. To state it in the simplest language of religion, modern man must know that he is a child of God and that the God of life in all its parts and the God of the human heart are one and the same." He continues, "Such an assurance will vitalize the sense of self, and highlight the sense of history, with the warmth of a great confidence. Thus, we shall look out upon life with quiet eyes and work on our tasks with the conviction and detachment of Eternity."[45]

Our knowledge of God grows as we live our way into life. Finally the deepest insight about God breaks upon the consciousness with startling forcefulness: "Ultimately there must be no distinction between the God of Life and the God of Religion. All events in life take place, somehow, within the divine context."[46] Nothing can occur outside the reaches of the knowledge and control of God because it is from God that all things in life take their meaning and reality.

---

44. Thurman, *The Centering Moment*, 108.
45. Thurman, *Deep is the Hunger*, 144.
46. Thurman, *Meditations of the Heart*, 23.

It is for this reason that God becomes the answer to all the issues, problems, and contradictions of life.

God is not far away, coming to us only on rare occasions or in rare situations; God is present in life. God is present as Creator, Sustainer, Person, and Father. "What we most want to know about God is whether He is present in the commonplace experiences of ordinary living, available to ordinary people under the most garden variety of circumstances. That God is not far from any one of us is the essence of the Gospel which Jesus proclaimed."[47]

For an authentic and meaningful life in the world, Thurman suggests, a person needs three things: a sense of history that has deep logic, consistency, and purpose; a sense of self as spectator, participant in life, and child of God; and a sense of presence that relates one to God on all the levels of experience.

Thurman's preaching and theology reflect his deep awareness of the Presence of God in his life. That faith and awareness have deep roots. He recalls the time when he was a small boy in the home with his mother and grandmother. He learned from some of his classmates that a comet was passing across the sky at night. He had not seen it himself because he was not permitted to remain up after sundown. One night his mother awakened him, told him to dress quickly, and invited him to go with her to the backyard to see the comet (Halley's Comet). The sight before him was fear provoking. He stood in speechless awe and "beheld the great spectacle with its fan of light spreading across the heavens." His mother also stood in silence. Finally, he ventured a question from the fear churning within him. "What will happen to us if that comet falls out of the sky?" His mother did not answer right away, but when she did speak, her hand rested on his shoulder in a gentle gesture of assurance. She spoke with confidence, "Nothing will happen to us Howard; God will take care of us."[48] Thurman reflects:

> Times without number I have learned that life is hard, as hard as crucible steel; but as the years have unfolded, the majestic power of my mother's glowing words has come back again and again, beating out its rhythmic chant in my own spirit. Here are

---

47. Thurman, *Deep is the Hunger*, 147.
48. Thurman, *Jesus and the Disinherited*, 57.

> the faith and the awareness that overcome fear and transform it into the power to strive, to achieve, and not to yield.[49]

That rhythmic chant of his mother's words continued to work within his spirit across the years, becoming more and more his own inner music. It was at work within him in 1943, when he saw the germ of a meaningful possibility and applied to the President and Trustees of Howard University for a leave of absence to develop a new church in San Francisco. He told President Mordecai Johnson what he wanted to do and why it was important that he do it. Johnson reminded Thurman that he was not due a sabbatical for some time yet, and that the university could not therefore make any salary available to him even if the leave of absence was granted. Johnson queried him, "How on earth can you support your family? How will you manage? How will you live?" Thurman answered, fed by a faith deeply set and well tested by his struggles in life, "I don't know. All I know is, God will take care of us."[50] His mother's faith had become his own tested experience.

The Contradictions of Life Are Not Final. One of the most persistent facts in life is the fact of contradictions within human experience. In a quest to make sense of life, it is important that we see the contradictions as what they are—real, thoroughgoing, puzzling, and sometimes devastating. Human nature is an instance of illustration. Everyone knows what within themselves is positive and creative, on the one hand, and what is negative and destructive, on the other hand. The very quality of experience is always affected by how contradictions influence, limit, overrule, or cancel each other. Thurman uses human history to illustrate contradictions:

> We have no really authentic records of a time when there was peace in the world; the most that you can say is that we have records of those moments of treacherous quiet between armistices. Yet the human spirit constantly affirms its interest in, and the necessity of the logic of, peace. Even at the times of the most terrifying wars—right in the midst of them—there are individuals, there are movements, there are broodings, stirrings,

---

49. Thurman, *Jesus and the Disinherited*, 57.
50. Thurman, *Footprints of a Dream*, 31-32.

> that have to do with a dream, a way of living, feeling, thinking, that presupposes that the human spirit ultimately is made for peace.[51]

Thurman insists that there is a basic resoluteness in humanity bidding to expect a better tomorrow, a sense deep within that there is always another answer beyond some evident contradiction that has been experienced. He uses this argument as partial explanation for the rationalizing tendency of the human mind.

> There seems to be basic to human experience a kind of incurable optimism about the ultimate destiny of man; this is true even for people who regard themselves as confirmed pessimists. Sometimes blindly, sometimes with scarce hope of vindication, often with wild irrationality, the spirit of man dares to affirm ultimate hope. If in the present circumstances or the present world there seem to be no grounds for such assurance, there is the tendency to make immediate transfer to another period or even another form of existence or another world. This quality in human life is very important, for it is the ground of hope in times of despair, the incentive for dreams of a better day when desires are out of joint; and the "Hallelujah!" to life when worlds crash and dreams whiten into ash.[52]

We especially need optimism in facing the radical tension between good and evil within ourselves. We see and feel evil, while at the same time we see and feel good. It is an experience of felt contradiction. Persons of alert faith, Thurman insists, will refuse to accept the contradiction as final. They will dare and endure the struggle, setting their will firmly on the side of the good for which they live, always hoping, always expecting good.

---

51. Howard Thurman, "The Powers of the Spirit and the Powers of This World," a mimeographed address, Howard University School of Religion, Thirty-Fourth Annual Convocation, November 14, 1950, 2. **ED:** Howard Thurman, "The Power of the Spirit and the Powers of This World, 14 November 1950," in Fluker, ed. *The Papers of Thurman, Volume 4*, 22.

52. Howard Thurman, *Deep River: Reflections on the Religious Insight of Certain of the Negro Spirituals* (New York: Harper and Brothers, 1945, 1955), 82-83.

The assurances of optimism must also be at work when one confronts the fact of death. Among the many circumstances of life, death is at once the most dramatic and unusual. In the midst of life there is always death—inescapable, persistent, imminent—and our attitude toward death is profoundly influenced by our experience of life. "Death not only affects man by involving him concretely in its fulfillment, but man seems to be aware that he is being affected by death in the experience itself. There is, therefore, an element of detachment for the human spirit, even in so crucial an experience. Death is an experience in life and a man, under some circumstances, may be regarded as a spectator of, as well as a participant in, the moment of his own death. The logic here is that man is both a space binder and a time binder."[53]

Thurman tells us that his first experience of seeing someone die took place when he, a seven-year-old child, watched his own father die. At that young age he did not understand what he was witnessing, but he never forgot the scene and the details of the experience. His father's sickness had lasted only five days. Howard stood with his mother beside the bed and watched his father's sick body fight for air. He heard the guttural noises in his father's throat and listened as his mother called out to her dying husband to see if he was still conscious of their presence. "Saul," she questioned, "can you hear me?" Saul's head slowly nodded. She asked further, "Are you ready to die?" Her tone was one of evangelical concern. Thurman reports that: "With an effort supreme, he said, 'All my life I have been a man, I am not afraid of death, Alice. I can stand it.'" Finally his body was caught up in a great spasm. Howard and his mother struggled to hold Saul down on the bed. "Suddenly, it was all over. My father was dead."[54]

The experience of his father's death caused him to learn to deal with the differences it made in his early life. After careful thought, wide exploration, and the distillation of truth in his heart, Thurman is unwilling to accept the fact of death as a final fact in anyone's experience of life. He writes, "We come to regard all experience as taking place within a certain compass, and, in a sense, we are outside looking on. Why should death be any different? It is quite

53. Thurman, *The Negro Spiritual Speaks of Life and Death*, 17.

54. Thurman, *Footprints of a Dream*, 15.

unconvincing to say that death swallows life." Then Thurman rings the bell of hope, "The coming of spring is one of the happiest symbols in the experience of the race, a perennial reminder that death is but one aspect of experience, a phase of life in transition and a lag in the vast creative process of life itself. It is small wonder that, in the Christian tradition, spring and Easter merge into a glorious expression of the aliveness of life."[55] With further concern for the Christian tradition, Thurman points with joy to Jesus as a dramatic instance against the finality of death for humanity: "The answer of the world to his goodness and his revelation was death. But the ages have discovered what is one of man's oldest spiritual insights: death is an episode in, not the end of life. Perhaps the greatest discovery that we can make concerning Jesus is that, at long last, death could not touch in him that which gave to his life its great significance."[56]

Thurman isolates three basic attitudes which humans take toward the fact and experience of death: "One attitude is to dread it; another is to ignore it; and still another is to accept it."[57] Dread is the prevalent attitude because death appears to be so final. "The whole range of activities and functions that have characterized what is generally meant by life are stopped, cut off, finished. One by one, the duties end; one by one, the lights go out. . . . All men live the eternal in time. But not all men are aware of this aspect of their lives."[58]

In one of his pointed meditations on the theme of death Thurman discusses the possibility of "A Good Death."[59] That meditation constitutes his thought about how the end of one's own life here in the world can be a good end: "Life and death are felt as a single respiration—the ebb and flow of a single tide. Death is not the invasion of an alien principle, it is not an attack upon life by an enemy. Death is not the Grim Reaper, the black-cowled skeleton with blazing eyes, galloping on a white horse. No! Life and death are identical twins. Therefore it is a man's privilege and wisdom as it is to make a good

55. Thurman, *Deep is the Hunger*, 164-165.
56. Thurman, *Deep is the Hunger*, 177.
57. Thurman, *Meditations of the Heart*, 66.
58. Thurman, *Meditations of the Heart*, 66, 67.
59. Thurman, *The Inward Journey*, 24-25.

death, even as it is to make a good life."[60] Thurman adds, "A good death is made up of the same elements as a good life. A good life is what a man does with the details of living if he sees his life as an instrument, a deliberate instrument in the hands of Life, that transcends all boundaries and all horizons. It is this beyond dimension that saves the individual life from being swallowed by the tyranny of present needs, present hungers, and present threats."[61]

We die as we live—drawing upon that to which we have yielded to our spirit and related ourselves. If we have yielded our spirit to God and related to God as a child, we have the right and the resources to "die unshriven" according to Thurman. He continues: "It is urgent to remember that death is not the worst thing in the world. Again, death is an event in life. It is something that occurs in life rather than something that occurs to life. The distinction is important and urgently significant. If death is an event in life, than it must take its place alongside an endless series of events, none of which exhausts life or determines it. This is the basis of every fundamental hope about immortality or what is generally called life after death."[62] The apparent contradiction of life that we call death is not final. Rightly viewed, death is not to be dreaded as the worst thing in the world. "It is a final tribute to the character of an individual's living if he can die 'unshriven' but full-blown as he has lived. Such a man goes down to his grave with a shout."[63]

Howard Thurman's most extensive statement on the subject of death as an aspect of life is *The Negro Spiritual Speaks of Life and Death*, his Ingersoll Lecture on Immortality which he delivered in 1947 at Harvard University. Although brief, due to the nature of the occasion, the lecture was hailed as a major contribution to that lecture series. In that lecture he carefully explicated the hope of the early slave singers and he also articulated the philosophy of faith at work within that hope. Deeply influenced by the strains and insights of the Spirituals since he was a boy, Thurman drew upon his heritage as an African American, those who shaped the spirituals as creative religious thinkers in their response to life.

60. Thurman, *The Inward Journey*, 24-25.
61. Thurman, *The Inward Journey*, 25.
62. Thurman, *Meditations of the Heart*, 142.
63. Thurman, *Meditations of the Heart*, 142.

It is the faith and theology of Howard Thurman that no contradiction in life is final or ultimate. He eagerly contends that the evil that threatens and contradicts life now will ultimately have an end.

> At long last a man must be deeply convinced that the contradictions of life which he encounters are not final, that the radical tension between good and evil, as he sees it and feels it, does not have the last word about the meaning of life and the nature of existence, that there is a spirit in man and in the world working always against the thing that destroys and cuts down. Thus he will live wisely and courageously his little life, and those who see the sunlight in his face will drop their tools and follow him. There is no ultimate negation for the man for whom it is categorical that the ultimate destiny of man on this planet is a good destiny.[64]

This aspect of Thurman's theology holds an implied universalism, a line of thought reaching all the way back to Origen (CE 185-255) who was the first major Christian thinker to develop the notion of a cosmological universalism.[65] Thurman's thought on this relates also to the more recent philosophical and biological speculation of Pierre Teilhard de Chardin.[66]

As for Thurman's treatment of eschatology, his reasoning is an extension of his dynamic worldview of God as the source of all life and therefore the ground and future of all that lives and exists. The following passage reflects his belief:

> The goal of life is God! The source of life is God! That out of which life comes is that into which life goes. He out of whom life comes is He into whom life goes. God is the goal of man's life, the end of all his seeking, the meaning of all his striving.

---

64. Thurman, *The Inward Journey*, 106.

65. See especially Origen's treatise "On Prayer," in ed. by John E. L. Oulton and Henry Chadwick, *Alexandrian Christianity, Vol. II, The Library of Christian Classics* (Philadelphia: The Westminster Press, 1954), 303-304, 317.

66. See particularly Teilhard's books, *The Future of Man* (New York: Harper and Row, 1964), 306-308; and *Man's Place in Nature* (New York: Harper and Row, 1966), 115-121.

> God is the guarantor of all his values, the ultimate meaning—the timeless frame of reference. That which sustains the flower of the field, the circling series of stars in the heavens, the structure of dependability in the world of nature everywhere, the stirring of the will of man to action, the dream of humanity, developed and free, for which myriad men, sometimes in solitariness in lonely places or in great throngs milling in crowded squares—all this and infinitely more in richness and variety and value is God. Men may be thrown from their courses—they may wander for a million years in desert and wasteland, through sin and degradation, war and pestilence, hate and love—at last they must find their rest in Him. If there is that which at anytime, anywhere in the universe, can ultimately withstand the divine urgency—then whatever it is that shows such strength is co-equal with God. Such a position to me is not only untenable, but is also a denial of the basic ethical monotheism that for me is the most satisfactory explanation of the meaning of life.[67]

When Thurman speaks or writes about "the goal of life" he is concerned about what is ultimate. His thesis that God is both source and goal of life locates all that lives within an essential process and it posits a meaning toward which life moves. Given this philosophical presupposition, Thurman asserts that the very nature of one's life demands a final destiny with God. Thurman's eschatology sees God in total control, being celebrated at the last by all creation and all humanity, with all distance, division, and evil having been overcome. It is his faith that nothing "can ultimately withstand the divine urgency"; and he asserts this with great stress on the word "ultimately." This universalism implies that the contradiction between heaven and hell cannot be ultimate but must also be finally overcome. Thurman admits the certainty and seriousness of the biblical doctrine of judgment, but believes that the issues involved in judgment are so serious that the apparent contradiction demands a resolution that honors both God and humanity.

---

67. Thurman, *Deep River*, 74-75.

The Christological Question

It is at the point of Christology that Howard Thurman's theology is weakest and problematic. Measured against the essential nature and substance of New Testament preaching and teaching, Thurman's preaching and theology are admittedly non-kerygmatic. There are aspects within the arena of the kerygma about which he rarely speaks, if ever. As for Christology, Thurman does not deal with the work of Christ for us or in us but rather lays stress upon the work of God for us and in us and treats the life of Jesus before us as revelation and essential norm.

References to Jesus as religious subject (rather than religious object) appear constantly in his preaching and writings. For Thurman, Jesus is the supreme example of faith and loyalty to God, the one we are to watch and follow. He explains, "Regarding Jesus, there is a mixed tradition in Christianity, a tradition that has two streams flowing down it. Sometimes they run along together, then break, then come back together." Thurman describes one stream as where Jesus is understood as "the divine moment in human life, that he is the word made flesh, that he is the incarnation of God; he is the great, dramatic 'for instance' of the divine meaning; he is God; he is the illustration of how the infinite becomes finite; he is Redeemer and Savior. Around that concept has his complete mastery over nature, ideas of his mastery over death, ideas that have been cumulative in the history of the Christian movement and ideas which have appeared in creeds."

The other tradition places Jesus himself as "the subject of religious experience and that he, born out of the womb of Israel, felt that in himself the true meaning of Judaism blossomed and flowered. From birth to death he lived within the framework of Judaism. What he did with life, others can do—if they are willing to use the tools that are at hand. When that emphasis is given to Jesus, he becomes the source of inspiration . . . because those who come after him have so much in him and make so little of it. In a man's confusion and frustration, it may be easier to worship Jesus than to walk in his steps."[68] Thurman follows the second view and raises it as his major norm for interpreting Jesus. While he understands Jesus as pivotal

68. Thurman, *Footprints of a Dream*, 82.

guide and Son of God, Thurman reserves the ultimate term "God" for the Creator of life and Father of the human spirit.[69]

Referring to Jesus, Thurman comments that "He is in reach, and he can give me a tested series of formulae for the guidance of my own life because of the shared commitment which is ours. The study of his life thus becomes a necessity of my commitment. Any personal behavior, then, that is out of harmony with his life and teaching becomes exposed to the swift judgment of what seems to me now to be his spirit."[70] Thurman continues:

> Slowly his mind becomes my mind, and then the amazing discovery that the mind that is more and more in me is the mind that was more and more in him. The mind that was in him becomes more and more clear to me to be the mind that is God. All of this may be achieved without any necessity whatsoever of making a God out of Jesus.[71]

Thurman never appeals to the question of Jesus' nature but rather to his life or history. He refuses to attempt an abstraction of doctrine or dogma from Jesus' selfhood, yet he believes that Jesus' relation authenticates his claim upon others to follow him. This limited view is neither Confessional nor Reformational, but Thurman insists that for him it is both rationally valid and theologically central. So he does not speak of the "work" of Jesus Christ but of his life and uniqueness, as in the following instance: "Jesus of Nazareth had what seems to me to have been a fundamental and searching—almost devastating—experience of God. This experience was so fontal and so fundamental to the very grounds of his being that he had to deal with the implications of this experience whenever he raised any question about the meaning and function of his own life."[72]

Always in his discussion of Jesus, whether in preaching or in print, Thurman lays stress upon Jesus as religious subject rather than as religious object. He speaks of the Cross not in terms of Atonement but as the supreme instance of human rejection of divine values and,

---

69. Thurman, *The Creative Encounter*, 135-137, 147-148.
70. Thurman, *The Creative Encounter*, 83.
71. Thurman, *The Creative Encounter*, 83.
72. Thurman, *Temptations of Jesus*, 16.

at the same time, the supreme instance of unselfish and redemptive love.

Traditionally understood, the kerygma of the New Testament involves four major concerns: the life of Jesus, his death, his resurrection and exaltation, and the promise of his return. The summons to repent and believe is based upon the meaning of it all for the life of the hearer. The recital of these themes and a summons to act on their meaning with faith was the burden of the preaching of the early believers. It has been argued that the apostolic proclamation did not deal with much detail regarding the events of the life and ministry of Jesus but that it dealt more particularly with the significance of his death, his resurrection, and exaltation. This argument has been used by some to indicate that proper stress in Christian preaching must be upon the death, resurrection, and exaltation of Jesus rather than upon his life and ministry[73]—the Christ of faith as over against the Jesus of history. But surely the details of his life and ministry were not minor considerations because they were what made the other results possible; they are foundational for a kerygma.

Thurman's hermeneutic bias is plainly non-kerygmatic, but he insists that it avoids serious intellectual obstacles that confine the Christian faith to an exclusive dogma. His own approach permits a universalism that is crucial for his system of relational theology. Thurman's nonuse of the kerygma with universals rather than dogmas, some have labelled as reductionism and syncretistic liberalism.[74] In this respect he departs from the apostolic tradition. According to Thurman, Jesus lived his life and appeals to us in our living; it is for others to discern the doctrines that relate to this. This is much like a line from Alfred North Whitehead, who wrote, "Christ gave His life. It is for Christians to discern the doctrine."[75]

---

73. See the discussion in Robert H. Mounce, *The Essential Nature of New Testament Preaching* (Grand Rapids: Wm. B. Eerdmans Publishing Co., 1960), 79-81. Charles H. Dodd sees the life and ministry of Jesus both assumed and highlighted in the primitive kerygma. See his *The Apostolic Preaching and its Development* (New York: Macmillan Co., 1944), 21-22.

74. See, as an instance, Joseph R. Washington, *Black Religion: The Negro and Christianity in the United States* (Boston: Beacon Press, 1964), 111.

75. Alfred North Whitehead, *Religion in the Making* (New York: The Macmillan Company, 1926), 56.

Thurman bypasses the doctrines and highlights Jesus' experiences, and makes a great case for learning from his temptations[76] from his devotional centeredness and prayer life. He often lifts the prayer life of Jesus to our view. "I am always impressed by the fact that it is recorded that the only thing that the disciples asked Jesus to teach them how to do was to pray."[77] The fundamental attitude was trust toward God. Thurman also ranks Jesus' loving attitude toward people. Both of which ruled out fear, deception, and hate on his part. This forms the burden of his book *Jesus and the Disinherited*. The revolutionary character of Jesus' achievement and insights is sensed only against the background of environmental factors that were at work where he lived. Jesus settled the major questions having to do with survival on God's terms. Thurman has taken the teachings of Jesus and has analyzed them with regard to the oppressed of today, going beneath the surface of the New Testament statement about Jesus to point out the universals at work in his experience.

To the extent that his work helps us to better understand Jesus as religious subject, Thurman is to be thanked although aspects of his vision and some of his views are limited and partial when measured against the New Testament kerygma. It is possible to honor his contribution without overlooking the absence of the kerygma from among his major theological concerns.

---

76. Thurman, *Temptations of Jesus*, 5.
77. Thurman, *Disciplines of the Spirit*, 88.

Chapter Seven

Thurman as Practical Mystic

Howard Thurman has often been referred to as a "mystic," a label that is not without its connotative problems. In his 1961 Rufus M. Jones Memorial Lecture he was quick to admit that "There is a medley of confusion as to the meaning of mysticism."[1] Early in his ministry he pressed through the welter of diversity and confusion and worked out a reasonable definition of mysticism for his understanding and service. In keeping with his own central concerns and experience with God, Thurman's working definition of mysticism includes a personal attitude toward God, a recognition of the role of God within the inner life, and one's response to life through his experience with God. "For our purposes then, mysticism is defined as the response of the individual to a personal encounter with God within his own spirit. Such a response is total, affecting the inner quality of the life and its outward expression and manifestation."[2] The mysticism of Howard Thurman involves a religious experience with a balanced inner and outer manifestation, one that is life affirming and not life denying. In his life and work he has always attempted to strike that balance.

Experiences of inner realization of God came to him early in life. "When I was a boy in Florida, very often at night I would walk along the beach of the Atlantic Ocean. Dark night, bright stars.

1. Thurman, *Mysticism and the Experience of Love*, 5.
2. Thurman, *Mysticism and the Experience of Love*, 6.

My little life so insignificant. I could sense not only the vastness of the universe, but the order of it. It sometimes seemed utterly impersonal, but I was aware of some vast order, some limitless and boundless structure of rationality."[3] Reflecting on many early experiences like these Thurman suggests that "there seems to be, in the very nature of the human mind, the insistence that everything everywhere belongs. This sense of the wholeness in the universe gives us an immeasurable sense of security. And this is God, very God."[4]

Thurman would spend periods of time alone in his rowboat fishing. He describes his experience, "There was no sound save the lapping of the waves against the boat. There were times when it seemed as if the earth and the river and the sky and I were one beat of the same pulse. It was a time of watching and waiting for what I did not know—yet I always knew. There would come a moment when beyond the single pulse beat there was a sense of Presence which seemed always to speak to me. My response to the sense of Presence always had the quality of personal communion. There was no image. There was no vision. There was God."[5]

These two reflections from *The Inward Journey* reveal Thurman's inner life and his experience of God's Presence:

- There is a unity that binds all living things into a single whole. This unity is sensed in many ways. Sometimes, when walking alone in the woods far from all the traffic which makes up the daily experience, the stillness settles in the mind. Nothing stirs. The imprisoned self seems to slip outside its boundaries and the ebb and flow of life is keenly felt. One becomes an indistinguishable part of a single rhythm, a single pulse. . . . And yet there always remains the hard core of the self, blending and withdrawing, giving and pulling back, accepting and rejoicing, yielding and unyielding—what may this be but the pulsing of the unity that binds all living things in a single whole—the God of life extending Himself in the manifold glories of His creation?[6]

3. Thurman, *The Growing Edge*, 58.
4. Thurman, *The Growing Edge*, 59.
5. Thurman, *Disciplines of the Spirit*, 96.
6. Thurman, *The Inward Journey*, 51-52.

- There is the rest of detachment and withdrawal when the spirit moves into the depths of the region of the Great Silence, where world weariness is washed away and blurred vision is once again prepared for the focus of the long view where seeking and finding are so united that failure and frustration, real though they are, are no longer felt to be ultimately real. Here the Presence of God is sensed as an all-pervasive aliveness which materializes into the concreteness of communion; the reality of prayer. Here God speaks without words and the self listens without ears.[7]

The mood of the mystic pervades almost all of Thurman's written work. As a basically religious personality and a person of intense inner life, the mystic mood has marked his major experiences and ministry. As for his writings, the mystic mood stands coupled with two other very passionate strains that are a part of his living: prophetic vision and poetic powers. These three traits are especially noticeable in his many books of meditations.

The writing of meditations grew out of Thurman's custom as a pastor to write a weekly aid for meditation during worship services at The Church for the Fellowship of All Peoples in San Francisco. Placed in the Sunday Bulletin, the meditation was used during a reflection period that came just before the regular morning service of worship. The meditations became so popular during the first year of use that they were collected and a little book with fifty meditations was published in 1947 under title *Meditations for Apostles of Sensitiveness*. Written as occasional pieces, the meditations were not a connected series of observations about any one aspect of life but shed light upon many, many aspects. That first edition was so widely received that within a year a second edition with an additional fifty new meditations was published. In 1951 Harper and Brothers published a still larger third edition under title *Deep is the Hunger*.

Thurman continued his custom of preparing meditations for the Sunday Bulletin after he left Fellowship Church to become Dean of the Chapel at Boston University. As before, the meditations were gathered and published as books. *The Inward Journey* began in this way and was published in 1961. So did *The Centering Moment* book of prayer meditations published in 1969.

---

7. Thurman, *The Inward Journey*, 112.

Thurman's meditations reveal to us the heart of a mystic. They also reflect the skills of a person who has the rare ability to articulate the features of spiritual experience and share them as by a calculated detachment. Written with the lyrical touch, Thurman's meditations contain no fantastic diction nor unwarranted stress. His lines are models of simple but dignified prose reflecting clear thought, respect for truth, poetic style, and firm conviction. He seems to have no problem either with form or content. Every expression is controlled by the central insight of the meditation. Without any bid for fancy, his words make the mind and spirit take wings while the life takes roots. His lines hold a sense of proportion, a quality of thrust, and an edifying tone. The reading of his written work allows both a religious experience and a cultural moment. The meditations are rich in intellectual content and can be studied for their theology, philosophical content, or poetic style; they can be sifted for psychological depth, personal impressions, or rhetorical delicacy. Thurman is there in every writing, transparent, as it were, always without intruding or obscuring, always without any display of superior attitude or the tone of one who talks down.

The meditations are sometimes outrightly autobiographical in background, telling some aspect of Thurman's own struggles, search, and findings. The stored-up emotion from those personal experiences is used creatively so that the reader can identify with the concern. Thurman has learned well how to make words serve his will, convey a mood, and carry a message. His published meditations certainly show this. Seldom "dated" in content, his meditations are generally universal in applicability.

The Inward Journey, Thurman's favorite among his writings, shows the range and depth of his art as no other writing from his pen. There is great literary merit and religious profundity in the way Thurman has dealt with the spiritual quest, using, among so many other materials, some sentences from Fenelon,[8] a phrase from Abraham Heschel,[9] a line from an African American spiritual,[10] a parable

8. Thurman, *The Inward Journey*, 46-47, 71-72, 134-135.

9. Thurman, *The Inward Journey*, 19-20. See Thurman's treatment of Heschel's phrase, "radical amazement."

10. Thurman, *The Inward Journey*, 24-25. The line is, "I want to die easy when I die.

from Jesus,[11] a statement from the Book of Tobit,[12] the poetry of T. S. Eliot,[13] Paul's Hymn to Love in I Corinthians 13,[14] a prayer from St. Francis,[15] and the constraining lines of Psalm 139,[16] to mention only a few "thought-starters." Elizabeth Yates, his biographer, tells us that "It is his favorite among his own books and the one to which he turns most often for his own renewal."[17]

Thurman's interest in mysticism is not academic but personal. It grows out of his own experience of being. When he studied with Rufus M. Jones it was to explore the history of mystics and mystical movements under attentive guidance. It was also to seek further validation of what had been his own unique experiences as a boy, youth, and adult. His subsequent achievement in this area has been so marked that in a recent study of American mysticism Howard Thurman was cited as the leading living Protestant mystic.[18]

Thurman's mysticism is practical and productive. It has had to be so, and for very personal reasons: being Black placed him in a social context that kept him surrounded by threats to his sanity, equilibrium, and well-being. He explains:

> I have sought a way of life that could come under the influence of, and be informed by, the fruits of the inner life. The cruel vicissitudes of the social situation in which I have been forced to live in American society have made it vital for me to seek resources, or a resource, to which I could have access as I sought means for sustaining the personal enterprise of my life beyond all of the ravages inflicted upon it by the brutalities of the social order. To live under siege, with the equilibrium and tranquility of peace, to prevent the springs of my being from being polluted

11. Thurman, *The Inward Journey*, 64-65.
12. Thurman, *The Inward Journey*, 69-70.
13. Thurman, *The Inward Journey*, 68-69, 72-73.
14. Thurman, *The Inward Journey*, 88-102.
15. Thurman, *The Inward Journey*, 104-105.
16. Thurman, *The Inward Journey*, 140-155.
17. Yates, *Howard Thurman*, 212-213.
18. Hal Bridges, *American Mysticism: From William James to Zen* (New York: Harper and Row, 1970), 51-60. See also Wayne E. Oates, *The Psychology of Religion* (Waco: Word Books, 1977), 112, 119.

> by the bitter fruit of the climate of violence, to hold and re-hold the moral initiative of my own action and to seek the experience of community, all of this to whatever extent it has been possible to achieve it, is to walk through a door that no man can shut.[19]

The first twenty-three years of his life were lived in the South, and Thurman has confessed that his experience there "left its scars deep in my spirit and has rendered me terribly sensitive to the churning abyss separating white from Black."[20] That experience sensitized him for the unrelenting necessity he has felt to work at achieving human community.

The practical orientation of his mysticism can be credited largely to Thurman's desire to be a true disciple of Jesus. He could so easily identify with Jesus: Jesus was poor, disinherited, dispossessed, and a member of a minority race held captive by a dominant majority. Thurman's analysis in his book *Jesus and the Disinherited*, of what a disinherited person knows, feels, and experiences, is so authentic because he wrote from inside the problem. The example and teachings of Jesus helped him to sense more deeply his God-given dignity and he thus won release from the hounding fear of whites. It was his relationship with Jesus that helped him develop a thoroughgoing honesty that rejected deception as a means for survival. The example and teachings of Jesus helped Thurman to learn the art of agape love—which helped him to rise above hatred. Thurman still proclaims that Jesus and his teachings are always fundamentally relevant "to those who stand, at a moment in human history, with their backs against the wall."[21]

There is a fundamental psychology in Thurman's discussion of the historical Jesus. He sifts the record to see how Jesus lived in history—and to assess his teachings against the background data of his life. Thurman discovered insights that helped him to settle the social question of how he would handle himself as member of a minority group, the political question of how he would regard the system of the dominant majority under which he had suffered, and the personal or spiritual question of how God works in connection

19. Thurman, *Mysticism and the Experience of Love*, 5.
20. Thurman, *The Luminous Darkness*, x.
21. Thurman, *Jesus and the Disinherited*, 11.

with a believer's problems and concerns. Having drawn principles from the life and teachings of Jesus for his own life, Thurman then translated those principles into the circumstances of African Americans, and even applied them to Jews and other minorities of today. After more than twenty years of being in print, Thurman's study about *Jesus and the Disinherited* continues to promote clear thinking about Jesus and his significance for self and society.

> The great contribution that Christianity or the religion of Jesus is making to the contemporary struggle of the Negro for full participation in the common life is to be found in the kind of resource that it declares to be available to him in his struggle. It provides him with a way of thinking, not only about himself and himself in relation to the white man, and the white man in relation to himself and the Negro, but also with a technique which, if properly used, can create an inclusive community—the dream of the democratic society.[22]

It can be said that Thurman's thinking, speaking, and writing on this subject laid the foundation quite early for what is being discussed within recent years as a "Black theology." This marked him as a kind of pioneer in this area of theological development, which shaped a relevant and resourceful theological viewpoint about his life and for his life. His thinking began to serve him first in a reactionary way. This led to a reorientation of the gospel in terms of his own Blackness and social location. The more he studied the life and teachings of Jesus, especially during his seminary years, Thurman saw increasingly that Jesus was uniquely relevant to the pain and peril of being Black in a white racist society.

He was not limited to mere reactionary thought. As Thurman himself tells it, the matter of focus was settled in this way. He had just graduated from seminary and was at the post office gathering his mail before leaving. George Cross, his Systematic Theology professor, also happened to be there at the same time. They exchanged a few quietly spoken words about the young preacher's intended future. Then Cross ventured some final advice to his gifted student.

---

22. Howard Thurman, "Christ's Message to the Disinherited," *Ebony*, Centennial Issue, September 1963, 60, 62.

"I think, Howard Thurman, you have the ability and the gift to make a creative contribution to American religious thought. You are sensitive, and you are a Negro. No one could blame you if you did battle on the racial problem but, as your friend, I say to you that to do that would be a waste. This must be done but your gifts are in another dimension."[23] There was more talk, much more, especially to explain the advice.[24] But the conversation was rounded out with this significant note of encouragement. "You, Howard Thurman, should address yourself to the tireless hunger of the human spirit. Doing so, your greatest capacities will be released."[25]

Cross's words continued to echo in the young man's brain, answering something about which he had been questioning himself. Thurman would later work on the race question and the social issue of segregation, but from the highest perspective, and he would be utilizing more religious resources.[26] He would not serve a mere reactional function, but a relational and redemptive role. Howard Thurman was being tutored by the Spirit of God to be an exponent of a "Black theology" with a relational thrust and ethical creativity.

---

23. Yates, *Howard Thurman*, 78-79.

24. **ED:** Yates, *Howard Thurman*, 79. George Cross, "No white man has the right to say this, for he does not know what it is to be a Negro, but all social questions are temporary." (Yates mistakenly identifies George Cross as Dr. Strong.) Harvey, *Howard Thurman & The Disinherited*, 146, Cross did not "recognize the kind of white privilege implicit in such a statement."

25. Yates, *Howard Thurman*, 79.

26. **ED:** Thurman, *With Head and Heart*, 60, "I pondered the meaning of his words, and wondered what kind of response I could make to this man who did not know that a man and his Black skin must face the 'timeless issues of the human spirit' together." Eisenstadt, *Against the Hounds of Hell*, 105-106, "Cross was correct. He didn't have the right to say what he said. . . . The conversation resonated with Thurman because Cross had identified a real tension and division with Thurman's understanding of his mission and ministry. He did have an extraordinary gift for addressing 'timeless issues of the human spirit." But the 'race problem' was equally urgent. Thurman would spend the rest of his life pondering how to bridge the gap between the perennial questions of religion and the immediate needs of African Americans. He realized early that his God abhorred dichotomies."

Thurman was one of the earliest leaders of the church who lifted the view and outlined the specific theological content of Black heritage, particularly documenting the spirituals as the earliest repository of the African American's creative religious thought.[27] With reference to enslaved African singers, Thurman wrote back in 1947:

> And this is the miracle of their achievement causing them to take their place alongside the great creative religious thinkers of the human race. They made a worthless life, the life of chattel property, a mere thing, a body, worth living! They yielded with abiding enthusiasm to a view of life which included all the events of their experience without exhausting themselves in those experiences. To them this quality of life was insistent fact because of that which deep within them, they discovered of God, and his far-flung purposes. God was not through with them. And He was not, nor could He be exhausted by, any single experience or any series of experiences. To know Him was to live a life worthy of the loftiest meaning of life. Men in all ages and climes, slave or free, trained or untutored, who have sensed the same values, are their fellow-pilgrims who journey together with them in increasing self-realization in the quest for the city that hath foundations, whose Builder and Maker is God.[28]

Thurman's discussion highlights a distinct process of the hand of God in the life of Black people. His theological work is in the nature of a witness. It witnesses against a culture that rejected Black children of God and subjected them to horrors worse than death. But his theology is also a witness for a style of life that is relational in spirit. In this way, he has been pointing a finger of protest while offering an alternative to division and segregated living.

It has been said that "theology is the action of a people who are reacting responsibly to their everyday world, the environment of relatedness with its past, present, and future in which they live."[29] Black Theology does not deport itself as a strictly formal science,

27. Thurman, *The Negro Spiritual Speaks of Life and Death* and *Deep River*.

28. Thurman, *The Negro Spiritual Speaks of Life and Death*, 56.

29. G. Ernest Wright, *The Old Testament and Theology* (New York: Harper and Row, 1969), 17.

as the suffix—ology—would tend to suggest; it is rather a set of studied observations, truths, and affirmations that have been found pertinent for faith and practical social use. Black Christians do not see social circumstances as a phenomenon unrelated to anything else in history. They are rather concerned to sift their own heritage, discover their own identity in the light of divine truth, and pursue the mission that this life situation tends to make plain. Black Christians' experience has fitted them for redemptive service—much like Israel as a Suffering Servant nation. Joseph R. Washington has ventured to assert that God has called the African American to be "humanizing agents" to help effect transformation in both the church and the world.[30] It is for this reason that a Black Theology must not only be reactional, but relational in concern.

Understood in such a context, it should be said that Martin Luther King, Jr., was fashioning a Black Theology as he made his intellectual and moral "Pilgrimage to Nonviolence."[31] Like Thurman, King grew up with an abhorrence within himself against the segregation system in the South. He had experienced the oppressive and barbarous acts that grew out of such racial partitioning. Through early encounters he became conscious of racial injustice, economic injustice, and the apparent lack of social concern in the wider church toward those who were socially despoiled and blighted. His own concern for techniques to deal radically with social evil was nurtured through the writings of Henry Thoreau, the example of Mohandas K. Gandhi, and the theological writings of Walter Rauschenbusch. But it was in Jesus that young King found the right spirit for his concern and action. Martin Luther King, Jr., became a Christian leader with a social vision. He cannot rightly be accused as lacking "any real theological understanding"[32] because it was in the interest of a practical Black Theology that his thinking and planning focused. Even where syncretism appears in his religious statements it was in the interest of an adequate theological response to a sad social situation; it was

30. Joseph R. Washington, *The Politics of God* (Boston: Beacon Press, 1967), 153-227.

31. Martin Luther King, Jr., *Stride Toward Freedom: The Montgomery Story* (New York: Harper and Row, 1958), 90-107.

32. This criticism is made by Joseph R. Washington, Jr. in his book *Black Religion*, 5.

his faith seeking a way to deal with threat, separateness, segregation, and hate in a land where his steps as a Black person were forever at risk by such real terrors. In King's own words, he was concerned about a "morally and practically sound method open to oppressed people in their struggle for freedom."[33] He learned that method by studying the Gandhian technique of nonviolent resistance. He found the spirit for his activity in the life and example of Jesus. Far from lacking a relevant theology, King helped to shape one—and his commitment in the sphere of practical action showed that theology as relevant because it kept him forever asking to be related even with his enemies.

The pioneering work of Howard Thurman also helped Martin Luther King, Jr., in his quest, especially the book *Jesus and the Disinherited*, while he was thinking through a philosophy of nonviolence during the early months of the Montgomery struggle in 1956. Lerone Bennett, Jr., one of King's biographers, reports that King read and reread Thurman's book during that time.[34] Given King's philosophical turn of mind, he needed a synthesis of the critical, theological, and practical for his civil rights social action. Thurman's thought helped him particularly at that point of need.

King found precedent in Thurman's discussion of the love ethic. It is of interest to compare King's discussion of the philosophy of nonviolence in *Stride Toward Freedom*, particularly on the theological level, with the earlier articulation of the same theme by Howard Thurman, especially in *Jesus and the Disinherited* and *The Creative Encounter*.[35] Both developed a theological position that was markedly relational in spirit and brought to bear upon the problem of racial and color divisions, an attitude influenced by Christian concern to be relational and redemptive through the wisdom of suffering but courageous love. Properly informed by the teachings and life of Jesus, neither one lost his social concern; nor did King or Thurman minimize their view to a mere reactionary Black consciousness. Their social thought keeps God in evident view.

---

33. King, *Stride Toward Freedom*, 97.

34. Bennett, Jr., *What Manner of Man*, 74-75.

35. King, *Stride Toward Freedom*, 101-107; Thurman, *Jesus and the Disinherited*, 89-109, and *The Creative Encounter*, 125-153.

Here are three provocative paragraphs on the social issue as Howard Thurman views it.

- Implicit in the Christian message is a profoundly revolutionary ethic. This ethic appears as the binding relationship between men, conceived as children of a common Father, God. The ethic is revolutionary because the norms it establishes are in direct conflict with the relationship that obtains between men in the modern world. It is a patent fact that attitudes of fellowship and sympathetic understanding across lines of separateness such as race, class, and creed are not characteristic of our age. Whatever may be the concomitant reasons therefore, we are faced with the naked truth that twice within a quarter of a century our world has been involved in two wars and at the present moment most of the countries that have survived are themselves armed camps. This tragic picture indicates, at least, that we have not found a way by which to implement the insights of the Christian ethic or that the ethic itself has been rejected.
- The religious implications of the ethic demand that the individual place at the center of his life a completely unswerving commitment to a God who is conceived in terms of supreme worthfulness. This conception of God finds its manifestation at many different levels of life. The far-reaching significance of this fact becomes at once the guarantor of whatever universal validity there is for the ethic itself. In the final analysis, life must sustain the ethic or it is a snare and a delusion. Practically stated, it raises the question and answers it in the affirmative as to whether or not a man who undertakes to live in the world on the basis of the Christian ethic can expect to be sustained and strengthened in his great endeavor.[36]
- The bearing of all of this upon the intricate relationships between Negroes and white people in the United States is not far to seek. If it be true that the normal relationship between men is activated kinship, grounded in a common dynamic origin, then attitudes of

36. Howard Thurman, "Judgment and Hope in the Christian Message," in *The Christian Way in Race Relations*, edited by William Stuart Nelson (New York: Harper and Brothers, 1948), 229-230. **ED:** Howard Thurman, "Judgment and Hope in the Christian Message, 1948," in Fluker, ed. *The Papers of Thurman, Volume 3*, 243.

> mistrust, of fear, of prejudice, whatever may be the extenuating justification for them, are a repudiation of the ethical meaning of life. He who undertakes to approach his fellow as a brother and will with courage, intelligence, and integrity fashion his life on the basis of such an imperious demand can depend on the God of life to sustain him even in his moment of greatest despair and frustration. The hardest task is to be found not in affirming this kind of conviction but rather in discovering techniques of implementation that will make so great a commitment a common part of the daily round of experience. Our hope is in a devotion to life in this dimension and our judgment is in the barrenness which we sustain in not living this religion.[37]

The Altar Stairs of Religion

Howard Thurman is a person open to religious vitality and insights wherever they appear in the world of religion. And given his mystic bent, he appears to have a constitutional demand to accept nourishment from any creative source that speaks to his need. He has dared to so live, believing that he has not thereby reduced the meaning and integrity of his own faith or obscured or altered the faith he actively promotes as a follower of Jesus.

I noted in the previous chapter Thurman's assertion that the contradictions of life are not final. This is not specifically a Christian affirmation but is based upon his belief that life is whole, sustained by a common ground. "At long last a man must be deeply convinced that the contradictions of life which he encounters are not final, that the radical tension between good and evil, as he sees it and feels it, does not have the last word about the meaning of life and the nature of existence, that there is a spirit in man and in the world working always against the thing that destroys and cuts down."[38] There is a spirit of affirmation here that forbids gloom, hopelessness, and pessimism. The lines radiate optimism. This appraisal does not arise from the exact statements of Scripture but from reasoning that

37. Thurman, "Judgment and Hope in the Christian Message,", 234-235. **ED:** Thurman, "Judgment and Hope in the Christian Message, 1948," in Fluker, ed. *The Papers of Thurman, Volume 3*, 247.

38. Thurman, *The Inward Journey*, 106.

refuses to view God as basically partial, immoral, amoral, or demoniacal.[39] It is a faith that the structure of the universe and the nature of the living process is not stacked against humanity but actually serves the human family. It is a statement that life is meaningful although not yet complete in its present form and offerings. For Thurman:

> There is something present in the spirit of man, sometimes even taking the form of great arrogance, sometimes quietly nourishing the springs of resistance to a great tyranny—there is something in the spirit of man that knows that the dualism, however apparently binding, runs out, exhausts itself, and leaves a core of assurance that the ultimate destiny of man is good. This becomes the raw material for all hope, and is one of the taproots of religious faith for the human spirit.[40]

It is interesting to study Thurman's way of openness in relating with those who differ from his own Christian orientation. Aware that every worshipper "brings to his religious experience certain structural and ideological equipment or tools, [and that] this equipment is apt to be very determinative in how he interprets the significance not only of his religious experience but also the significance of experience itself,"[41] Thurman maintains a distinction in his thinking between the way we observe and the way we participate in religious experience.

Thurman recalls an experience from his visit to India in 1935 that is illustrative of what he means at this point. He spent a full day in conversation with Kshiti Mohan Sen, the head of the Division of Oriental Studies at Santeneketan, Tagore's university in North India. Sen was a noted scholar on medieval mysticism in Hinduism. The morning portion of their discussion ended with a lunch break. Sen noted that Thurman was amused.

> **Sen:** "I see you're smiling. I think we're smiling about the same thing."

---

39. Thurman, *Deep River*, 59-62.
40. Thurman, *Deep River*, 60-61.
41. Thurman, *The Creative Encounter*, 20.

Thurman: "I think so."

Sen: "Suppose you tell me first."

Thurman: "I was thinking how much time we have wasted sparring for position—you from behind your Hindu breastwork, and I from behind my Christian embankment. Occasionally we peered out at each other to be sure that each was somehow in sight of the other."

Sen: "Quite right. Let's be wiser when we return this afternoon."

When they reconvened for conversation in the afternoon, Thurman reflects: "We were able to communicate with each other in a manner that was for me profound and completely unique. In one sweeping assumption I gathered up in my thinking his Hindu fact and for me he did essentially the same with my Christian fact. We were thus released to communicate with each other as sharers of what each in his own way had discovered of his experience of God. We were no longer under the necessity to defend anything but were free to be to each other what was most fundamental to each."[42]

Thurman has embraced and been nurtured by the Christian revelation as a follower of Jesus, but he also believes that "the God of the Universe . . . has established other altar stairs that are foreign to [one's own] footsteps, up which men may climb to seek entrance into His Kingdom."[43] He continues:

> This feeling is at first very difficult to encompass because of the sectarian character of Protestantism. But sooner or later one must be alive to other religions. . . . In the presence of God the human spirit is naked, undisguised, and without pretense. Can a man believe profoundly in his own faith without establishing squatter's rights on other faiths? If it is true that the central act of the worship of God is the be-all and end-all of life, then cannot such an experience in which the individual comes to an authentic understanding of his own personality and the meaning of life, be experienced anywhere, by anyone, without regard to the

42. Thurman, *The Creative Encounter*, 21-22.

43. Thurman, *Footprints of a Dream*, 81.

> particular context out of which he comes? Can a man affirm this unity and at the same time walk with dignity within the context which is his?[44]

Such attention to the universals of religion brings Thurman into sharp contrast and disagreement with those who believe solely in the New Testament kerygma. Thurman does not preach the absolutism of the gospel. He has consciously avoided the delimiting facts of gospel particularity in the interest of universalizing the spirit of the gospel. While he does not simply borrow elements from other religions to make a stronger, fuller, or more universal faith, nor seek to equate the value levels of all religious systems, Thurman sees the central issue in religion as a one's openness to God in honest seeking, and the experience that results as of more importance than the system or context within which the experience occurs. In this way he does not sidestep the issue of religious pluralism but rather emphasizes the basic universal with which religion as an experience is concerned. For Thurman, that which is universal is never foreign but common; it is not dependent upon human systems but is structured in life itself; as a universal it unifies and does not divide.

Thurman does not exalt cultic forms. He does not overemphasize the logical expressions and doctrinal patterns of religious systems. Religion itself is not finality but it opens us to finality because it makes us conscious of God who is final. The disclosure of God is addressed to our religious consciousness, and we recognize God because we have an intuitional awareness of The Holy and a capacity for receiving God. For Thurman, religion is not, then, a product of culture but is rooted in the very nature of human life itself. The intimation of divinity can be colored and conditioned by culture, but the intimation itself does not arise from culture merely. Religion is not a product of humanity's self-consciousness but rather what one does with one's God consciousness. A mature religion is for Thurman a matter of personal relationship with a self-revealing God. Although he is quite aware of the historical aspects of religious life, Thurman is careful to never posit finality in any religious system. He sees the experience of the Holy taking place in many contexts because there is in all life a drive for the realization of God.

44. Thurman, *Footprints of a Dream*, 81-82.

Howard Thurman's statements about the aliveness of life, discussed in depth in the previous chapter, are reminiscent of the vitalism Henri Bergson (1859-1941) explicated in his book *Creative Evolution*.[45] The thought of both is dependent upon naturalism, the immediacy of consciousness, the instinct for inwardness, and the kinship of all living things through the elan vital.

In the thought of both there is strong belief in a radical vitalism, and both explain the principle of vitality in life as the givenness of God. Both stress upon the dynamic character of the spiritual order—and how people can experience the very energies at work in the world on the moral and religious levels of life as well as the natural and physical. A central motif in each of their writings has been the aliveness of life, and for both the idea of evolution has played a large part. It is very possible that in the theology of Thurman we see reflections of Henri Bergson. Thurman acknowledges that he found much in Bergson that commended itself to his thinking.

But there was another thinker to whom Thurman has confessed his greatest debt: Olive Schreiner (1855-1920).[46] In a recently published anthology of her writings, which he edited, Thurman paid tribute to the white South African woman novelist whose thoughts, dreams, and convictions were several decades ahead of her time and scene. Entitled *A Track to the Water's Edge: The Olive Schreiner Reader*,[47] Thurman's collection reflects Olive Schreiner's best thought. Filled with selections characterized by "a timeless effectiveness which goes straight to the aspirations, feeling tones, and dreams of the human spirit,"[48] the new anthology is Thurman's tribute to one who, next to Rufus M. Jones, contributed most by

---

45. Henri Bergson, *Creative Evolution* (New York: H. Holt and Co., 1911), 176-185.

46. **ED:** Much of what James Earl Massey wrote in this chapter regarding Olive Schreiner was published simultaneously in the journal of the Howard University School of Religion. James Earl Massey, "Howard Thurman and Olive Schreiner on the Unity of All life; A Bibliographical Essay," *The Journal of Religious Thought*, Volume XXXIV, Fall-Winter 1977-78, No. 2, 29-33.

47. Howard Thurman, ed. *A Track to the Water's Edge: The Olive Schreiner Reader* (New York: Harper and Row, 1973).

48. Thurman, ed. *A Track to the Water's Edge*, xxxviii.

spirit and writings to nourish his spirit "in strange and defiant ways."[49]

The two never met. Olive Schreiner died in 1920, five years before Thurman first learned about her work. Introduction to her thought came in 1925 when he heard George L. ("Shorty") Collins read aloud from her book *Dreams*,[50] one evening during an informal conference they were attending in Pawling, New York. The *Dreams* book fascinated Thurman, especially the allegory about "The Hunter" as a seeker for Truth.[51] Although the literary art form of the "dream" impressed him, the music of the meaning spoke most pointedly to his temperament. "It seemed," Thurman comments, "that all my life long I was being readied for such an encounter."[52] Quite apart from all else during the informal conference, being introduced to the thought of Olive Schreiner was for Thurman the most profound experience. He was so impressed by the encounter that he spent his late twenties and early thirties finding and reading all of her available works[53] and studying biographical treatments of her life.[54]

Olive Schreiner had a mind of compelling appeal. Thurman felt the power of that mind when he was twenty-five, still in seminary. Her work had a sense of vastness and depth. George Cross, one of his teachers at Rochester Theological Seminary, had been talking in one of his courses on the importance of the timeless in human experience; now, in Schreiner's writings, Thurman was reading and feeding on the timeless through her thought.

Thurman liked the way Olive Schreiner's mind worked, and he marveled over her clear and contagious prose pictures, the broad

---

49. Thurman, ed. *A Track to the Water's Edge*, xxxviii.

50. Olive Schreiner, *Dreams* (Boston: Little, Brown, and Co., 1900).

51. *Dreams*, 25-50; Thurman, ed., *A Track to the Water's Edge*, 84-95.

52. Thurman, ed. *A Track to the Water's Edge*, xi.

53. Thurman has listed the books he found and read: *The Story of an African Farm* (1883); *Dreams* (1890); *Dream Life and Real Life* (1893): *Trooper Peter Halket of Mashonaland* (1897); *Woman and Labor* (1911); *Stories, Dreams, and Allegories* (1923); *From Man to Man* (1926); and *Undine* (1929), It was only in later years that he finally acquired and read three other of her works: *A Letter on the Jew* (1906); *Closer Union* (1909): and *Thoughts on South Africa* (1923).

54. See S.C. Cronwright-Schreiner, *The Life of Olive Schreiner* (Boston: Little, Brown, and Co., 1924).

sweep of her vision, and the emotional creativity that churned in his own spirit. Her basic social philosophy impressed him, and he was especially alert to her evident freedom and that she had escaped being spoiled by the racism rampant in the colonizing community of which she was a part. In fact, this aspect of her life became a point for critical study on his part. Thurman felt under necessity to discover just how was it that this white woman born and reared in South Africa at such a time could "think as she thought and feel about man [Black man] as she felt."[55] In his editorial introduction to the anthology of her writings Thurman tells what he discovered during his search to know.

Olive Schreiner wrote with an acute sense of history and with a worldview of compelling logic. But it was with her "innate, instinctual sense of the unity of all life"[56] that he felt most especially involved. Thurman has explained this result:

> It was this emphasis in her writing that was the first external confirmation of what had always been an active ingredient in my own awareness of life. As a boy in Florida, I walked along the beach of the Atlantic in the quiet stillness that can only be completely felt when the murmur of the ocean is stilled and the tides move stealthily along the shore. I held my breath against the night and watched the stars etch their brightness on the face of the darkened canopy of the heavens. I had the sense that all things, the sand, the sea, the stars, the night, and I were one lung through which all of life breathed. Not only was I aware of a vast rhythm enveloping all, but I was a part of it and it was a part of me.[57]

Thurman further explains, however, that:

> It was not until I read Olive Schreiner that I was able to establish sufficient psychological distance between me and the totality of such experiences to make the experience itself an object of thought. Thus it became possible for me to move from primary

55. Thurman, ed. *A Track to the Water's Edge*, xii.
56. Thurman, ed. *A Track to the Water's Edge*, xxvii.
57. Thurman, ed. *A Track to the Water's Edge*, xxvii-xxviii.

> experience, to conceptualizing that experience, to a vision inclusive of all of life. The resulting creative synthesis was to me religious rather than metaphysical, as seems to have been true in Olive Schreiner's case.[58]

It should be said that such a "vision inclusive of all of life" has been dynamically active at the center of Howard Thurman's life and writings. Just as Olive Schreiner carried such a vision with her throughout all her years, and sought to translate it responsibly in her dreams and deeds, Thurman has done likewise, having identified himself as a bearer of the same dream. Thurman did not learn the vision from Olive Schreiner; his discovery of her thought rather served to make the vision conceptually articulate. The dream of oneness had been in his heart since his years as a boy growing up in the segregation-ridden Florida town of Daytona Beach.

Tracing the "footprints" of this dream in Thurman's writings is not at all difficult. Here is a strategic passage from a meditation used originally by Thurman for the congregation of Fellowship Church in San Francisco:

> I am aware that all the race, in some very meaningful sense, breathes through me—that I am a part of the very pulsating rhythm of existence. I am not a thing apart; I am not a separate unit; I am deeply involved in the collective experience of aliveness and of human aliveness. If I am cut off so that only my little life breathes through me, only my little hopes course through my mind and spirit, only my little thoughts penetrate my brain, then life for me is not worth living. I must have a sense of deep corporate vitality; nothing less than that will satisfy. Therefore I must manage somehow to keep the lines of communication open between me and the human family. How wonderful it is if I can do this by love, by warmth, by kindling flame of abiding fellowship! Often, if it cannot be done that way, there is a resort to hate, to antagonism, to belligerency. The shouting of defiance is the call of my heart for kinship. If a man cannot become the center of an increasing affection, in his desperation he becomes the core of a great rejection. For

58. Thurman, ed. *A Track to the Water's Edge*, xxviii.

> better or for worse, there is but one family under God and I am a member of it.[59]

The theme of the unity of all life is found in many places in Thurman's books, but it is given its most extended and systematic treatment in Thurman's book *The Search for Common Ground*, which he subtitled "An Inquiry into the Basis of Man's Experience of Community." *The Search for Common Ground* is actually a sequel to his earlier 1965 study *The Luminous Darkness*. In *The Luminous Darkness* Thurman gives his insights regarding the problem of racial, social, and political segregation in the United States, together with a proposed theological solution. In *The Search for Common Ground* he gives a philosophical treatment of the social and political need for community, together with a reasoned statement about the rich potential for fulfillment illustrated by insights drawn from biology, physics, anthropology, myth, the dreams of prophets, and the common age-old aspirations of the human spirit. Both books are alike in spirit and focus although they differ in the style of treatment. In both works he discusses how the experience of vital religion deepens and widens and energizes the human spirit for the business of achieving harmony between all manifestations of life. Basic to Thurman's treatment is the thesis made explicit also in Olive Schreiner's works: that the thrust of life itself is for community, unity, and harmony—and that no person should put themself over against what life itself is seeking to fulfill in time and space. In both books Thurman argues this thesis with fierce but worthy logic.

Across many years now, Howard Thurman has made a point of prefacing his sermons and lectures with brief and perceptive readings from the pen of Olive Schreiner, the insights seeming "to stand by themselves and in their own right," and as I noted earlier, bearing "a timeless effectiveness which goes straight to the aspirations, feeling tones, and dreams of the human spirit."[60] Moved by an impulse that is religious rather than metaphysical, Howard Thurman has continued to live by the insight that life is a unity. Like Olive Schreiner, he, too, has a special faculty for seeing the world as a whole. He affirms: "The religious experience as I have

59. Howard Thurman, *Meditations of the Heart*, 115.

60. Thurman, ed. *A Track to the Water's Edge*, xxxviii.

known it seems to swing wide the door, not merely into Life but into lives."[61]

It is as a sensitive, perceptive, experienced Black person that Thurman has written: "[We] are made for one another. In this grand discovery there is a disclosure of another dimension: this experience of one another is not enough. There is a meaning in life greater than, but informing, all the immediate meanings—and the name given to this meaning is religion, because it embodies, however faintly, a sense of the ultimate and the divine."[62]

Olive Schreiner had mined from the same vein of vision when she wrote: "Between spirit that beats within me and body through which it acts, between mind and matter, between man and beast, between beast and plant and plant and earth, between life that has been and the life that is, I am able to see nowhere a sharp line of severance, but a great, pulsating, always interacting whole. So that at last it comes to be, that, when I hear my own heartbeat, I actually hear in it nothing but one throb in that life which has been and is—in which we live and move and have our being and are continually sustained."[63]

Howard Thurman has been at work for many decades. He has done his work with such discipline and depth that he now stands as one of the most respected and insightful leaders on the church and social scene. He has been at work living a life, declaring his witness, and shaping belief. He has been a creative religious leader, an innovator who pioneered successfully in developing the first interracial, intercultural, interfaith church in the United States. He has been busy erasing lines of demarcation between all humanity—lines of ignorance, prejudice, hatred, fear, illusion, and religious pride.

Thurman was an early Black advocate of nonviolence, urging mistreated and exploited African Americans to use the Gandhian style of nonviolent direct action as a method for altering their situation in the United States. Thurman was an early fashioner of a Black theology, a theology relevant as an articulate reaction against a false Christianity, as well as about true relations based upon Christian love. His idea of God did not demand but inspired. Conscious of

---

61. Thurman, *The Luminous Darkness*, 111.

62. Thurman, *The Luminous Darkness*, 112.

63. Olive Schreiner, *From Man to Man* (New York: Harper and Brothers, 1927), 155. See also Thurman, ed., *A Track to the Water's Edge*, 151-152.

the psychological needs of Blacks, Thurman's theology speaks to the point of self-respect in the sight of God as a child of God. This word has inspired self-respect, confidence in God as Creator and Source of life. He has given the African American an idea of God that is honest and relevant to the social situation in which Blacks have found themselves.

Thurman expands on the difference in how one describes their belief in God based on their social location:

> How a man describes his belief in God when his life is serene and his place and position are safe and secure may differ radically from what he has to say when the storm is raging and the winds are wild and unrestrained. It is my conviction that what a man has to say about the meaning of God when he lives in a society which he largely controls and in which he is accepted may be quite different from what he has to say about the same God if he lives in a society in which he is always marginal and of no account. It is for this reason that I am convinced that the test of any religion, as far as its impact upon mankind is concerned, turns on what word does it have to share about God with men who are the disinherited, the outsiders, the fringe dwellers moved from the citadels of power and control in the society.[64]

But Thurman's idea of God is as universal as it is particular, as relevant to whites as to Blacks, to non-Christians as to Christians. At once philosophical, liberal, relational, and universal, Howard Thurman's theological concerns are essentially ecumenical and offer a creative approach to the problem of human polarities. His theology celebrates God, life, unity of humanity, and an impartial God.[65] It celebrates a life sustained and directed by God, a life in which God is not without witness or without unique work. It celebrates a beloved community in which the experience of love is a necessary deed and a safe place.

---

64. Thurman, "Introduction," in *Why I Believe There Is a God*, xi.

65. See the discussion of this aspect of Thurman's theology as stated by Benjamin E. Mays, *The Negro's God: As Reflected in His Literature* (New York: Atheneum Press, 1968 reprint of 1938 edition), 174-176, 186.

Thurman the practical mystic peers into one's future encounter with God in the final days:

> A man dare not face his God on the Day of Atonement, seeking a right relation with Him, unless he has already exhausted himself in redeeming all the broken relations that he has with his fellows. There is an august impertinence and an utter arrogance in coming before God seeking for one's self at His hands what one has refused to give to those who walk the common way from day to day. "Forgive us our debts as we forgive our debtors": this is the timeless utterance, the password that relaxes the Angel with the Flaming Sword who guards the entrance to the Holy of Holies. No man can be happy in heaven if he left his brother in Hell.[66]

66. Thurman, *The Inward Journey*, 137-138.

Chapter Eight

Thurman and Massey in Conversation

The following dialogue was gathered on tape during an extended interview with Howard Thurman on May 8, 1971, at the Center for Continuing Education, on the University of Chicago campus in Chicago, Illinois. Dr. Thurman was in Chicago to fulfill an assignment as guest preacher for the Sunday morning service at Rockefeller Chapel on May 9. The dialogue provides the reader with an overview of Thurman's reactions to certain aspects of the author's assessment of his pilgrimage and theology. The dialogue was an extemporaneous conversation, but some central questions had been framed by the author to aid in a logical progression and natural flow of subject matter.[1]

MASSEY: Dr. Thurman, I recall a newspaper article about you in the January 3, 1970, *Afro-American*. The article was describing a celebration that some Morehouse alumni had for you in San Francisco.[2] The

---

1. ED: Thurman and Massey edited this conversation into this final form. Massey noted this would happen in his letters to Thurman in preparation for the taped interview. It is also very evident having listened to the original tape of the session. See Massey, James Earl. Letter to Howard Thurman. 23 February 1971. *JEM Papers*; Massey, James Earl. Letter to Howard Thurman. 23 March 1971. *James Earl Massey Papers*. Anderson University and Church of God Archives, Nicholson Library, Anderson, IN.

2. *The Afro-American*, January 3, 1970, 14.

article began with the statement, "How does it feel to know that you are a kind of living legend?" Then the writer went on to mention that two great American universities have named social halls after you, and that Morehouse College, your alma mater, is naming a new dormitory after you. The writer also mentioned that some schools of religion now offer courses dealing with your religious thought. I would like to know, just how does it feel to be a "kind of living legend"?

THURMAN: Well, first of all, I must say it is very difficult to think of myself as that, but I think that I understand what you mean in asking the question.

Actually, I have no sense of identification with the things that are said about me in that way. It is as if those things being said have rather happened to somebody else. I move toward them in my thinking with a kind of detachment. I feel about "the legend" as I feel about some things that I have written. For instance, I live with my book of meditations *The Inward Journey*. The book is always with me. I carry it everywhere. I have worn out a couple of bindings. There are times when my need is very great, and I turn to sections in that book and read them in the Presence of God. And—strange thing! It is as if somebody else wrote that book because I am only aware of being nourished by it.

This whole effect reminds me of the time when our group was touring in Burma back in the Thirties. We were going down a country road just outside of Rangoon. We came upon a certain tree, and underneath that tree there was a stone with a cup and a bowl of fruit. Some Buddhist monk had placed it there. The logic was: any passerby who travelled that way was heir to the supplies if he was famished and thirsty and needed them. He would not need to know. I feel that the things that come through a man—through the outpouring of his mind or spirit—are gifts, and those gifts belong to anyone who is nourished by them. I also believe that such a person nourished by another man is never under any obligation either to honor, praise, or to thank him.

Now I recognize that this is not the normal thought, that it is a bit off center, but this is my honest conviction. So you can see why I try to keep from identifying myself with any gift a man might have gained through me. The gift is something that happens through me, yes, but only through me. I can hold no proprietorship over the gift at all. What the gift does to another is not mine to claim. It is a man's possession. If there is any claim I can make upon any gift it is the extent to which that gift nourishes me. It is in this sense that I would have you understand my claimed "detachment" from so much attributed to me by means of "the legend." I am confident that you know I am not trying to sound pious in saying all of this.

MASSEY: Your discussion about "gifts" and "claims" is quite illuminating. I would have to conclude that such a view would tend to keep you steady when you don't see full results from the work you do.

THURMAN: From my point of view, the gift in a man, and the work he does, are a part of the givenness of God in him and through him. Any man who views life in this way must be careful about making claims about that which is not his own.

Now I must confess that one of my greatest personal spiritual struggles I have had has been to keep from making a primary issue of results. I must admit that the most psychologically normal thing is to work in life with one eye on results. The story of my life is much like the story of any other man's life, that is, walking the tightrope of letting results take care of themselves while I give my attention to making as much of an opening as possible for what God wants to flow through me. My job is done when the opening is made so the thing God is doing can flow through. But there are times when I fail to stay on that tightrope, because there is something so reassuring about knowing that you succeeded in some quest, that you hit the bullseye, that your working at something paid off.

You remember that story Jesus told about the businessman who went on a trip. We have termed it the Parable of the Talents, but I think we have missed the point of the whole story. At any rate, a man was going on a trip. He knew he was going to do some heavy spending while away, so he called three of his servants and gave each one a certain sum to handle for him until his return. He left instructions that upon his return they were to report to him about their use of the money. When the man got back he summoned the three men. The first man reported an increase through his use of the money allotted to him. So did the second man. The third servant could not match the report of the others, but he made a speech trying to cover his own lack of industry. He finally ended the speech and said, "here is your money—exactly what you gave me!" Jesus said that the man was thrown off the estate into outer darkness and wailing and gnashing of teeth. Why? We usually say that it was because he didn't show an increase, but I rather think he witnessed such a fate because he didn't work with what he had been given. That is how I feel about my life. I have felt under necessity to work at life. It has been a lifelong struggle, however, to keep my eyes on life and not on the results I would expect.

MASSEY: Looking at life that way also saves you from despair.

THURMAN: That's right. But here is another benefit. This view of life also keeps you from being jealous of people and envious of their recognition, their output, or whatever relates to their "success."

I would like to say that in this sense I have been especially blessed: that I have never been driven by ambition—in the usual sense of the term. There has never been a thing I wanted to have at any cost. There has never been a certain institution I wanted to run. There has never been any place where I have just had to go. Now my lack of this kind of "ambition" is not through any virtue that I have succeeded in whittling out of the raw stuff of life. It just happens to be the way I am put together. If there has been any one ambition that I feel as a constraining factor it is the desire to keep myself available to the gift that flows through. I think this is very important.

MASSEY: Dr. Thurman, in terms of your theological thought, I have discussed with you my approach in teaching about your methods as a master preacher. I have also had to deal with your theology in my classes on preaching in the seminary where I teach. I am interested to know whether any other professors and instructors around the country who are teaching about your religious thought have shared with you in discussion before attempting the task? Just how many of them have asked you questions to determine whether their views and assessments are reasonable, warranted, and balanced?

THURMAN: Well, to tell the truth, excepting you, none of the others sat down with me to discuss anything at length. They just decided to teach about my thought, and they have done it. Actually, I just bumped into the knowledge of what they were doing by accident.

MASSEY: As I understand it, at least four of us are at work teaching about your theological thought: Hazaiah W. Williams, of the Graduate Theological Union Center for Urban Studies, in Berkeley, California; Edward McCreary, at Virginia Union Theological Seminary, in Richmond, Virgina; J. Deotis Roberts, of Howard University School of Religion; and myself. At least two of this group, Williams and McCreary, have structured formal courses dealing explicitly with your theology. I am not sure just to what extent Roberts has taught on your views, but he has written an assessment of your theological position in an essay he prepared for a recent anthology dealing with the impact of the Negro on Western civilization.[3] I would have thought that all of us would consult with you before attempting to teach about your views.

THURMAN: I did talk very briefly last year with McCreary while I was at Virginia Union for the annual Summer Seminar. You were there. You and I talked at length, but McCreary and I only got to talk for a few minutes. He told me about his teaching project, which surprised me. I asked whether he had access to all of my writings, and when he informed me that he did not have them all, I promised to see that they were sent to him.

It might be that Hazaiah Williams proceeded with his work believing he was sufficiently familiar with my thought. You see he knew me back in the Boston University days. As a matter of fact, he came to California at my request. There is a very interesting story associated with the whole venture.

Williams was a senior during my first year at Boston as Dean of the Chapel. I asked The Church for the Fellowship of All Peoples to invite him out to become the first full-time director of religious education there. He accepted the offer, which put us together in both personal and professional roles. I must tell you how I managed the matter of his finances for that first year. This part of the story is a kind of aside, but it is of interest to show how some rather obscure happenings can finally fit into a pattern and bring forth meaningful fruit.

It happened like this. I had been invited to preach at a church in Minneapolis. The minister there was a good friend of mine. One of the families in that church invited me to have dinner with them at the country club to which they belonged. Well, I was somewhat self-conscious about the whole affair because under ordinary circumstances I would not be able to enter the door of that club if I were not with them. So I said to myself: I must explain to this couple just how I feel about their invitation—and why. I also reasoned about

3. J. Deotis Roberts, "The American Negro's Contributions to Religious Thought," in Joesph S. Roucek and Thomas Kiernan, eds., *The Negro Impact on Western Civilization* (New York: Philosophical Library, 1970), 86-89.

a way to let that couple "make up" for the situation. So I told the couple my thinking—and interestingly, they said they understood. They even agreed to "atone" for the way things were. I outlined to them our church's need for an underwritten salary for a full-time religious education director. I agreed to go to dinner with them if they would agree to give that director's salary for the first year. They agreed; that is how Williams got out to California. He stayed with the church for about a year and then went on to other posts in the Bay Area.

But to get back to the matter of extensive discussion with those who are teaching about my thought, the only thing I hope is that those who undertake to structure and do the courses will have available to them everything that I have written.

And let me say this: when you sent me those pages of bibliography listing my written works across the years, I was shocked.[4] I was shocked because such a listing would never have crossed my mind. I had never thought of doing such a thing for my writings. But here again you can see some connection with what we were talking about earlier: my mind just doesn't move in the "results" category.

By the way, when I learned that Roberts was doing a course on my thought, I sent a copy of that bibliography you prepared to him.

MASSEY: I have been reading Dr. Benjamin E. Mays's recently published autobiography, *Born to Rebel*. In one of the chapters, I ran across a statement about his experience, together with you and James Nabrit, in meeting the Fisk University debate team in contest in 1923. Mays tells us he made a painful discovery on that trip—namely rank discrimination on the part of the Fisk president at that time. When he realized that there were no "colored" judges acceptable to the college president, Mays was furious. He therefore told you and Nabrit that under the circumstances you men just had to win that debate. You did win it.[5] Just how extensive was your debate activity when you were at Morehouse College?

---

4. <u>**ED:**</u> The bibliography they are referring to was likely the one included here: James Earl Massey, "Bibliographical Essay: Howard Thurman and Rufus M. Jones," *The Journal of Negro History*, Volume LVII, No. 2, April 1972, 190-195. The actual bibliography is found on pages 193-195.

5. Benjamin E. Mays, *Born to Rebel: An Autobiography* (New York: Charles Scribner's Sons, 1971), 93.

THURMAN: Actually, I only debated for one year, my senior year. I just did not have the time for it. I was working a pretty full twenty hours a week to be exact. I not only had too little time for it but perhaps had too little inclination—given the facts of my situation. I was not an ascetic, detaching myself from all things social or extracurricular, but the time that I had available had to be used with a great deal of discretion. Interestingly though, at night, after the big things in town, the fellows would come by my room to report. They knew that I was interested. They also knew I would be there studying.

MASSEY: So you were still at the center of things even though you did not get into a great deal of activity.

THURMAN: I would suppose so. But with regard to debating, it was a good experience for me. I well remember the incident that Dr. Mays recounts.

MASSEY: What was the age difference between the two of you at that time?

THURMAN: Well now, I imagine Mays was about five or six years older. I imagine so. He came to Morehouse almost fresh from Bates. He was a bit older than the other young instructors who were coming to teach at Morehouse. He and I grew close in friendship because of some common interests. He lived in a room at the dormitory and ate in the dining room. He was married at the time but his wife was away teaching in South Carolina. Benjamin Mays brought to bear upon our school life an additional element besides his good teaching. Educated in the North, he had had the experience of being educated in an entirely different kind of social environment than most of us knew. When our studies brought us into contact with him, the ceiling of our hopes were raised in a quite new way. As a Negro, Southern born, he knew what it felt like to be segregated, and he knew what distortions segregation had produced in most of us. But he also tasted the joy of real possibilities beyond the Southern way of life, and when he spoke to us about such things we envisioned possibilities for ourselves beyond the limited boundaries of self-service, segregation, and the Southern style of social life.

For a long time, as you well know, there was a ceiling over the hopes of the Negro. He lived within a closed circuit. If a Negro aspired to be a professional, the professional ceiling was established as the preaching and pastoral ministry, medicine, dentistry, and teaching. It was later that law and social work entered the picture.

The great contribution made to my generation by men like Bennie Mays, Lorimer Milton, and "Smokey Joe" Caroll was that they heightened our morale by broadening our understanding of the stage of American life.

Bennie Mays was a good teacher, particularly in mathematics. We visited together often. As a matter of fact, he and I were closer during those Morehouse years than at any other time in our lives, even closer than when we served on the same faculty of the School of Religion at Howard University. I would have to add that this was because in later years our responsibilities were so separate and our worlds were increasingly different.

MASSEY: Dr. Thurman, in treating your early boyhood, I took notice that you grew up in a home atmosphere controlled and nurtured by strong women. You were very much nurtured by women: grandmother, mother, and I am especially interested in your relationship as a growing boy with Mrs. Mary McLeod Bethune. One of her biographers listed you as a member of her Better Boys Clubs.[6] I would like to know, since you have not written about this elsewhere, just what was your relation to Mrs. Bethune? What is your assessment of Mrs. Bethune as a person, community leader, and friend? What characteristics challenged you as a boy growing up in a town where she was one of the more militant figures in the community?

THURMAN: Well, there are several things that can and should be said about Mrs. Bethune. First of all, the very fact that she was the principal of a school put her in a separate category. In those days, we Negroes were always on the hunt for the hero or a heroine. There was always a spotlight on any Black person who had won some stature. The person helped us to sense our own identity and worth. Mrs. Bethune was not only principal of the school she started, but she was black. You must remember that during this period, there was a lot of "hanky-panky" about color distinctions among Negroes, some being black, others being "high yellow," and so forth. Well Mrs. Bethune was very black, and this put her automatically within the reach of everybody in the Negro community. It might sound ridiculous in 1971 to talk this way, but this is the story of those years.

Mrs. Bethune would come to all the Negro churches in the town, usually visiting on whatever afternoon or night the pastor would

6. Holt, *Mary McLeod Bethune*, 114.

assign. We called those occasions "off nights," because nothing else was planned of a religious nature. She would come to the churches, make speeches about her school, discuss her dream for the school and Black people. She would also sing—she was quite a singer. After a bit we would pass the hat and collect money for her work. Sometimes people would send foodstuffs from their gardens to the school, sometimes fresh, sometimes canned.

I remember the Sunday afternoon services that she led. She called them Temperance Services. These were open to all the public—including whites. I recall that it was during such Temperance Services that I first noticed that she did not allow segregation at her meetings. For example, sometimes rich white people would come over from the beach, some of them heavy contributors to her work, but she would never provide special seats for them. You sat where you sat. Remember: that was over fifty years ago! She had strength—and pride. She bore a contagious mystique.

Then, too, Mrs. Bethune could think on her feet. I was very impressed by this ability on her part. I am reminded at this point of how much of an impact this ability on her part made upon me. As you know, I earned money as a boy doing various chores around town. I would collect discarded newspapers and magazines from certain homes and take them for disposal to the city dump. One day I leafed through one of the magazines I was to discard, *The Atlantic Monthly* it was, and saw on a certain page of that heavy, enameled paper a full-page advertisement of a Hamilton watch. In the center of the page was a reproduction of Rodin's "Thinker." I tossed the rest of the magazine on the fire, but kept the picture of "The Thinker." The picture affected me profoundly. In fact, I was so enamored of it that I tried to reproduce the pose and stance—even the furrowed brow, resting my chin on the flat side of my fist, believing that these were hallmarks of thought and real profundity. I practiced the pose whenever I had a spare moment and something against which I could lean. One day I was leaning against the fence perfecting my stance when my sister called me to do an errand for my mother. I was so engrossed that I told my sister to tell my mother that I was busy thinking! Needless to say, I did not repeat that again.

MASSEY: I believe you referred to that experience in one of the chapters of your new book *The Search for Common Gound*. It is interesting to hear you tell about it now in connection with the impact of Mrs. Bethune upon your aspirations during boyhood.

THURMAN: Yes, I did refer to that boyhood experience in my new book. There is something else I want to say about Mrs. Bethune at this point. I mentioned that she bore a contagious mystique. As the years unfolded, as life was kind and she became a national figure, she projected this mystique on a national canvas.

I remember the time when she visited with Mrs. Thurman and me during my time at Howard University. She and Mrs. Thurman worked quite closely in a Negro Women's organization. One morning Mrs. Bethune was standing in front of the mirror in our hallway. She touched her face, pulled here and there, and as she saw that I was noticing it all, she said, "Howard, Black is beautiful! Black is beautiful!" The expression is now in current use, but she was saying it even then. This is why her contagion was so persuasive. She had identity and she projected it. I was caught up in this along with a lot of other people in town.

MASSEY: I can well understand. In 1955, you went back to Daytona Beach to give the eulogy at her funeral. Was this by her request or the request of the family or the administrators at Bethune-Cookman College?

THURMAN: I understood from President Moore that it was what she wanted. It would be like her to have asked for this.

You know, as I think about that request she made for me to speak at her memorial service, I am reminded about her frequent calls upon me across the years to be a religious service to her. I feel particularly honored by God to have had that privilege. It is an interesting thing, really, because of all the things a Negro leader is usually called upon to do—speak on race topics and related issues, I have been called upon to do things which have to do with the religious life, especially during my last twenty-five years or so. I consider that a compliment to my ministry and my gift from God.

As I think about it, I recall that about a year or so before Martin King was killed I got a call from [Ralph] Abernathy to come to Chicago—they were in this very city—and speak to the Southern Christian Leadership Conference leaders while they were in their annual session. I was in San Francisco, holding the phone as Abernathy said, "Doc [meaning Martin Luther King, Jr.] told me to call you, Dr. Thurman. He wants to know if you can come and meet with us here in Chicago. Doc wants you to meet with us and use one of the night sessions to help us deal with our inner lives. Can you come?" He paused only briefly, then added, "We are meeting to work out our strategy. We don't want you to get mixed up in that. We need to have somebody to dig around our roots and help us deepen them, and we feel that you are just the one to help us do this." Abernathy was calling me on Thursday. The meeting opened on Friday. I just couldn't go, but the very invitation warmed my spirit. It had to do with the very thing toward which my life leans and finds focus.

Mrs. Bethune used to call upon me for much the same ministry for her and the National Negro Women's Organization she headed. If I remember correctly, she had me come twice from San Francisco to Washington, DC to do worship series for the women. I have always prized such opportunities and assignments. I have always felt especially blessed in receiving them. As for other assignments and requests dealing with race, I do have ideas about all of these things—and also very deep feelings about them, but dealing with them is not the same as handling the issues of religious experience.

I remember the time, early in my seminary days, when I did give myself to the business of speechmaking about race concerns. Those were the years when I needed money for an education. One year, my first year, I made speeches every Sunday night at one church after another because I was determined that I was not going to be corralled into the busboy job that was always doled out to Negro seminary students—although even a few white seminarians had such jobs too. We lived at the dormitory and we ate at the YMCA. On my first morning there, the lady in charge said to me, "Now, Mr. Thurman, your white coat is over there," pointing to a pile of uniforms. And I promptly replied, as politely as I could, "No, I'm not working this semester." But I knew that I didn't have any money reserves, so I had to figure out a way to support myself so that I could spend the semester in study and thought. So, I finally signed myself out to churches as a speaker on race concerns. I went out every Sunday night from October until May. I was really beating the bushes. I would say a few things and the people would pass the hat. I had lived in the South. I knew the life lived there, and I knew how to make a good speech about it all. I became known as a kind of "specialist" on the subject, and I would often leave with the people feeling deeply guilty about their race prejudice.

On the last Sunday night of my circuit that first year, I was in a little town in New York State when a man came up to me and said, "Well, this is your last night. School closes next week." I said, "Yes." Then he said, "You know, I liked the speech tonight as well as the one last Sunday night." And I said, "What was that?" He went on to say, "Why yes! I have covered your circuit during every speech you have given since last October." He pulled out a little black book and traced the dates and the places. Then he explained, "You see, this has been my assignment from the Klan!" The man not only told me my subjects and where I had used them, he also told me the number of people attending the meetings and where I had spent the nights!

When I got back to the seminary, I began to do some serious thinking about what I had been doing. My attitude was not right. I had been vindictive even enjoying it when I could see the people writhing under guilt. Yet I considered my work quite amoral. The longer I thought about it the more I could see that I couldn't go on in that way. I knew that that was not true preaching. I put the question to myself of whether I would truly preach or do something else. This was the first and last year that I have ever talked in a worship setting on race prejudice.

Do not misunderstand me. My decision was not out of fear of the Ku Klux Klan. The fact that the Klan was breathing down my neck only precipitated the necessity to think the whole thing through as a preacher.

Although I have explained the relation of that Klansman's comments to my final decision, let me also confess that there were times in my speaking work when I had reason to be afraid. At that time, back in the 1920s, Western New York was one of the most highly organized Klan territories in America. It was hard to find a town there where most of the men did not belong to the Klan. I was to go to a certain town but the minister came into Rochester on Saturday in order to especially see me about the engagement. He said, "Brother Howard, you better not come to our church this weekend because the Klan just doesn't want you in town." I said to him, "How do you feel about it?" He said, "Well, you know how some men are. This can be very dangerous for you. But, if you still want to come, I would be very glad for you to be with us." I said, "I'll be there. Meet me at the inner-urban station." I went. He picked me up at the station. That Sunday when we pulled up in front of the church in his car we noticed that the long sidewalk leading up to the church door—the church sat way back from the street—was lined with men standing on both sides of the walk. We didn't know what the men were going to do. The pastor was very disconcerted. I won't discuss how I felt! The men did nothing really; it was just a scare tactic. But times like those do make you think.

But, getting back to Mrs. Bethune: she had also faced times like those. The whole town knew how she had stood up against pressures and scare tactics. I was caught up in my regard for her courage and bravery like every other Negro in town. Her story is the story of a psychic and spiritual impact on the Black community in the places where she worked. And the fact that she was an educator only heightened the regard accorded her.

You know, speaking of the role of Black educators in the psychic and spiritual history of the Black community in America, somebody someday ought to write that story in a way that it is not yet available. The impact of the Black colleges and Black educators upon the Black community in our land, particularly the South, is a romantic story. It is hard to interpret what has been happening at the leadership levels within the Black community now without knowing that story. It is appalling to consider the ignorance of the average white American about this.

When I was teaching at Morehouse, a friend of mine from Penn State came through Atlanta. He was going on to New Orleans and he stopped over for a day to see me. He arrived at the railroad station, hailed a waiting cab, got in, and stated his destination as Morehouse College campus. The driver, white, said, "You must be in the wrong town, I have been a taxi driver here for some twenty-seven years and I have never heard of any Morehouse College." But if my friend had been in a cab driven by any Black driver! If only the story of such an impact upon the Black community by its schools could be told as we know it!

MASSEY: I recall an article by you that touches on this concern. If I remember correctly, it was an article published in the *Journal of Negro Education* some years ago. I believe the title was "The New Heaven and the New Earth."[7]

---

7. Howard Thurman, "The New Heaven and the New Earth," *The Journal of Negro Education* (Vol. XXVII, No. 2) 115-119. <u>**ED:**</u> Howard Thurman, "The

THURMAN: I had forgotten that. Yes, you are right. I did deal with certain aspects of the Black man's encounter with higher education. I remember pointing out some of the frustrations occasioned within the Negro by college training in so many, many instances. There were many years when I could never find or talk with any Negro that has college training who was not at the same time discouraged. The fruits of his learning were soured by his social experience of being segregated against. The level of his living had not been changed by education—except among his own people. There were certain vocational goals at that time that you just could not hold with any sense of realism in expectancy. They were unrealistic in terms of what the wider society would allow. Those goals were unrealistic despite the fact that they were like fires kindled inside as a result of prolonged exposure to what higher education offered. There was more at work to occasion the frustration to which I gave attention, but I also dealt with how the frustration had to be faced and handled. The problem had to be understood before it could be counteracted. And it had to be counteracted if students were to be graduated emotionally healthy.

One of the first steps in dealing with that frustration on the part of the Negro college students was to find teachers who were free within their thinking and had points of view that could not be contained within the segregated structure known as "the Negro college." Such persons did not accept the system of segregation, nor would they see it as necessary or reasonable. They broadened the area of the Black student's awareness. They did this not only educationally in terms of subject matter and classroom concerns, but also in terms of morale, raised hopes, the structuring of an honest service motive—which they demonstrated, and their distinctive image as professionals skilled in their tasks. This was particularly true if the teachers were not only conversant with the extenuating circumstances of the Negro education experience but had been educated for the most part in Northern or Eastern institutions as further training to teach. Such teachers would bring with them the distinct flavor of a different kind of environment which they would share. But also brought with them the living proof that they had

---

New Heaven and the New Earth, 1958," in Fluker, ed., *The Papers of Thurman*, Volume 4, 201-207.

been able to compete with the wider world and present themselves as achievers.

This is how I interpreted Bennie Mays, as I mentioned earlier. Such teachers heightened our morale and gave us belief in our cause. There were other factors at work within the situation to mitigate against frustration, but it is hard to overemphasize the crucial importance of the trained and dedicated Black teacher in doing so.

By the way, that article grew out of an address I delivered at a Special Convocation at Virginia Union University back in November 1957. The American Baptist Home Mission Society was commemorating its One Hundred and Twenty-Fifth Anniversary. Many of the Black colleges developed through the backing of such missionary organizations. This, too, is a story in itself, but especially the dilemma posed by the structure of the institutions the missionary movement established and supported. The missionaries were willing to go only so far, even in the name of their ethical imperative. This set of facts presents an involved drama that needs to be more widely known and understood.

There is so much about Black college life and mystique that needs to be told, so much has not been touched at all. Think, for example, of Alcorn A&M College in Mississippi. This year the College celebrates its centennial. It began back in 1871 as a school for white boys, supported by the Southern Presbyterians. The many buildings were built by the slaves—the dormitories, the chapel, the president's house. And then by some act of God, that school built by slaves for the sons of their masters became a Black school.

MASSEY: Was not Hiram R. Revels, the first Negro elected to the United States Senate, the first Black president of that school?

THURMAN: Yes, he was. And the story of how it all came about—in Mississippi—shows us the hand of God working in the picture.

MASSEY: I recall a brief article setting forth a bit of the history of Alcorn A&M College in a recent issue of *The Negro History Bulletin*.

THURMAN: The article was in the April issue.[8] Such stories need to be told, and told widely. And with the sensitivity possible only to one from the inside. The story should be told by a Black man as one

8. George A. Sewall, "A Hundred Years of History: Alcorn A. & M. College Observes Centennial 1871-1971)," *Negro History Bulletin* (Vol. 34, No. 4), April 1971, 78-79.

who knows the kinds of impact such a school has had upon the Black community in Mississippi and elsewhere. Alcorn College antedates Tuskegee by about ten years, and it has played a meaningful role in establishing a pattern in the scope and operation of agricultural and mechanical institutions among and for Blacks.

MASSEY: Our discussion about Mrs. Bethune led us down a broad avenue filled with the traffic of many related matters.

THURMAN: Yes, indeed! She was quite a woman, a woman in a quite unique spot at a most strategic time in my life as a boy. But anyway, such was the impact of Mrs. Bethune upon me. Interestingly, your putting of the question to me made me think about her in ways I had not ever formulated before now.

There was another aspect of consideration that your question has dredged up in my mind. As one of the three strong women with whom I was associated in my boyhood—the other two being my mother and grandmother, Mrs. Bethune and I could relate without undo difficulty on my part. I could relate to the impact of her inspiration and personality without having to do a transfer because I grew up in a matriarchal home. As you know, my father died when I was very young, and I was left as the only male in the household. I have thought quite a lot about what effects his absence has upon my life. I have often wondered what differences might have been for me if I had not grown up without a father.

At any rate, the impact of Mrs. Bethune was more than the mere impact of a Black woman. It was the impact of what we then called, "a big Negro," meaning a Black person of considerable stature in mind and personhood. She was one of the last such big Negroes. She was like a mountain peak. There were so few like her. It seems today as if there are still so few. But it is not essentially the case. It is not that our day has fewer great persons, fewer mountain peak Negroes, it is rather that the valleys around them have been raised.

MASSEY: Dr. Thurman, I am not surprised that Mrs. Bethune left on record a request that you give the eulogy at the memorial service in her honor. You have not only distinguished yourself as one who grew up in the town she loved, but you have a distinctly unique way of eulogizing. Your comments have a way of bringing the meaning of a person's life into clearer focus. I have observed this on your part in many settings. I especially recall the published version of the sermon you gave at the American Embassy in Lagos,

Nigeria, memorializing John F. Kennedy after his assassination.[9] I recall the published version of the memorial tribute you gave after Martin Luther King's death over a Los Angeles, California, radio station.[10] And, more recently, there was your eulogy delivered at Riverside Church in March during the funeral service for Whitney M. Young.[11] I recall at least one constant refrain that each eulogy held in common. It went something like this: The time and place of a man's life on earth is the time and place of his body, while the meaning and significance of his life is as vast and far-reaching as that man's gifts, times, and committed powers can make it. It is at once a statement of basic orientation at a time when meaning is in need of being underscored. I have always appreciated the way you eulogize.

THURMAN: I appreciate your comments. I see that you have screened my eulogies as carefully as you have worked with the rest of my published work.

MASSEY: It has been my judgment that your theological thought is clearly in evidence at such times of human stress helping to transform the hour of felt loss into an occasion of realized meaning about life itself.

THURMAN: I must agree with you in your judgment.

MASSEY: I was especially impressed by the way Elizabeth Yates treats your approaches to funeralizing in her biographical study about you.[12] The readings you select for use are apt and pointed in their insight. Your eulogies are warm and tender without slighting in any way the raw fact of death. It is not easy to affect a sense

---

9. Howard Thurman, "Sermon Preached by the Reverend Dr. Howard Thurman," at the American Embassy, Lagos, Nigeria, Sunday, November 24, 1963, in memory of the late President John F. Kennedy, in William M. Fine, ed., *That Day with God* (New York: McGraw-Hill Book Co., 1964) 135-141. **ED:** Howard Thurman, "Eulogy for John F. Kennedy, 24 November 1963," in Fluker, ed., *The Papers of Thurman, Volume 5*, 103-107.

10. **ED:** Howard Thurman, "Martin Luther King, Jr.: Litany and Words in Memoriam, 7 April 1968," in Fluker, ed., *The Papers of Thurman, Volume 5*, 176-188.

11. **ED:** Howard Thurman, "Eulogy for Whitney Young, 16 March 1971," in Fluker, ed., *The Papers of Thurman, Volume 5*, 219-223.

12. Yates, *Howard Thurman*, 135-141.

of comfort, but I believe that you usually succeed. Your eulogies make it clear that you appreciated the person about whom you are speaking. This in itself serves to reveal your sense of kinship with the bereaved family. But your handling of the subject of death as but an episode in life reminds every listener that the person's life being remembered has not been exhausted finally by death.

THURMAN: I can only thank you for your regard. As you know, I have done quite a lot of thinking about the subject and experience of death. This kind of thought has been forced upon me because of my unabating interest in the subject and my experience of life itself. Life is indeed alive. The separateness of the many, the near infinite, particularized forms of life only underscores the ruggedness of the life those forms all share in common, and all that lives seems to forever work toward fulfillment, order, wholeness. My interest in the very stuff of life has made it imperative that I also consider death, since death appears at first sight to be a kind of contradiction that opposes life. It is my honest conviction that the apparent contradiction to life that we call death is not a final contradiction. I believe that there are levels in every man that are so deeply set in the process of his life that the final privacy and stability of his life cannot be ultimately threatened even by the experience of dying. Death does not ever swallow life in any ultimate sense. Death is a part of the life process. The logic of this view is that death is seen always as an aspect of experience, a transitional phase in the process of life. One might even speak of death as a kind of lag in the vast creative process of life. Your treatment of my thought on this subject, I must say, is essentially true to my inner witness. Life is rooted in God, and God sustains and supports life in all its forms. Ultimately, even death will exhaust itself since it cannot be an external fact. Death is not a final contradiction. Death is but one of several literal facts of the external world. It is a part of the orderly disorder that we experience with our senses, but the life rooted so deeply with our spirits draws its strength and sustenance from the boundless ebb and flow that is the givenness of God. This affirmation is categorical for me.

MASSEY: Speaking of affirmations, Dr. Thurman, I am especially impressed by the logic and faith explicated in your recent book about *The Search for Common Ground.* I consider that book as a sequel to your earlier work *The Luminous Darkness. The Luminous*

Darkness gave your psychological insights into the American social and political problem, together with a stated concern to apply a theological solution. *The Search for Common Ground* gives your philosophical insights into the social and political need for community, showing the rich potential for fulfillment through illustrations drawn from biology, physics, myth, the dreams of prophets, and the common aspirations of the human spirit. How do you view this assessment?

THURMAN: I agree with it, very much indeed. I must say that you have understood my thought very well indeed.

Actually, both of those books of mine are alike in spirit although they differ in both style of writing and treatment. In both I have tried to indicate the ground of hope, as I see it. I believe with all my heart that all of life is in process, and that there is a basic tie that binds all that lives, reinforcing and blessing and even in a sense guaranteeing what is fundamental for the total fulfillment of that process. At the same time, however, I have been concerned to show in a practical fashion to what extent the responsibility for social change and community rests with men of faith and radical commitment.

MASSEY: Even the most casual reader of either book will catch the strength with which you state your affirmation. Was it not *Time* magazine that spoke about the "Fierce Logic"[13] of your argument in *The Luminous Darkness*? I liked the way you dealt with segregation in that book. First, you anatomized it, telling it "like it is," then you went on to anathematize it as a situation that causes a sense of desolation and despair.

THURMAN: The ground of hope in that whole situation is the striving of the whole human race buttressed by the vitality at work within the context of the life process itself. I wrote about this in my new book in rather formal terms but the concept unfolds as a personal statement of my own faith and "working paper" of life. *The Search for Common Ground* is an outgrowth of a personal search within life and a severe questioning of life—and an awareness of The Answer at work within the total process at levels deeper that I can fully trace. My new book is a pointer.

MASSEY: In my opinion, *The Search for Common Ground* comes close to being a systemic explication of your philosophical theology.

13. *Time,* August 27, 1965, 85-86.

Your title reminds me a bit of Karl Jaspers, who employed the expression "common ground" in much the same manner as you.[14] Your statement, however, impresses me as fresh and intensely personal, logical and compellingly handled. As for your vision of the future, I view it as authentic.

I consider the discussion you give of the Afro-American's identity crisis across the recent past as must reading for our time. The argument is so carefully set; and frankly, I have not encountered such compelling prose in a long time. I am commending you on both the mechanics of writing and the grasp of the subject matter itself.

THURMAN: Thank you for that assessment. *The Search for Common Ground* grew slowly across many years as I took a long and hard look at my reactions to the experiences of life. I discerned, very early in my life, a tendency—an inner demand, rather, to see things "whole," consummated, in pattern. I have been particularly concerned about the insistent notion of humans in community: all this, mind you, has been related to the awful sense of living as a victim of segregation and prejudice while sensing, at the same time, that the unity fundamental to all life urged me to structure my living for the work and ideal of community. I had to constantly inquire, therefore, into the basis of community. I had to ask myself—and to ask of life, is there a common ground upon which to stand affirming oneself as a unique person while relating to oneself with the rest of unfolding life in the world? I can state the question a bit differently because I thought about the question from many angles and approaches: my search led me to seek answers to why there has been a pull toward community within me when the general and specific drift of society threatened it all and did not seem to aid or reinforce that pull. This made for a personal crisis in my thinking as well as in my experience as a Black American. I began to search everywhere for some empirical sanction for the tendency I knew was at work within me. I had to know, once-for-all, if my concerns to see and make things "whole" was a mirage and vain dream or something of promise working for change and life as it was meant to be. The questioning led me into many areas of exploration: biology, the query of accounts of creation, prophetic and classical literature, animal life, anthropology,

14. Karl Jaspers, *Philosophical Faith and Revelation* (New York: Harper and Row, 1967), xxv, 321.

and personal and group histories. The book documents my findings and my faith.

The material in the first five chapters was amassed and assessed with my basic thesis always in mind: the basis for man's experience of community must be rooted in the very life process itself. There must be a common ground for understanding, relation, and community. My problem was to document this on more than one level of life process. The book shows the levels on which my mind worked. As I finished the first five chapters, my mind came to a kind of "dead end." It was a long time, a long time indeed, before I was alert enough to see how my basic thesis was to be related to the current social tensions between Black men and white men in American society. The actual moment of vision about that relation came while I was on a sea voyage on the Pacific Ocean with Mrs. Thurman early in 1970.

The doors of insight finally opened early one morning, about 5:00 a.m., as I sat alone in the rear of the ship dining room. I had gone there purposely at a time when there would be no traffic. I was intent to tie all of my concerns together in final form on the manuscript pages. I began to see the mood of Black articulateness back here in the States as a necessary phenomenon, a pivotal point around which a positive self and race awareness was actively and necessarily at work.

Actually, the Black man's life in America was never one in which he felt himself an accepted part of the larger primary structure of society as a whole. This fact left a residue in the individual and collective psyche of the Black man because he knew that he was always at the mercy of the white world. This tragic fact is a most signal clue to the present phenomenon of the Black man's rejection of white determination to control his life and fortune here.

The present scene, highly polarized between Black and white, is both a by-product and a corrective possibility—and within it are the basic dynamics that can make for a new social structure. There was a time in America when the will for exclusiveness was confined primarily to white society. Whites would not open the door to Black men. The Black man was knocking at every door asking to be let in. He knew he was a vital part of the life here even though he was being segregated against and denied his rights. Now we are at the point in time in our society when the Black man is insisting upon his exclusiveness. In the earlier period, white was the absolute; now, Black is an absolute among Blacks. This new feature is a stage of the development of a sense of identity for some—or so it should be. The sense of identity should give a sense of our roots, which is essential to feeling "at home," but identity must not become a trap that ensnares like white supremacy ideas trapped white Americans. It is my considered judgment that what has been happening on the level of identity among Blacks, particularly among young Blacks, is a stop gap, a stirring at the center of the human will in preparation for a thrust across barriers that forbid community. I see the strong quest for identity as the concern for an established center out of which the men who will have found themselves can function without fear and relate with a sense of meaning to other men.

The social crisis in our land is not yet over, and will not soon be over. But it is crucial that the Black man has rejected the arbitrary social classifications arising from the prejudices of the larger white society. The message of life itself has gotten through to Negroes—the message that that which lives must be true to itself in order to be its best in relation. I have often described this aspect of my thought on identity very categorically, saying that the only person who can be at home everywhere is the person who is at home somewhere. That is one of the basic concerns stated in the final chapter of *The Search for Common Ground*.

What I have written in the chapter is in part a kind of testimony to the worth of the Black idiom in American society. The Black idiom belongs here, and it is as indigenous to the society as any other idiom being honored here. In fact, if you go back far enough in the life of any American you would be listening to a foreign tongue. The Black man in America is as grounded in the uniqueness of the American experience as those from any other idiom and area. It is necessary that this be affirmed, and that affirmation—done without any fear, shame, or sense of absoluteness—can be one of the creative ingredients in the new residue now building up in the collective psyche of the nation and society.

MASSEY: Dr. Thurman, I regret to say it, but the clock before us shows that we have utterly disregarded the schedule we intended to keep. We have pursued some of the most important concerns in our talk, and I am especially thankful that we took the time to deal with them, even if only briefly. You have been gracious in so giving of yourself for all this, and your enthusiasm in responding has made this occasion of interview a fundamental experience of sharing.

THURMAN: It has given me far more than I have given you. It has been delightful to share my thoughts with you in this way.

Chapter Nine

Afterthoughts

At thirty years after his death in 1981 and more than a century after his birth in 1899, Howard Thurman's name and influence remain at an imposing height and are still growing. A commanding figure during his long and significant ministry, Thurman's work shows a combination of demonstrated giftedness, widening grace, and stubborn grit. A man of warmth, wisdom, wit, and humor, his appeal was engaging and inspirational. His sermons are still being heralded by many, and his books are readily available in libraries scattered across the landscape of many English-speaking countries.[1]

There were many things about Howard Thurman that impressed me, but central among them was his unique ability to pass his experience through his thought and shape relevant theology in so doing. Thurman was always seeking to sense in his experiences some inner logic connected with truth, the truth out of which he could see and share what he called "my own testimony, my own witness to truth." Thurman sensed that theology cannot be separated from the totality

1. ED: James Earl Massey's unpublished manuscript on Howard Thurman was dated 1977—while Thurman was yet alive and they were yet in conversation. Found in Massey's papers were later undated and unpublished reflections on Howard Thurman. This closing chapter of the Massey book on Howard Thurman weaves together some of those comments. They reflect a more seasoned Massey. This chapter begins with the only paragraph of his notes that identifies a time period—2011.

of one's own humanity, that the process and findings of the searching mind are related to the destiny of the soul. He knew that knowing is not a distraction if it arises from being, from realized life. Again and again he was wont to quote Robert Browning's "Paracelsus," that thoughtful line that . . . "to know rather consists in the opening out a way whence the imprisoned splendor may escape, than in the effecting entry for a light supposed to be without."

Thurman's appeal for personal experience was not a selfish venture. His approach to theology was autobiographical, to be sure, but his findings show something more than the arid results of self-absorption. His approach was individual, and necessarily, but he was above the cult of individualism. As he often said while speaking, "The only light a man has is the light that falls across his path." This distinction is seminal and imperative for interpreting Thurman's personhood, methods, and thought.

His writings relate to his inner biography. His basic theology was the synthesized essence of his own search and findings. He confessed this again and again in his writings. His book *The Creative Encounter* (1954) was Thurman's view of how religious experience and social witness imply or require each other. "This volume," he explained in the preface to the book, "is the testimony of a personal quest with many indications of seeking and perhaps little evidence of finding."[2] But that was a characteristically modest disclaimer. In the foreword to his later study *The Search for Common Ground* (1971), Thurman explained, "When I completed the manuscript, I was struck by the feeling that here I had set down the case in rather formal terms, for what reveals itself is my lifelong working paper."[3] The fact is that Howard Thurman's writings are more often than not a statement of his theology as derived from a sifting of his own experience with life. He gives us his life in his literature. He put his realizations on record and into print. Personal experience is the main province from which a theology is drawn and shaped, and to which it must be addressed again and again for validation and effect.

I knew Howard Thurman long enough and close enough to understand what he meant by insisting on this approach to the shaping of a theology—and I saw the validity of this approach in his life

2. Thurman, *The Creative Encounter*, 12.

3. Thurman, *The Search for Common Ground*, xi.

and work. But I was never without the caution that must attend such an approach. A caution was necessary because truth is not always best treated or traced by exploring the tracks of one's own heart and mind; inspecting the self can become a trap, with superficial and insignificant results. The circle of one's own experience can become a stopping place where one is out of touch with the truth rather than brought closer to it. Given my biblical orientation, I always viewed personal experience under the light of Scripture wisdom. I was never fully comfortable to search my mind and heart except under the light of the revealed Word. I have always believed and moved within the concern that the true source of theology is the biblical witness and not in the heart and mind of the seeking thinker.

I would like one day to write more comprehensively about the mind and meaning of Howard Thurman. There is so much about him that needs to be said, especially crucial is to make his living thought emerge in context. I have been at home with his mind and believe that I see how his experience and thought interacted upon each other. As I think back upon our friendship, one of the highest compliments he ever paid me was to refer to me as a "blood brother of the mind and of the spirit."

Thurman had a unique lyrical gift. His works will continue to impress and inspire, not only by their subject matter but also by their style. There is in Thurman's writings a richness of sentiment as well as theological depth; his ability to express himself and the truth with such memorable style and immediacy was his genius for balancing emotion and fact. His statements had character and spirit, with an openness to the world of fact that was strengthened by an outlook on the world within. Thurman was a constituted spokesperson readied by insight and outlook to share his sense of reality with others. Although introspective and shy by nature, he was blessed with the ability to give himself on purpose. He could make himself felt as he threw himself outwards and externalized sharing of his thought. Those who saw and heard him would see and hear his truth, ready to identify themselves with his vision. To be in his company was to experience the forcefulness, however gentle, of a rising tide. Those who shared with him in conversation or study found themselves looking more sharply at things and into them, seeing parts, and seeing them whole, seeing philosophically and yet feeling personal at the same time. In this sense he was right to insist that personality and theology relate, since our humanity brands our thought. In so speaking, Thurman was urging us to keep all things subordinated to the whole of life and not seek to exclude what is personal from what is prophetic. He insisted that object and subject belonged together, that any detachment spells death to understanding and experience. He did not lose himself in any disturbing prepossession with himself; he was moved always by the need to see subject and object in relation, to see the inner and the outer as one. In true fashion as a mystic, then, Howard Thurman was insisting that life is at once personal and supra-personal, and that theology develops best when the private and the personal are experienced in the arena with truth.

Jane Steger, from whose book *Leaves from a Secret Journal* Howard Thurman often recited, once referred to William Blake as one whose "whole being must have been standing on tiptoe, reaching up to a higher shelf of thought than any of us shorter people could reach for ourselves."[4] Howard Thurman was also a "tiptoe person." He stood tall, and he passed down to us those higher level gifts of his thought and spirit. As for his thought, it was like a river, moving always out to sea, a strong river filled with currents—all strong, persistent, determined, obedient to its sources and destiny. He lived a long and fruitful life, always giving of himself.

When he died in April 1981, I was one of several "sons" his wife Sue asked to take part in the service celebrating his life and work. The service was in two parts, the memorial service held at the church, and the service of committal held at the cemetery. During the memorial service, fifteen friends and colleagues gave tributes and personal reflections. The committal took place the following day, and it was a private service conducted for the family and very close friends. I was one of five people who spoke comfortingly to the family about the meaning Howard Thurman's life had held for us—and how he would be remembered.

An interesting story emerges in connection with Howard Thurman's final illness and death. When he was taken to the hospital and it was discovered that his appendix had ruptured, one of the physicians attending to him was a former student of mine at Anderson College. Having heard me mention Thurman's name in connection

---

4. Jane Steger, *Leaves from a Secret Journal* (Boston: Little, Brown, and Company, 1926), 24.

with course work reading, this young man was surprised when he looked down at the wristband of the patient being wheeled from the operation and saw the name "Thurman, Howard." The name stirred his memory. Intent on decorum but stirred by the occasion, the young doctor asked, "Are you the Howard Thurman?" Thurman answered a bit groggily, "Yes!" Wanting to be sure, the doctor asked further, "Did you write *Jesus and the Disinherited*?" Again Thurman answered, "Yes!" But the doctor wondered if the patient being wheeled along was fully at himself, so he asked still another question: "Do you know a Dr. James Earl Massey?" To which Thurman again answered, "Yes, I do!" And with that statement, the doctor's feelings were so full that he fell silent—wondering how it could be that someone whom he had heard so much about, and for whose life he felt so indebted, could be with him now—under his care in the intensive care unit.

The doctor immediately placed a long-distance call to my home in Anderson. I was out when the call came, but my wife Gwendolyn was there, and they talked for some time about the strange experience. Gwendolyn filled me in when I got home from my trip, and I called the hospital, talked with the doctor friend, and then called Mrs. Thurman to see what I could do to assist her at such a time.[5] I stayed on the phone across the weeks after he was released to go home, but both the doctor and Sue had informed me that it was only a matter of time before we would lose him.

The day before Thurman died, I talked by phone with Sue. I asked if she thought it might comfort him to see me at his bedside. She replied, "I really don't think so—unless he comes back this way!" He was in a coma. Thurman died early the next morning. I later learned that my doctor friend had been seeing him each week, visiting at the house, and helping Sue Thurman in various ways; Dr. T, as we called him, had grown close to him. After the death, Mrs. Thurman asked the young man if he would agree to be one of the pallbearers. When I saw Thomas Hignell at the funeral he embraced me for a long moment, tears flowing from his eyes, as he

---

5. **ED:** For published versions of this story see Massey, *Aspects of My Journey*, 293-294, 341-342; James Earl Massey, "Others follow in His Footsteps," in George K. Makechnie, *Howard Thurman: His Enduring Dream* (Boston: The Howard Thurman Center, Boston University, 1988), 72-73.

spoke wonderingly about the grace that brought him into contact with Howard Thurman—and the opportunity he had to serve him in a time of need, fulfilling a debt he felt he owed because of what Thurman's thought and counsel and friendship had helped to make me his mentor. Again and again we have evidence like these that "There is a divinity that shapes our ends." There is, and for it we thank God and serve each other.

There have been times of hearing when no voice was speaking, and occasions of insight when the most ordinary things were before my eyes. Although I did not conceptualize such happenings at the time, I later understood that Life was having its say, and I was being taught to look and listen. From early childhood I had lived these experiences, but I had not shared them with anyone. I have again and again had experiences of sensing something more than I see around me, and Someone other than myself. My social surroundings and personal problems have always been less burdensome because I have sensed a helping Presence. I have sometimes wondered if this sense of presence is a gift or if it is a common heritage that some discover only when they are awakened by need to seek it.

Whatever the right answer to this, I know that it was only after meeting Howard Thurman that I began to sift my memories and study the rich deposit of those early and frequent experiences of sensed Presence. Thurman helped me to interrogate those experiences, categorize them, and extract from them basic messages about how God relates to my life and living. All of this helped to broaden the base of my conscious thought about the ways of God with us, and as a rather direct corollary, the ways of fellow believers with each other. To a degree that no one else had ever done, Howard Thurman helped me see my life in the context of what I had been sensing in my life. He encouraged me to probe experience at a level of mind that would be at one with what I was experiencing at the level of spirit. So as I grew into the years, I was thus helped to make sense out of my opportunities and environment, my crises and concerns.

SECTION THREE

Editorial Postlude—Curtiss Paul DeYoung

Howard Thurman died on April 10, 1981. He was eighty-one years of age. James Earl Massey and his wife Gwendolyn stayed in contact with Sue Bailey Thurman. As a gift to help her deal with her grief, James Massey sent her an audiocassette tape of him playing the piano.[1] Sue Thurman wrote:

> What a wonderful surprise and pleasure to receive the gift of Bach Choral preludes played by pianist, James Earl Massey! If Howard had ever told me (and I am not quite sure that he knew himself) you were a serious musician, while wearing as you do the robes of a distinguished clergyman, I was never aware of the extent to which you belonged in this artist's company. . . . (we played) your cassette as background music for one of Howard's most creative meditations. The two together made a fine combination. I wish this could have been done in his lifetime. It would have been a heartwarming experience for him who loved you in a very special way from the moment he first met you. . . . My thanks to you and the gracious girl who cares for you, for your love and concern for me and my family,

1. Massey was preparing for a career as a concert pianist, when at sixteen years of age he felt called to ministry. In his early adult years, he also studied at the renowned school of music, the Mozarteum in Salzburg, Austria. See Massey, *Aspects of My Journey*, 52, 91-95.

> as we carry on here in the spirit of our dearly beloved one, "whom we have loved long since and lost awhile." Only in the physical sense as his spiritual presence is always with us. With warmest and best love to both of you always, Sue Thurman[2]

Howard Thurman approached life and spoke of death as a mystic. He once reflected, "I don't think a person who is sick can ever die until somewhere in his organism a decision is made, a conclusion is arrived at which says that all of me, the totality of my organism is at last contained in the event."[3] Peter Eisenstadt notes that Thurman the mystic wrote about his death in an unpublished chapter of his autobiography: "I am at ease knowing that nobody like me ever lived before. I am at ease because there is a nonspatial and nontemporal dimension of my personality that has to do with life and is not bound by death. I function freely outside an interval of time in which I happen to be living at the moment: I can hark back thirty years, or project thirty years, leaping to the past, leaping to the future. I can be aware of my dying right up to zero. Part of me will be watching Howard Thurman, the time binder and space binder, being delivered from a particular time and a particular space. I shall be a participant in my dying as I have been in my living."[4]

In 1978, Howard Thurman spoke about death to a gathering at the Interdenominational Theological Center (ITC) in Atlanta, Georgia. Walter Fluker was there and shares: "In his distinct and mesmerizing cadence, he spoke about the mystery of life and death and the 'double-search, the hunt' for his elusive God. He indicated that he had questions for God that were unanswered. In language reminiscent of the epigraph of his autobiography, 'Always we are on the outside of our story, always we are beggars who seek entrance to the kingdom of our dwelling place.' In his last dramatic sentences, after a long, silent, waiting moment with his hands folding and unfolding in prayer

---

2. Thurman, Sue Bailey. Letter to James Earl Massey. 12 October 1981. *James Earl Massey Papers*. Anderson University and Church of God Archives, Nicholson Library, Anderson, IN.

3. Howard Thurman, *Walking with God: The Sermon Series of Howard Thurman, Volume 1: Moral Struggle and the Prophets*, eds. Peter Eisenstadt and Walter Earl Fluker (Maryknoll: Orbis Books, 2020), 159.

4. Eisenstadt, *Against the Hounds of Hell*, 390.

fashion, trying to grasp the elusive meaning that haunted him, he exclaimed to his breathless audience, 'I shall find Him—how long I do not know—but I shall find Him somewhere under the old oak tree.'"[5]

In a hospitalization a few months prior to his death, the staff and Thurman's family thought he had died while they sat with him. Unexpectedly Thurman woke up from "the fight that I was having with death." Thurman said he was searching for God in the universe with two questions: "Why is there Black and white? Why is there male and female." He told God, "I am going to follow you through the ends of existence until you give me an answer to these questions." His wife Sue Bailey Thurman said that "he stayed the hand of death while he encountered 'the particular man' and the 'universal man' within himself and wrestled them to the earth, until he won the consent of both—to Life, to Death, and Back to Life."[6]

And so it was that Thurman, in the last few weeks of his life, continued his pursuit of God for answers to the central questions of his life's work, now mostly operative in the realm of the spirit. Philosopher Sam Keen noted in a conversation with Thurman two weeks before his death, Thurman asked: "Why was I born a Black man and you a white man? What in the universal way of things required me to be the particular person that I am? Why should the ultimate secret of my life be kept from me?"[7] Boston University Dean George Makechnie added: "Only days before his leave-taking, when Howard Thurman the particular man was to become Howard Thurman the universal man, he confided in me that he was still searching for answers to certain questions which the contradictions of life posed. . . . 'Why, over the entire world, are the disinherited oppressed by oppressors who themselves are so well provided for; and how and by whom is the crucial decision made about who may live out his or her life span fully and who must die prematurely?'"[8]

5. Walter Earl Fluker, "Introduction," in Walter Earl Fluker, ed. *The Unfinished Search for Common Ground: Reimagining Howard Thurman* (Maryknoll: Orbis Books, 2023), 6.

6. Fluker, "Introduction," 7.

7. Fluker, "Introduction," 7.

8. Geroge K. Makechnie, "Epilogue," in George K. Makechnie, *Howard Thurman: His Enduring Dream* (Boston: The Howard Thurman Center, Boston University, 1988), 88.

James Earl Massey learned of the death of his mentor on the day of his death, April 10, 1981. He wrote in his autobiography that "Mrs. Thurman explained that her husband's body would be cremated after the funeral, and she wanted Kelly Miller Smith and me to conduct a private service for the family and selected friends just before the body was released to the cremation process. Smith and I agreed, and we then went over to Fellowship Church where the body of Dr. Thurman was lying in state. There we found Jesse Jackson and several others gathered. A vast crowd was present for the memorial service on Thursday, and the order of service was replete with tributes and personal reflections from colleagues personal and professional who all spoke at their best." Massey reflected, "The memorial service that Thursday highlighted aspects of Dr. Thurman's life, which was expected, but it was during the private service of committal on Friday morning when I felt the 'balm of Gilead' blessing my spirit. Those of us who spoke personally to the family did so as family members ourselves, and we experienced an intimacy that only family members know. Paradoxically, my experience of that final service helped me gain a sense of closure, even while my heart was feeling a greater openness. Somehow, even my mentor's death was influencing my life."[9]

On Sunday, June 24, 2018, I visited Dr. James Earl Massey at a medical center in Tuscaloosa, Alabama. I did not know when I arrived that I would spend the last hour of his life with him in that hospice room. I should have known. Twice in the month prior to my visit I had a premonition that he would die while I was with him. Each time I pushed these thoughts out of my mind. I was not ready for him to die. And I did not feel like I was the one worthy enough to share that moment with him.

Despite great pain, he was fully present and filled with much grace for that hour as I finally became aware that this was the end of his earthly life. We spoke of the mundane and the eternal. It was a moment both traumatic and sacred for me.

James Earl Massey the mystic was also engaged in another conversation. He would close his eyes and drift off into quiet words. It was clear that we were not alone in the room and he was conversing with the Divine Presence. Then he said, "The time is very near." In

---

9. Massey, *Aspects of My Journey*, 342-343.

a final act of grace, he sat up, held my hands, and smiled. But he was clearly looking past me. He saw where he was headed. And he transitioned into the arms of God. What a sacred moment. And as Dr. Massey said of Dr. Thurman, "Somehow, even my mentor's death was influencing my life."

In this volume we have engaged with Howard Thurman and James Earl Massey—two luminous lives—through biographical reflections, theological assessments, conversational encounters, and mystical moments. Howard Thurman mentored up close James Earl Massey and a generation of Civil Rights Movement leaders including Pauli Murray, James Farmer, Martin Luther King, Jr., Otis Moss, Jr., Jesse Jackson, Sr., Barbara Jordan, Whitney Young, James Lawson, Vernon Jordan, Vincent Harding, and others. In addition to this number, Thurman mentored, as he had mentored Massey, a generation of mystics and Thurman scholars including Walter Earl Fluker, Zalman Schacter-Shalomi, Paul Smith, Mozella Mitchell, Luther Smith, Derrick Bell, Jr., and others. Of course, many others were mentored from a distance through his sermons and writings. Howard Thurman still mentors from beyond the grave through his writings . . . and through those mentored by his mentees, like James Earl Massey who mentored me. The combined impact of Howard Thurman and this mentoring legacy is beyond measure.

Howard Thurman's life ended and yet lives on. He influences us from the other side, prompting us to pursue God for answers to the enduring questions of why our one human family remains so fragmented. May this journey of the mystic-activist Howard Thurman—"Dr. T"—as recounted by his mystic-activist son James Earl Massey, inspire us to live lives where we hear in ourselves and in others "the sound of the genuine"[10] and embrace a "faith (that) holds within its grasp the past and the future as a single moment in time."[11]

10. Thurman, *The Luminous Darkness*, 99, 111; "The Sound of the Genuine, 1 May 1977," in Fluker, ed., *The Papers of Thurman, Volume 5*, 281-286.

11. Thurman, *The Inward Journey*, 23.

Bibliography

James Earl Massey's 1977 Bibliography

Howard Thurman Books:

The Greatest of These (Mills College, CA: Eucalyptus Press, 1944).

Deep River: An Interpretation of Negro Spirituals (Mills College, CA: Eucalyptus Press, 1945).

Meditations for Apostles of Sensitiveness (Mills College, CA: Eucalyptus Press, 1947).

The Negro Spiritual Speaks of Life and Death (New York: Harper and Brothers, 1947).

Jesus and the Disinherited (Nashville: Abingdon-Cokesbury Press, 1949).

Deep is the Hunger (New York: Harper and Brothers, 1951).

Meditations of the Heart (New York: Harper and Brothers, 1953).

The Creative Encounter: An Interpretation of Religion and Social Witness (New York: Harper and Brothers, 1954).

Deep River: Reflections on the Religious Insight of Certain of the Negro Spirituals (New York: Harper and Brothers, 1955). Revised edition of the 1945 edition, with illustrations by Elizabeth Orton Jones.

The Growing Edge (New York: Harper and Row, 1956).

Apostles of Sensitiveness (Boston: The American Unitarian Association, 1956).

Footprints of a Dream: The Story of the Church for the Fellowship of All Peoples (New York: Harper and Row, 1959).

The Inward Journey (New York: Harper and Row, 1961).

Mysticism and the Experience of Love (Wallingford, PA: Pendle Hill Pamphlet 115, 1961).

Temptations of Jesus: Five Sermons (San Francisco: Lawton Kennedy Printer, 1962).

Disciplines of the Spirit (New York: Harper and Row, 1963).

The Luminous Darkness: A Personal Interpretation of the Anatomy of Segregation and the Ground of Hope (New York: Harper and Row, 1965).

The Centering Moment (New York: Harper and Row, 1969).

The Search for Common Ground: An Inquiry into the Basis of Man's Experience of Community (New York: Harper and Row, 1971).

The Mood of Christmas (New York: Harper and Row, 1973)

A Track to the Water's Edge: The Olive Schriner Reader, edited by Howard Thurman (New York: Harper and Row, 1973).

Howard Thurman Contributions to Books:

"Finding God," in *Religion on the Campus*, edited by Francis P. Miller (New York: Association Press, 1927), 48-52.

"Good News for the Underprivileged," in *The Negro Caravan*, edited by Sterling A. Brown (New York: The Citadel Press, 1940), 685-692.

"Fascist Masquerade," in *The Church and Organized Movements*, edited by Randolph Crump Miller (New York: Harper and Brothers, 1946), 82-100.

"God and the Race Question," in *Together*, compiled by Glenn Clark (Nashville: Abingdon-Cokesbury Press, 1946), 118-120.

"Judgment and Hope in the Christian Message," in *The Christian Way in Race Relations*, edited by William Stuart Nelson (New York: Harper and Brothers, 1948), 229-235.

"The Religion of Jesus and the Disinherited," in *In Defense of Democracy*, edited by T. H. Johnson (New York: Putnam, 1949), 125-135.

"And When Thou Prayest," in *Sermons from the Ecumenical Pulpit*, edited by Max F. Daskam (Boston: Starr King Press, 1956), 86-90.

"Exposition to the Book of Habakkuk," in *The Interpreter's Bible*, Volume 6, edited by George A. Buttrick et al (Nashville: Abingdon Press, 1956), 979-1002.

"Exposition to the Book of Zephaniah," in *The Interpreter's Bible*, Volume 6, edited by George A. Buttrick et al (Nashville: Abingdon Press, 1956), 1013-1034.

"The Meaning of Purpose in Religious Experience," in *Religion Ponders Science*, edited by Edwin P. Booth (New York: Appleton-Century, 1964), 266-278.

"Sermon Preached by the Reverend Dr. Howard Thurman," at The American Embassy, Lagos, Nigeria, on Sunday, November 24, 1963, in Memory of the Late President John F. Kennedy, in *That Day with God*, edited by William M. Fine (New York: McGraw-Hill Book Co., 1965), 143-147.

"Introduction," in *Why I Believe There Is a God: Sixteen Essays by Negro Clergymen* (Chicago: Johnson Publishing Co., Inc., 1965), v-xi.

Howard Thurman Single Sermons, Addresses, and Articles

"Peace Tactics and a Racial Minority," in *The World Tomorrow*, December 1928, 505-507.

"Keep Awake!" *The Christian Century Pulpit*, June 1937, 125-127.

"What Shall I do With My Life?" *The Christian Century Pulpit*, September 1939, 210-211.

"Religious Ideas in Negro Spirituals," *Christendom* (Vol, IV. No. 4) Autumn 1939, 515-528.

"The Great Incarnate Words," *Motive*, January 1944, 24.

"The Fellowship Church of All Peoples," *Common Ground*, Spring Issue 1945, 29-31.

"Interracial Church in San Francisco," *Social Action*, February 15, 1945, 27-28.

"The Quest for Stability," *The Woman's Press*, April 1949.

"I Will Light Three Candles," *Parents*, December 1949, 26.

"The Powers of the Spirit and the Powers of This World," Mimeographed Address, Howard University School of Religion, Thirty-Fourth Annual Convocation, November 14, 1950.

"For a Time of Sorrow," *The Christian Century*, July 26, 1953, 867.

"The Church and the Administrator," *California Elementary School Administrators Association Yearbook*, 1953, 162-164.

"Deep River," Book Condensation Feature, *Pulpit Digest*, January 1956, 81-97.

"The Christian Minister and the Desegregation Decision," *Pulpit Digest*, May 1957, 13-19.

"The New Heaven and the New Earth," *The Journal of Negro Education*, Volume XXVII, No. 2 (1958), 115-119.

"Putting Yourself in Another's Place," *Childhood Education*, February 1962, 259-260.

"The Search for God in Religion," *The Layman's Movement Review*, November-December 1962.

"Human Freedom and the Emancipation Proclamation," *Pulpit Digest*, December 1962, 13-16, 66.

"Mysticism and Ethics," *The Journal of Religious Thought*, Summer Supplement 1970, 23-30.

"Who Can We Believe In?" *The Journal of Religion and Health*, Volume 12, No. 2, April 1973, 111-119.

"The Search for Common Ground," *Perspective: A Journal of Pittsburgh Theological Seminary*, Vol. XIII, No. 2 (Spring 1972), 127-137.

Howard Thurman Book Reviews

Review of William Douglas Chamberlain's *The Manner of Prayer*, in *The Journal of Religious Thought*, Volume 1, 1943-1944, 179.

Review of Douglas V. Steere's *On Beginning from Within*, in *The Journal of Religion*, October 1944, 284-285.

Review of Richard I. McKinney's *Religion in Higher Education Among Negroes*, in *Religion in Life*, Autumn 1946, 619-620.

Review of J. Deotis Roberts's *Liberation and Reconciliation: A Black Theology*, in *Religious Education* (November-December 1971), 464-466.

Selected Secondary Sources (Arranged by year of publication)

Tobias, Channing. "Some Outstanding Negro Christians: Howard Thurman—Preacher," *The Missionary Review of the World*, June 1936, 295-296.

Jenness, Mary. *Twelve Negro Americans* (New York: Friendship Press, 1936), "A Leader of Students," 145-160.

Mays, Benjamin E. *The Negro's God: As Reflected in His Literature* (Boston: Chapman and Grimes, 1938), viii, 174-176, 186.

Religious Leaders of America, 1941-1942, edited by J. C. Schwartz, 1054.

"Fellowship Church," *Time*, July 26, 1948, 40-42.

Torrence, Frederic R. *The Story of John Hope* (New York: The Macmillan Co., 1948), 329, 383.

"Trumpet Ready in the West," *The Christian Century*, September 12, 1951, 1040-1045.

Tendulkar, D. G. *Mahatma: Life of Mohandas Karamchand Gandhi*, Volume IV, 1934-1938 (Delhi and Bombay: Government of India, Publication Division, 1952), 48-51.

New York Times, March 22, 1953, 79.

"Great Preachers," *Life*, April 6, 1953, 128.

Burden, Jean. "Howard Thurman," *The Atlantic Monthly*, October 1953, 19-22.

"Offering of the Heart," *Yankee*, December 1953, 19-22.

"Great Negro Preachers," *Ebony* (Vol. IX, No. 9), July 1954, 29.

Current Biography, 1955, 602-604.

Henderson, Dorothy, *Biographical Sketches of Six Humanitarians Whose Lives Have Been For the Greater Glory* (New York: Exposition Press, 1958), see "Creative Encounter: Howard Thurman," 160-184.

Dexter, Harriet Harmon. *What's Right with Race Relations* (New York: Harper and Brothers, 1958), 165-167.

Bardolph, Richard A. *The Negro Vanguard* (New York: Rinehart, 1959), 218. 221, 222.

Burr, Nelson R. *A Critical Bibliography of Religion in America*, Vol. IV, Parts 3, 4, and 5 (Princeton: Princeton University Press, 1961), 833-834.

"Dolls for Democracy: Toys Aid Thurman's Campaign for Understanding," *Ebony*, December 1961, 93-96, 98.

Sullivan, A. J. "About Encounters: A Sketch of Howard Thurman," *Bostonia*, Fall Issue 1963, 6-10.

Holt, Rackham. *Mary McLeod Bethune: A Biography* (Garden City, NY: Doubleday and Co., Inc, 1964), 114.

Yates, Elizabeth. *Howard Thurman: Portrait of a Practical Dreamer* (New York: The John Day Co., 1964).

Washington, Joseph R., Jr. *Black Religion: The Negro and Christianity in the United States* (Boston: Beacon Press, 1964), 105-112.

Reimers, David M. *White Protestantism and the Negro* (New York: Oxford University Press, 1965), 132-133, 162-164.

Oppenheim, Bernice. "Dr. Howard Thurman," *Bostonia*, Summer Issue 1965, 18.

"Fierce Logic," *Time*, August 27, 1965, 85-86.

Jones, Edward A. *A Candle in the Dark: A History of Morehouse College* (Valley Forge: Judson Press, 1967), 199, 234, 236, 238, 240, 257-258.

Cameron, Richard Morgan. *Boston University School of Theology, 1839-1968* (Boston: Boston University School of Theology, 1968), 137.

Logan, Rayford W. *Howard University: The First Hundred Years, 1867-1967* (New York: New York University Press, 1969), 184-187, 289.

Robinson, Wilhelmina S. *Historical Negro Biographies* (New York and Washington: Publishers Co., Inc., 1968), 251-252.

Boulware, Marcus H. *The Oratory of Negro Leaders: 1900-1968* (Westport, CT: Negro Universities Press, 1969), 184-187, 289.

"Morehouse Pays Tribute to Dr. Thurman," *The Afro-American*, January 3, 1970, 14.

Trueblood, Elton. *The New Man for Our Time* (New York: Harper and Row, 1970), 65, 75-76.

Bridges, Hal. *American Mysticism: From William Jones to Zen* (New York: Harper and Row, 1970), 8, 51-60, 142.

Mays, Benjamin E. *Born to Rebel: An Autobiography* (New York: Charles Scribner's Sons, 1971), 93, 185, 186.

Roberts, J. Deotis. "The American Negro's Contribution to Religious Thought," in Joseph S. Ronek and Thomas Kiernam, editors, *The Negro Impact on Western Civilization* (New York: Philosophical Library, Inc. 1970), 86-89.

Massey, James Earl. "Christian Theology and the Social Experience of Being Black," *Christian Scholar's Review*, Vol. 1, No. 3 (Spring 1971), 203-216.

Massey, James Earl. "The Relational Imperative: Black Theology and Redemptive Relations," in *SPECTRUM: International Journal of Religious Education*, July-August 1971 (Vol, 47, No. 4), 15-17.

Massey James Earl. "Bibliographical Essay: Howard Thurman and Rufus M. Jones, Two Mystics," *The Journal of Negro History*, Vol. LVII, No. 2 (April 1972), 190-195.

Lovell, John, Jr. *Black Song: The Forge and the Flame: The Story of How the Afro-American Spiritual Was Hammered Out* (New York: The Macmillan Co., 1972), 504-506.

Goodwin, Mary E. "Racial Roots and Religion: An Interview with Howard Thurman," *The Christian Century*, May 9, 1973, 533-535.

Bibliography (post James Earl Massey book)

Howard Thurman Books

With Head and Heart: The Autobiography of Howard Thurman (New York: Harcourt Brace Jovanovich, 1979).

For the Inward Journey: The Writings of Howard Thurman, selected by Anne Spenccer Thurman (Richmond, IN: Friends United Meeting, 1984).

Fluker, Walter Earl, and Tumber, Catherine, eds. *A Strange Freedom: The Best of Howard Thurman on Religious Experience and Public Life* (Boston: Beacon Press, 1998).

Fluker, Walter Earl, ed. *The Papers of Howard Washington Thurman, Vol. 1, My People Need Me, June 1918-March 1936.* (Columbia, SC: University of South Carolina Press, 2009).

Fluker, Walter Earl, ed. *The Papers of Howard Washington Thurman, Vol. 2, Christian, Who Calls Me Christian, April 1936-August 1943.* (Columbia, SC: University of South Carolina Press, 2012).

Fluker, Walter Earl, ed. *The Papers of Howard Washington Thurman, Vol. 3, The Bold Adventure, September 1943-May 1949.* (Columbia, SC: University of South Carolina Press, 2015).

Fluker, Walter Earl, ed. *The Papers of Howard Washington Thurman, Vol. 4, The Soundless Passion of a Single Mind, June 1949-December 1962.* (Columbia, SC: University of South Carolina Press, 2017).

Gowler, David B. and Jensen, Kipton E., eds. *Sermons on the Parables* (Maryknoll: Orbis Books, 2018).

Fluker, Walter Earl, ed. *The Papers of Howard Washington Thurman, Vol. 5, The Wider Ministry, January 1963-April 1981.* (Columbia, SC: University of South Carolina Press, 2019).

Eisenstadt, Peter and Fluker, Walter Earl, eds. *Walking with God: The Sermon Series of Howard Thurman, Volume 1: Moral Struggle and the Prophets* (Maryknoll: Orbis Books, 2020).

Eisenstadt, Peter and Fluker, Walter Earl, eds. *Walking with God: The Sermon Series of Howard Thurman, Volume 2: The Way of the Mystics* (Maryknoll: Orbis Books, 2021).

Eisenstadt, Peter and Fluker, Walter Earl, eds. *Democracy and the Soul of America* (Maryknoll: Orbis Books, 2022).

Eisenstadt, Peter and Fluker, Walter Earl, eds. *The Inner Life and Social Responsibility* (Maryknoll: Orbis Books, 2023).

Books About Howard Thurman

Brown, Amanda. *The Fellowship Church: Howard Thurman and the Twentieth-Century Religious Left* (New York: Oxford University Press, 2019).

Brown, Lerita Coleman. *What Makes You Come Alive: A Spiritual Walk with Howard Thurman* (Minneapolis: Broadleaf Books, 2023).

Dixie, Quinton and Peter Eisenstadt. *Visions of a Better World: Howard Thurman's Pilgrimage to India and of the Origins of African American Nonviolence* (Boston: Beacon Press, 2011).

Dorrien, Gary. *Breaking White Supremacy: Martin Luther King and the Black Social Gospel* (New Haven: Yale University Press, 2017).

Eisenstadt, Peter. *Against the Hounds of Hell: A Life of Howard Thurman* (Charlottesville: University of Virginia Press, 2021).

Ellison, Gregory C., ed. *Anchored in the Current: Discovering Howard Thurman as Educator, Activist, Guide, and Prophet* (Louisville: Westminster John Knox Press, 2020).

Epperly, Bruce. *Prophetic Healing: Howard Thurman's Vision of Contemplative Activism* (Richmond: Friends United Press, 2020).

Fluker, Walter. *They Looked for a City: A Comparative Analysis of the Ideal of Community in the Thought of Howard Thurman and Martin Luther King, Jr.* (Lanham, MD: University Press of America, 1989).

Fluker, Walter Earl, ed. *The Unfinished Search for Common Ground: Reimagining Howard Thurman's Life and Work* (Maryknoll: Orbis Books, 2023).

Gandy, Samuel Lucious, ed. *Common Ground: Essays in Honor of Howard Thurman on the occasion of his Seventy-fifth Birthday, November 18, 1975* (Washington, DC: Hoffman Press, 1976).

Gowler, David B. *Howard Thurman and the Quest for Community: From Prodigals to Compassionate Samaritans* (New York: Paulist Press, 2024)

Harvey, Paul. *Howard Thurman & The Disinherited: A Religious Biography* (Grand Rapids: William B. Eerdmans Publishing Company, 2020).

Hunt, C. Anthony. *Come Go with Me: Howard Thurman and a Gospel of Radical Inclusivity* (Baltimore: Wyndham Hall Press, 2019).

Johnson, Alonzo. *Good News for the Disinherited: Howard Thurman on Jesus of Nazareth and Human Liberation* (Lanham: University Press of America, Inc. 1997).

Johnson, Kipton E. *Howard Thurman: Philosophy, Civil Rights, and the Search for Common Ground* (Columbia, SC: University of South Carolina Press, 2019).

Makechnie, George. *Howard Thurman: His Enduring Dream* (Boston: Howard Thurman Center, 1989).

Mitchell, Mozella G. ed. *The Human Search: Howard Thurman and the Quest for Freedom, Proceedings of the Second Annual Thurman Convocation* (New York: Peter Lang, 1992).

Neal, Anthony Sean. *Howard Thurman's Philosophical Mysticism: Love against Fragmentation* (Lanham: Lexington Books, 2019).

Pollard, Alton. *Mysticism and Social Change: The Social Witness of Howard Thurman* (New York: Peter Lang, 1992).

Smith, Luther E. *Howard Thurman: The Mystic as Prophet* (Richmond: Friends United Press, 1991).

Young, Henry James, ed., *God and Human Freedom: A Festschrift in Honor of Howard Thurman* (Richmond, IN: Friends United Press, 1983).

Books and articles written by James Earl Massey that speak of Howard Thurman

The Soul Under Siege (Anderson, IN: Warner Press, 1970), 104.

"Bibliographical Essay: Howard Thurman and Rufus M. Jones, Two Mystics," *The Journal of Negro History*, Vol. LVII, No. 2 (April 1972), 190-195.

The Responsible Pulpit (Anderson, IN: Warner Press, 1974), 109.

"Howard Thurman and Olive Schreiner on the Unity of All Life: A Bibliographical Essay," *The Journal of Religious Thought*, Vol. XXXIV, No. 2, Fall-Winter 1977-78, 29-33.

Concerning Christian Unity (Anderson, IN: Warner Press, 1979), 51-52, 63, 87-88.

Designing the Sermon: Order and Movement in Preaching (Nashville: Abingdon Press, 1980), 78, 82.

"Thurman's Preaching: Substance and Style," in Henry James Young, ed., *God and Human Freedom: A Festschrift in Honor of Howard Thurman* (Richmond, IN: Friends United Press, 1983), 110-121.

The Soul Under Siege: Dealing with Temptation, Second Edition (Grand Rapids: Francis Asbury Press, 1987), 100.

A Bridge Between: A Centennial History of Campus Ministry at Tuskegee University 1888-1988 (Tuskegee, AL: Tuskegee University Press, 1988), 53.

"Others follow in His Footsteps," in George K. Makechnie, *Howard Thurman: His Enduring Dream* (Boston: The Howard Thurman Center, Boston University, 1988), 72-73.

"Howard Thurman," in William H. Willimon and Richard Lischer, eds., *Concise Encyclopedia of Preaching* (Louisville: Westminster John Knox Press, 1995), 484-487.

The Burdensome Joy of Preaching (Nashville: Abingdon Press, 1998), 27, 38-39, 50-52.

Sundays in the Tuskegee Chapel: Selected Sermons (Nashville: Abingdon Press: 2000), 16-17, 122.

"Reconciliation: Two Biblical Studies," in *A Mighty Long Journey: Reflections on Racial Reconciliation*, eds. Timothy George and Robert Smith, Jr. (Nashville: Broadman & Holman Publishers, 2000), 212-214.

Aspects of My Pilgrimage: An Autobiography (Anderson, IN: Anderson University Press, 2002), 64-66, 198, 268-270, 278-279, 284, 293-294, 341-343, 350, 355, 424-425.

African Americans and the Church of God Anderson, Indiana: Aspects of a Social History (Anderson, IN: Anderson University Press, 2005), 53.

"Faith and Chrisitan Life in the African-American Spirituals," in *God the Holy Trinity: Reflections on Christian Faith and Practice*, ed. Timothy George (Grand Rapids: Baker Academic, 2006), 57-63.

1 & 2 Timothy, Titus, Philemon: Immersive Bible Studies (Nashville, Abingdon Press, 2012), 40, 54.

"The Church, Preaching, and Christian Music," in *Worship, Tradition, and Engagement: Essays in Honor of Timothy George*, eds. David Dockery, James Earl Massey, and Robert Smith, Jr. (Eugene, Pickwick Publications, 2018) 307-317.

Views from the Mountain: Select Writings of James Earl Massey, eds. Barry L. Callen & Curtiss Paul DeYoung (Glendora, CA: Aldersgate Press, 2018), 341-342.

Online Sources

The Howard Thurman Papers Project: The Papers of Howard Thurman: Home

Howard Thurman & Sue Bailey Thurman Collections, Howard Gotleb Archival Research Center, Boston University: Howard Thurman & Sue Bailey Thurman Collections » BU Libraries | Boston University

The Howard Thurman Digital Archive, Emory University: Thurman Research Resources · The Howard Thurman Digital Archive

James Earl Massey Papers, Anderson University & Church of God Archives: James Earl Massey Papers · Collections of Notable Individuals in the Anderson University & Church of God Archives · Omeka @ Anderson University

Index